THE DAY OF HIS COMING

THE DAY OF HIS COMING

COMING

The Man in the Gospels

*

GERHARD GLOEGE
Professor in the University of Bonn

FORTRESS PRESS · PHILADELPHIA

Library of Congress Catalog Card Number 63–13876

—

Translated by Stanley Rudman from
Aller Tage Tag
Kreuz-Verlag Stuttgart, 2nd edition 1960

—

This book has a companion on the Old Testament:
A Thousand Years and a Day
by Claus Westermann, also published by Fortress Press

© SCM PRESS LTD 1963
FIRST PUBLISHED 1963
PRINTED IN GREAT BRITAIN

CONTENTS

THE EVE OF HIS COMING:
JESUS OF NAZARETH

PREFACE

THIS is my first book without footnotes. This abstention from academic discussion and the normal citation of references did not come easily to me. I should like to make it clear, therefore, that this book is in a certain sense—albeit very indirectly—the work of many hands. As a rule I have refrained from quoting the names of scholars who are still alive. My debt to modern scholarship is indicated in part by the bibliography in the German edition. The expert will recognize where my account goes its own way— perhaps even stubbornly so. Anything controversial is the result not of personal prejudice, but of the total impression which the text of the first three Gospels has conveyed to me and which I have tried to expound not as an Existentialist, but existentially. Those who are acquainted with my previous work will come across important changes. Questions which I have left open will be discussed in a second volume, dealing with Paul and the early Church.

Does my book have an apologetic aim? Of course. What serious book doesn't? The subject of this 'apologetic', however, is neither the teaching of the New Testament nor the dogma of a church, but the Jew, Jesus of Nazareth. His figure is the touchstone by which everything else must be measured—including Paul and John, not to mention the Reformers. If we really seek the historical Jesus in earnest, we shall not be disturbed by the battle-cries of Liberalism and Orthodoxy, Modernism and Conservatism. Our objective survey of the past points us, paradoxically, to the future.

THE DAY OF HIS COMING

THE NEW TESTAMENT, like the Old, is not a book but a library. It is not, of course, a library of the same size and scope as the Old Testament which is three times the length of the New, even without the Apocrypha. It contains twenty-seven books, the longest of which—St Luke's Gospel—is roughly comparable in length with the historical books of the Old Testament, while the shortest—the Second and Third Epistles of John—take up less room than the fragments of Obadiah's prophecies.

The spaciousness of the period covered by the books of the Old Testament, the stretch of centuries taken for their composition, is compressed into a few years in the case of the New Testament. The historian finds himself dealing with documents which were, in the main, completed within two or three generations. The length of time involved is so short that any succession of periods, such as that presupposed by the broad outlines of ancient Israel's history, is completely absent. There is no trace of slow gradual developments; at the most their beginnings are indicated. A great deal of what seems like a terminal point to later ages may only have been one element among others.

This compression is even greater if one considers the subject-matter. Apart from the Acts of the Apostles, which deals with other times and places, the one and only event considered is the fate of Jesus of Nazareth. All attention is concentrated on his 'day'. For in his day the thousand years which lead up to him are realized. The promises of God and the hopes of men, the threats of the prophets and the longings of the people, the needs of the world and the stifled expectations of the whole of creation, are fulfilled in what happens to Jesus. That is why his destiny is the goal of time in the 'day of his coming'. That is why, from a purely literary standpoint, the New Testament forms such a small library. The limited size of this collection reflects the limited time of the decisive day.

The day of Jesus is what gives meaning and unity to all that the New Testament says. This unity is not to be confused with uniformity or absolute harmony, of course. The New Testament is complex, and its unity is anything but uniform. The observant reader who has come across this difficulty has noticed something important.

To come to the New Testament with the modern idea that a 'book' must be a unity from the point of both style and content is inviting disappointment and even, maybe, confusion. There are differences and contradictions not only in historical or geographical details, but even in the important testimonies of God's decisive utterances. One thing is certain: there is not a single voice in the New Testament which does not serve to glorify God, not a hymn whose text is not 'Jesus of Nazareth'. But melody and rhythm, tone and volume are sometimes different. The New Testament is a polyphonal chorus in which every voice has a life of its own and therefore the right to express itself in its own way, and even on occasion to sing in opposition to other voices. The outsider, who only hears one individual statement after another, considers at times that he is perceiving only discords. Not only the statements about the man and the world but also those about God and Jesus are mutually conflicting. Not only do different books disagree—the fourth Gospel and the first three Gospels, or Luke and Matthew or James and Paul—but contradictions are to be found within a single group of writings, whether it is a Gospel or Paul's letters.

The teaching of the New Testament does not take the form of a thesis about man, the world, God and Jesus. The writers of the New Testament from start to finish are engaged in a dialogue; they talk with their contemporaries, with one another and with us. It is a conversation that is audible and sometimes quite loud. It had been in progress for a long time before we joined it. To regard the New Testament as a divine monologue is to make a complete mistake. The New Testament has the character of a dialogue from the very beginning. And this means that we, too, are involved. The conversation of these early Christian witnesses does not rush past us, like a film on the screen or a speech on the stage, like a commentary on the radio or television. The New Testament comes up to us. It involves us. For, whatever it may say, one thing is certain: it is talking about *us*, it is concerned with *us*. No one who approaches the New Testament can afford to remain a listener. He must jump on to the stage and enter the conversation. He will agree with one witness and disagree with another. He will have to say 'Yes' to one and 'No' to another. There is only one thing he cannot do—that is, keep silent. The day of his coming loosens the tongue. It is 'the last day'. We are called and questioned as witnesses.

The following pages seek to show how modern life and modern men are partners in the dialogue of the New Testament. The question is not *whether* we speak—for, whether we are aware of it or not, we are already involved in the conversation—but *what* we shall say. In order that this dialogue might be clear and articulate and unambiguous we shall make use of the critical methods of historical research and refer to the results of modern scholarship: for neither author nor reader would be concerned with the New Testament, if they did not know that they were called to an independent, reasoned judgement. It would be a great help towards understanding what will concern us in the following pages if we could agree to jettison the old assumption that the New Testament is a book which contains a systematic treatise of divine utterances about men or human utterances about God, all of which chime in perfect harmony! Instead, let us proceed on the assumption that the New Testament is an invitation to us to take an interest in a history in which from now onwards we are involved.

Because this history is no myth, but the history of a real person like ourselves, a history which occurred at a specific time and place and evoked a response from the world, we shall inquire into the historical setting first. For the 'day of his coming' is an actual day in the midst of passing time.

BETWEEN THE TESTAMENTS

THE TRANSITION from the thousand years of the Old Testament to the single day of the New Testament is accompanied by peculiar twists and turns; the changeover was not immediate or direct. The people of God had never lived an isolated existence; even though they were a race apart they were always surrounded by others. But in the last three hundred years before the birth of Jesus they had to pass through a special danger zone, which can be described in two words: Hellenism and the Roman Empire. The former danger was more internal, the latter more external. Sandwiched between Hellenistic cosmopolitanism and Roman imperialism they had to overcome the attacks and enticements of this new world. And, in addition to this, the people of God themselves also underwent a great change—outwardly and, what is more important, inwardly: Judaism came into being. From the standpoint of Jesus' day, it was a period of transition.

This break is reflected in the literature; between the books of the Old and New Testaments there is a gap. The reason for this was that writings which originated in this period were less highly regarded; they were not generally recognized as Holy Scriptures. They were, in fact, refused entry into the canon. After the catastrophe which overtook the Jewish State in AD 70 Rabbinic Judaism tried to remove them. We owe their preservation—though only fragments have survived in some cases—to the interest of the Christian Church and its unorthodox offshoots. The 'establishment', the synagogue, marked the historical gap by a break in its literature.

The New Testament cannot be properly understood, if this double break in the history and literature is ignored. It is important to know what happened, what was thought, what believed, what written and what experienced in the period in between. The one day is not only the fulfilment of the thousand years but also of that strange period, which, for many people, lies in the shadows of salvation-history, though it is historically well-lit and set in the brilliant context of Hellenism, the most modern period of antiquity.

I

THE HELLENISTIC WORLD

THE WORLD into which Jesus of Nazareth came was both geographically and culturally spacious. It was a modern world, marking the end or autumn of antiquity. It began with Alexander the Great and came to an end with Augustus. The formative culture was Hellenism, which stemmed from Alexander's time.

Hellenism binds together East and West, Asia and Europe. Chronologically speaking, its three hundred years (from the battle of Gaugamela in 331 BC to the battle of Actium in 31 BC) form the bridge between the Persian Empire and the Roman Empire. When Jesus was born, the world had become a single unit both inwardly and outwardly.

Since the conquest of Egypt and the Far East by Alexander the world in which the narrow strip of Palestine was situated had extended its borders. A homogeneous pattern of life had spread everywhere. The people of the three continents bordering the large basin of the eastern Mediterranean shared a similar outlook on life.

1. *The Persian Empire*

The outlines of this world had already been sketched before Alexander. He had simply taken them over. They had been created by the first Indo-Germanic Empire known to history: the Persian Empire. Cyrus II, the *Kōresh* of Deutero-Isaiah, 'shepherd' and 'anointed' of the Lord (Isa. 44.28; 45.1), a man of enterprise and energy, had conquered the Empires of the Medes, Lydians and Neo-Babylonians about the middle of the sixth century BC. In Northern Iran he had dethroned his Median overlord and in the west he besieged Croesus, a king of fabulous wealth whose coastal lands in Asia Minor had taken over the Greek city states. Without striking a blow he advanced as far as

Babylon, the capital of Nebuchadnezzar, in 539. His son, Cambyses, conquered Egypt, and Cambyses' successor, Darius I, extended Persian rule to the Indus in the east and Lake Aral in the north. East and west of the highland of Pamir, the roof of the world, were the steppes of Turkestan, which also belonged to the Persian Empire's sphere of interest.

The Persian Empire was a centralized, efficient, military and bureaucratic state. It had an excellent fiscal system and an excellent intelligence service at its disposal. Its twenty large satrapies were linked together as administrative districts by a network of roads used by both army and commerce. A proud symbol of this commercial system, which also provided for a state postal service and long distance communications, was the King's Highway from Sardis to Susa. More than 1,800 miles long, it linked the important Mediterranean port of Ephesus with the king's residence in the heart of the Empire.

It was the first state to create a uniform system of weights and measures and coinage. The basic unit of exchange in the currency of the Persian Empire was the golden 'daric'. The language of government and trade was the so-called 'King's Aramaic', a dialect in which certain parts of late Old Testament books (e.g. Daniel, Ezra) were written.

Persian religion had for a long time been a religion without temple or images. Ever since the time of Darius, the Great King and his court had paid homage to the Wise Lord, Ahura-Mazda, who had created heaven and earth, man and his destiny, and 'who made Darius King, one man to rule over many of his fellow-men'. The God Zarathustra, whose representative on earth the Great King was, decided Persian foreign policy. His priests taught that life was to be understood as a battle-field of two deities, the 'good spirit' and the 'evil spirit', later Ormuzd and Ahriman, who are locked in conflict like brothers fighting. Life is a struggle between light and darkness, good and evil, truth and falsehood. Man is called to work strenuously in thought, word and deed. As in the prophets of the Old Testament the world was understood, in the main, in terms of history. This view of the world's dramatic course struck a new note and had a decisive influence on Judaism and its apocalyptic. In fact, it also influenced the New Testament's view of the world. Within the framework of four aeons, each lasting three thousand years, the beginning and end of time meet.

The world is hurrying to its judgement, which is preceded by the resurrection of the dead, and followed by the renewal and transfiguration of the universe. An eschatology complete in itself is proclaimed. Its individual elements are the kingdom, the rule of law, the virgin-born harbingers of justice, the primal man, angels, demons, the course of history as a justification of God (theodicy), an appeal to men's sense of responsibility, and confidence in the final victory of the Good. All these elements had to be thrown into the great crucible of the new age just dawning, in order that they might fulfil their purpose later.

The ruling dynasty constantly moderated any exclusive claims by Zoroastrianism and, like all powerful dynasties in history, gave full rein to religious tolerance as a piece of wise statecraft. Within a year of the fall of Babylon Cyrus had sanctioned the return home of the Jews who were exiled there and had given permission for the temple at Jerusalem to be rebuilt. During the next hundred years, Nehemiah was made Governor of Judah, and Ezra, who was in charge of religious affairs, was appointed 'Minister for Church affairs' in Jerusalem. Such measures were intended to assist internal developments.

In foreign policy, however, plans threatened to get out of hand. The division of the Greek world into a free, European Hellas and an enslaved, Persian Hellenism in what we now call Asia Minor heralded the era of the Persian wars. For more than fifty years the small alliances of the Greek army and navy defended the freedom of their civilization against the attack of the greatest military power in the world. But after Athens' short-lived golden age under Pericles, the internal inability of the Greek city states to agree amongst themselves led to the Peloponnesian War. The defeat of Athens was no more than external confirmation of the death of its 'democracy'. In the course of the Enlightenment inspired by the Sophists the principle of justice had been exchanged for the unprincipled maxim 'might is right'. Athens, Sparta, and Thebes had surrendered the leadership to a nation which stood outside their circle: Macedonia.

2. *The Greek Revolution*

This external change in the relation of the great powers reflected an internal change. In all areas of public and private life ideas had begun to change—springing from belief in the supremacy of reason. Life was no longer understood as something growing, but as something manufactured. Planning took the place of growth. Theory became the arbiter of life. Political life was seized by a radical revolution of the spirit. Nationalism was replaced by the principle of a world state. Empire was to succeed the city-state and the *polis* was to become part of a larger unit.

Already, about 500 BC, Heracleitus, who declared that Logos (reason) governed the world, confessed to being cosmopolitan; he was a world citizen. A couple of generations later Euripides stated openly, 'What is the fatherland of the brave? The whole, wide world.' And even before the Stoics developed the idea of the world state, the young Macedonian, Alexander, had already realized it in his monarchy.

The new, Hellenistic-style king did not accept the old ways of thinking about the state. The great 'individual', an idea of the Sophists, controlled the fate of state and nation. The romantic notion of a Panhellenic war of revenge against the barbarians— revenge for the burning of Athens 143 years before—gave impetus to political decisions. Alexander inherited his father's plan to make an expedition to Asia which Philip had already begun to execute. The 'Greek Revolution' took shape in him.

In the spring of 334 Alexander crossed the Dardanelles as commander of the confederate Greek forces, numbering 30,000 infantry and 5,000 cavalry. Within four years the far superior fighting force of the Persians was broken and their empire conquered. The legend grew—anticipating historical reality: in the autumn of 331 on the battlefield of Gaugamela, not far from the ruins of Nineveh, the victorious troops were to acclaim him 'King of Asia'. The palaces of Persepolis went up in flames. Alexander allowed the body of Darius to be cremated according to traditional Persian rites; his murderer was cruelly executed in oriental fashion. The confederate forces returned home.

In Athens men began to realize that 'the world had changed'. Even before Alexander had penetrated as far as India, Aeschines, opposing Demosthenes in the trial *De Corona* (the 'Crown' case), had said: 'Surely in these days anything, however unexpected and amazing, could have happened. We have lived no ordinary human life; we have become the object of the most amazing stories among future generations.'

B

Alexander knew about the epoch-making significance of what he was doing and who he was. Indeed, it was his aim to change the world. World-conquest, not the establishment of a small kingdom, was his plan. His expeditions to the north-east beyond the Hindu Kush, towards present-day Samarkand and Tashkent and eastwards beyond the Kabul Pass to India (present-day West Pakistan), were not intended simply to secure what had been conquered. What he read on these expeditions, together with the papers he left behind, make his further plans clear. He intended to conquer the western half of the Mediterranean basin also.

Even if his sudden death put an end to the establishment of a world-wide rule, his example had made an impression on the minds of men. His attempt to rule the world led to the apotheosis of the ruler and the deification of the world ruler. From days of old it had been usual among the Greeks to make heroes of outstanding men. Those singled out in this way were received into the circle of the city gods with altars, festivals, month-titles and other honours. But from time immemorial the Orient had been the cradle of the cult of the ruler. In Mesopotamia the king was regarded as the son of the Most High god by adoption, in Egypt a son by birth. It was here, in Egypt, in fact—at the oasis of Siwa— that the oracle of the God Ammon, who stood in a position of highest esteem among the Greeks, second only to that of the Delphic Apollo, designated the conqueror as his son. No one misunderstood. The fusion of Greek and oriental ruler-worship by Alexander had a political motive as its first aim. It was intended to help in making the association of Hellenic democracy with world-monarchy more easy, and in reconciling the Greek concept of personal freedom with acceptance of a supra-personal order of rulers. The thoroughly secular character of his respect for the religious force of the Egyptian idea of world rule should not be underestimated, however. When, over 800 years before, the Pharaoh Raamses IV mounted the throne, the king's power was made the theme of a religious message of congratulation: 'Glorious day! Heaven and earth rejoice because thou art the great Lord of Egypt. The fugitives have returned to their cities and those who were in hiding have come forth again. The hungry are satisfied and happy, and the thirsty have drunk their fill. The naked are clothed in fine linen, and the unclean have white garments. Those who were

in prison are released and whoever was in chains is full of joy'
(cf. Luke 4.18f.). Alexander possessed no Virgil or Horace to
sing his divine renown, it is true, but the royal ceremonial of an
era long decayed and past was part of the king's experience. The
seizure of power by the world-king pointed to the birth of a new
world: the Hellenistic world.

3. *Mankind Becomes One*

The world began to grow aware of its common humanity. This
experience can hardly be overestimated. The dividing boundaries
of tribes, nations and races were in the melting-pot. The contrast
between Greeks and barbarians, expressed in language and
customs, began to disappear. Alexander deliberately attempted
to set it aside. The mass-wedding at Susa, in which he married
two princesses from the house of the Great King and allowed
about eighty of his generals to marry eminent Persian women, was
as much part of his policy as the reception of native Persians into
the Macedonian army. In all areas of life a policy of amalgamation,
as new to Greeks as to Orientals, was introduced; this led to a
new style of rule. The new age signified both Hellenization of the
Orient, and an Orientalization of Hellenism.

The Empire of Alexander, which stretched from the Balkans
to the Himalayas and from the Sahara to the Gobi desert, collapsed
after his death in the frequent but indecisive wars of succession
of his ambitious generals. But, once a common consciousness
had emerged and been experienced, it was no longer possible to
return to the old world. The place of world-empire was taken
by the Hellenistic system of confederate states. The most powerful
of these successor-states were the Ptolemaic Empire in Egypt
and the Seleucid Empire in Syria, which stretched beyond Persia
to the Indus at first. Both powers strove to possess the small
country of Palestine, which was so important strategically and
economically, because of the north-south axis of overland trade
running through it. After a hundred years of Egyptian rule the
Syrians conquered the country in 198 BC.

Meanwhile, the systematic invasion of almost all areas of civilization by the new spirit and its achievements continued. The
Hellenistic age saw the boom years of a passing antiquity. Ancient
areas of civilization were colonized. Throughout the East cities

named after Alexander sprang up. At their head both in time
and size stood the Egyptian Alexandria, founded by the King
himself. This great city of almost a million inhabitants at the
mouth of the Nile became, with its high buildings and well
laid out harbours, not only the trading exchange beween Africa
and India, but also the cultural meeting point between East and
West. As a centre of art and science, industry and trade, both
alongside and superior to the Syrian capital, Antioch, it was
'the world-city'. For the Jews of the Diaspora it proved to be
also a spiritual fortress alongside Jerusalem.

Everywhere there sprang up cities whose right-angled streets
and squares, arranged in part like a chess-board, reflected the
rational spirit of the times. Their public buildings, libraries and
observatories, theatres, sports stadia and swimming baths, aque-
ducts and street lighting were evidence of a practical approach
to life desirous of visible results. European names for cities, even
in Northern Syria, showed how a new Macedonia had arisen in
the midst of ancient areas of rule. In the heart of Asia, however,
the Greek kingdom of Bactria experienced a brief but powerful
period of prosperity. In this 'kingdom of the thousand cities'
(present-day North Afghanistan) Greek, Indian and Chinese
civilizations met and mingled, before streaming out into the world
of the Far East. The Hellenistic cities which were founded were
part of the greatest deliberate colonization movement carried out
by any state in history.

4. *The Civilization of the Spirit*

The spirit of this modern Hellenistic age was expressed in
great works of art and of science. The metropolis of learning was
Egyptian Alexandria, with its library of about half a million works.
The powerful spirit of learning here specialized in particular
theoretical and practical subjects. The period was hungry for this-
worldly realities, palpable, measurable and visible. Things foreign
and remote exerted a strong attraction: exotic, newly discovered
wonderlands of the earth, and the distant worlds of the heavens
above. Alexander, a pupil of the great Aristotle (d. 332), had
himself, like Napoleon later, conducted his military campaigns
in the style of scientific expeditions. He was accompanied by a
staff of scholars whose task it was to investigate the geography,

topography, botany, zoology and ethnography of the new territories, to evaluate the new discoveries and to make notes of their
results.

Among the individual disciplines mathematics, geometry, geography and astronomy were held in high regard. The centre of
this scientific activity was Alexandria; where Euclid wrote his
Elements about 325, where Archimedes of Syracuse studied, and
where Aristarchus of Samos (about 280—1800 years before
Copernicus) replaced the geocentric cosmology of Aristotle by
his heliocentric theory, although he was unable to implement his
discovery against the authority of Archimedes and the resistance
of the Stoic philosophers. It was at Alexandria, too, that the
Chief Librarian, Eratosthenes, building on the work of Aristarchus,
made a fairly accurate calculation of the orbit of the earth's planets
in the course of measuring the sun's position in Assuan (Syene)
and in Alexandria; he also drew up a map of the earth. About
200 BC Apollonius of Perga developed his theory of conic sections
in Alexandria.

In every branch of knowledge Hellenistic scholars arrived at
new conclusions by the application of cool, calculating reason.
The anatomists began with the dissection of corpses. Vivisection
was practised on criminals who had been condemned to death,
and in a repulsively playful mood the inquisitive monarch participated. In medicine scholars came near to discovering how the
blood circulates.

Theoretical physics, especially mechanics, demonstrated the
technical utility of scientific discovery. Hero of Alexandria constructed the first theodolite. By means of screws and cog-wheels
an exact measurement was possible, even without a telescope.
His mechanical and hydraulic apparatus made him the forerunner
of the inventor of the modern steam engine. In the fortress of
Pergamum there was a pumped water supply. On the island of
Pharos the fire from the lofty tower, the ancestor of the lighthouse,
showed shipping the entrance to the harbour of Alexandria. All
this indicates the innumerable applications of technical possibilities,
the innumerable signs of a new rational consciousness.

Older projects of exploration and discovery were resumed and
developed. The Phoenicians and the Persians, acting under
Egyptian orders, had already sailed round Africa in three years.
Pharaoh Necho of Egypt had formed the plan of linking the Nile

with the Red Sea by means of a ship-canal running east to west. A hundred years later Darius carried the project through—a feat which the Suez Canal inscriptions, more than two thousand years later, record as amazing. 'Nothing like this ever happened before.' Two hundred years later Ptolemy II tried to make the canal navigable once more. After unsuccessful attempts by the Persians and Carthaginians to sail round the black continent, Pythias, at the time of Alexander's campaigns in the East, had sailed round Western Europe from Marseilles and had penetrated as far as the shallows of the North Sea, where he observed the ebb and flow of the tide, and as far as the Orkneys and Shetlands.

The vitality of the period is shown particularly in the field of the plastic arts, especially by the art of the kingdom of Pergamum. The colossal altar of Zeus, whose marble frieze celebrates the victory of the Greeks over the fallen Gauls by representing the victory of the gods over the giants, is an expression of the utmost sophistication. In place of the calmness of Attic art, we find deliberate excitement and intentional commotion. This art is all for effect. At the same time that realistic naturalness which characterizes the intellectual activity of the period finds expression in it. Intellectual integrity and artistic virtuosity in the representation of the mythological material make the work of great interest for connoiss urs. Like the Hellenistic poet, the artist cannot be thought of w hout his library. In fact art began to become a professional occupation and the boundaries between genuine art and trash threatened to disappear.

Under the curse of the impulse to deify reason the Hellenistic spirit plunged deeper and deeper into crisis. The idea of a world-empire estranged political life from its great supporting traditions. Cosmopolitanism and individualism fed and nourished each other in turn. Great individuals began to dominate public life; powerful men, not always law-abiding, remarkable women, but sometimes scheming mistresses. Conscience, set free and left to the mercy of the ego, had to educate itself. But it floundered in the vastness of absolute freedom and unscrupulousness. The upsurge of the idea of freedom led to subjectivism and scepticism.

The question of truth was either stifled in academic technicality, resulting in a dead, dusty book-knowledge, 'Alexandrianism'— knowledge for knowledge's sake—or it was displaced by questions of utility, which resulted in scholarship being measured by its practicality and monetary value. The specialized disciplines flourished; true thought was crippled.

Education became shallow. Intellectual life grew barren. When the centre of gravity moved to Rome, which was constantly becoming more Hellenistic, culture was exchanged for a stereotyped civilization. Rhetoric, which was taught systematically, became the rival of philosophy. The child of Greek sophism, it was admirably suited to the requirements of the day. It possessed a flair for meeting contemporary needs and requirements, in short for anything that had market value. It offered something 'interesting', sensational and titillating. It was exciting and unfruitful at one and the same time. The various branches of knowledge were popularized in the train of rhetoric's victory.

Nevertheless there were intellectual forces working against such a general disintegration. One of the foremost of these was language. The numerous nations and their multitude of material interests were discovered to have a deeper unity in an all-embracing language. Since Alexander Greek had begun to be the language used when men of different countries met. The King's Aramaic of the Persian period was superseded by the international Greek of the Hellenistic age. This 'common' language—the Greek *koine*—was based on Attic, influenced by Ionic, a colonial Greek dialect. It was not a substitute for one's native language. But it required every non-Greek who wished to take part in the life of the community to be bilingual. It was spoken in government offices and business houses, as well as by soldiers and sailors on service. It gradually became the *lingua franca* of the whole world, which was now a single cultural entity. It linked East and West, slave and free, public and private life, office and home. It was spoken in the Emperor's court at Rome and equally in the markets and bazaars of the Orient. As a living, spoken language it talked its way automatically into the life of men, thus enabling those who wanted to do so to enter into the literary traditions of ancient Greece. It was this linguistic background, embracing both the religious and the non-religious world, which was to contribute to the rebirth in Greek of the Hebrew Old Testament—the Septuagint (LXX), which, in turn, influenced the language of the New Testament.

5. *International Economy*

For the first time mankind felt it was a unity. Its home (Greek *oikos*) was the whole wide world. The inhabited world—the *oikumene*—sheltered mankind within itself like a family. Mankind had to order its household—its economy—in accordance with external realities.

Not the least important contribution of Hellenism was in the sphere of commerce. The balance of political power had been the result of the disintegration of Alexander's Empire (301). None of the powers thought war a means of solving their political questions. Consequently a massive, silent moratorium produced an unexpected economic boom. By the side of poor and under-developed countries stood the Greek powers with their high rate of productivity. Urbanized Syria was full of caravan routes plying East-West trade, to and from Iran, India and China. Egypt, however, where state and monarch were identical under the Ptolemies, was the pattern of the standard planned economy and the prototype of future state-capitalism.

Economically independent, Egypt stimulated and exploited the growth of international trade. Almost all departments of its economic life were nationalized. Agriculture was carefully organized to give increased productivity. Industry was a state monopoly. Commerce and merchandise were subject to royal control. In farming particularly, the labour force of the whole population was mobilized—compulsorily, of course. Even the 'free' tenant had to settle his accounts under the eyes of the state official. The manufacturing process was painstakingly supervised at every stage.

A refined and subtle system of taxation made everyone—producer, trader, or consumer—directly or indirectly the object of taxation. Rewards acted as incentives. Private tax collectors, who worked in groups or companies, not only fleeced their victims as they wished (Luke 3.13) but also controlled the levy officials of the state. Not only the victim and the levy officials were power-less; so was the finance minister in the capital. These are the 'tax collectors' generally mentioned in the Gospels in the same breath as 'sinners' (Mark 2.15). In Egypt they were also 'the king's ears'—in other words, his spies, fiscal and political agents combined. They occur too, in the New Testament as 'sycophants'

(Luke 3.14; 19.8), i.e. professional blackmailers. These unscrupulous informers according to contemporary records were so ubiquitous that a 'bird in the air would report the voice of anyone cursing the king in secret'.

The 'commands of the gods and the king' bound the subjects. 'The patient populace were accustomed to obeying and being cudgelled, to being taxed and imprisoned' (Wilamowitz). No wonder, therefore, if the flames of revolt were smouldering beneath the ashes and from time to time set fire to a whole district. The country's new economic structure rested, it is true, on ancient traditions from the time of the Pharaohs, but was mainly a creation of the modern Greek spirit.

Another creation of this same spirit was the Hellenistic banking and credit system. The old credit institutions of Greece were of three kinds, those of the temples, those of the city-state, and private banks. These, like the deposit system, were transformed by an ever-changing economy. Trade also gave an impulse to everything connected with money and brought about a system of exchange based on more abstract principles. The Hellenistic banking trade flourished. Again it was Egypt whose centralization favoured extension and development at a time when the standard of living was rising. Spreading outwards from the state's central bank in Alexandria the whole country was covered with a network of branch banks and sub-offices in towns and villages. Loans and mortgages were guaranteed and transacted; all kinds of exchange deals and transfers of credit were undertaken. This written transaction of bank business was a new development. The system of transferring money from one account to another without the exchange of currency was particularly popular.

Naturally the general economic position differed from country to country. Severe vacillations in the market and the lack of balance in production and sales, supply and demand, were not the most suitable conditions for creating a stable, economic system. Rome was now becoming an increasingly powerful, but uncertain, factor in the world situation. Who could make any certain calculation while this significant unknown quantity in political life could not yet be clearly evaluated? Ultimately Rome's invasion of the East made the Hellenistic 'economic miracle' into an event of world history with an imposing reputation. Business and trade had been constantly injured by local wars of self-interest

between social groups, by strikes and open revolts, by civil wars
and foreign campaigns, by incursions of barbarian tribes from
beyond the border and especially by the scourge of sea piracy.
It was not accidental that later Virgil was to sketch a paradise in
which there was to be no pirate-ridden trade! Only the consolida-
tion of the Roman Empire under Augustus was able to curtail
this extreme anarchy by force. As part of its inheritance Rome
incorporated the economic activity of the Hellenistic world in
its total structure.

6. *Mass Society*

The 'autumn of antiquity' began to bring disintegration in all
walks of life. It is impossible to portray too fully the differences
within the world at that time or to describe its contradictions too
violently. Rulers and ruled, haves and have-nots, bourgeois and
workers, town and country, growing affluence and equally growing
poverty confronted each other at close quarters: Lazarus at the
door of the anonymous rich man (Luke 16.19–31). In between
these extremes innumerable other possibilities were to be found.
The spirit of enterprise and the desire for adventure gave rise
to a period of pioneering. But beneath the flood of colonists and
new settlers was a wide, unchanging river-bed, comprising the
settled population which did not readily accept the new spirit of
reasoning and planning, but stood by the old traditions of their
fathers, sometimes deliberately, sometimes without thinking.

Light and darkness intermingled here, wrapping world, time
and men in twilight. Side by side with selfishness, acquisitiveness
and the thirst for power there was a great deal of philanthropic
activity. Famine and earthquake evoked spontaneous help, which
was not confined by national boundaries and was a sign of a
genuine feeling of human solidarity. The pursuit of culture
constantly alternated with a loathing for civilization, especially
in the upper classes. Critical spirits put their finger on the trouble
spots in society. They tried to get rid of the conventional but false
veneer of civilization. The world became more honest, but also,
in a sense, more cynical.

In private life the institution of the family reflected every
possibility and impossibility of contemporary existence: happy,
healthy, homely contentment and insecure and broken marriages

and families. Women were gaining equality with men both before the law and in society. They could, as I Cor. 7.10 presupposes, institute divorce proceedings. Political activity, too, was open to them, as for instance in Asia Minor. In intellectual circles the emancipation of women was discussed and encouraged. But it was not only the common man who thought of women as nothing more than 'a necessary evil'.

This split-mindedness was particularly evident in the attitude taken towards children. The Hellenistic period was sated with an almost sentimental benevolence towards children, re-echoing with the praises of motherhood. The mystery religions, too, added their voice to the chorus. But in violent contrast to this was the practice of birth control, based on reason, hygienically managed and supported to some extent by medical authorities. The desire for a better standard of living suppressed the desire for children. The Greek Polybius (d.120 BC), who wrote a history of Rome, was already deploring the fall in the birth-rate and the decline in the population. The ancient world's cruel practice of exposing infants to die was still widespread. Even today the poor letter written in rough Greek from the labourer Hilarion in Alexandria to his care-worn wife, Alice, back home in the provinces, who was waiting anxiously for their baby's arrival, is extremely moving. The papyrus, dated 17 June, 1 BC, reads as follows: 'Don't worry if I stay on in Alexandria when the other workmen return. I beg and beseech you to look after the child. And as soon as we receive any money I will send it on to you. [This sentence is ungrammatical in the original.] When you give birth: if it is a boy, let it live; if it is a girl expose it . . .'

How similar is this divided world, with its city civilization, to ours with its speed and carelessness, its anxiety and longing for nature—and its helplessness in the face of almost every important question posed by a growing mass society! All our problems today are related to this, especially the central problem: How can man still remain man in mass society? How can he resist the deadly danger of having his life regimented in an apathetic and callous structure? A structure which threatens to become the world's doom.

The sign and seal of this regimentation of man in the Hellenistic-Roman world is represented by the slave problem. It is true that here and there humane treatment alleviated the position. In Egypt

the slave trade was strictly limited. A royal edict expressly forbade
the enslavement of free persons. Moreover, slaves had the right
to meet together. Their release was facilitated. The differences
which Paul, for instance, in Gal. 3.28 assumes, were being evened
out. Nevertheless, the slave market remained one of the most
important and darkest phenomena in the international trade of
the late Hellenistic world. The general barbarity of the times did
its worst. From the end of the third century BC onwards the
conduct of war, which had never been very humane, became
considerably more brutal. It was not infrequent for the population
of whole cities and districts to be brutally sold into slavery. The
problems of the proletariat—unemployment and falling wages—
were unnoticed by the intellectual free world. The word of the
Stoic Chrysippus (d. *c.* 204) expresses the blank indifference of
the whole epoch and its desire for nothing more than happiness:
'Foolish are those who despise wealth and health, leisure and
every material welfare and refuse to have anything to do with
them.'

Where, in such a world, was freedom? Where was man? The
greatest achievement of the ancient 'modern' was to raise questions
of a similar tendency to those posed by Berthold Brecht:

> Who built seven-gated Thebes?
> The books record the names of kings.
> Did the kings, then, drag the stones?
> And Babylon, destroyed so often—
> Who built it so many times?
> . . . Great Rome
> Is full of triumphal chariots,
> Who constructed them?
> Over whom did the Emperors triumph?
> Did men only live in palaces
> in much-hymned Byzantium?
> Young Alexander conquered India.
> On his own?
> Caesar defeated the men of Gaul.
> Without even the help of a chef?
> Every page a victory.
> Who made the victor's banquet?
> Every ten years a great man.

Who paid his expenses?
So many reports.
So many questions.

Behind these innumerable questions stands one silent question:
When will the day of man dawn?

2

THE THEOCRATIC STATE

1. *The Confessional Church*

UNDER THE PERSIANS: 539–332 BC.

Jesus lived amongst a people who were like a drop in the ocean of the world's nations. Their small strip of land was called 'Palestine' (i.e. the land of the Philistines) by the Romans on the downfall of the Jewish state. Almost every century the land changed rulers in the wars of the great powers.

And yet the beginning of the tragic history of Judaism was attended with great joy. The late prophetic oracle was fulfilled: 'The Lord will have mercy on Jacob and will again choose Israel and restore them to their own land' (Isa. 14.1). Cyrus had permitted the rebuilding of the Temple at Jerusalem. Under his successors the return home from Mesopotamia gained momentum. These first 'Zionists' saw the promises given by God to David wonderfully fulfilled. The dominant mood was no longer one of subdued apathy, 'We have escaped once again,' but one of glowing certainty, 'He has once again chosen us.'

A religious state (theocracy) came into being. The land of Judah was ruled from the rebuilt citadel on Zion. God himself resided in heaven; but he gave audience in the Temple. The theocratic state on earth was ruled by a council of elders. It consisted of twelve ministers, among whom the highest in rank, the Prime Minister so to speak, was the High Priest (Ezra 2.2). The constitution of this theocratic state was 'the law of the God of heaven' (Ezra 7.11). The Secretary of State, Ezra, had brought it back with him from Babylon. This was the document to which the rulers and people solemnly swore allegiance at a great church assembly (Neh. 8–10). Accordingly the new Jewish theocracy was formed on the model of the Babylonian temple-state, with its own forms of community, including its own coinage and soldiers.

Allegiance to the law—Torah—and the protection afforded by it were the chief factors which united all the citizens of the theocratic state. But these same factors also separated them from the non-Jewish inhabitants of the land, the 'Canaanites', and the half-Jewish half-castes, the Samaritans. The Jewish historian, Flavius Josephus (d. at the beginning of the second century AD), who wrote the history of his people while at Rome as the court favourite of the Flavian Emperors, called this arrangement a 'theocracy'. The nation became a church; politics and religion became to all intents and purposes identical.

The world continued to expand and develop, and in their own way after the Persian period the Jews too had experience of this. Objectively speaking, they had been brought for the first time for centuries into a political union with a large empire—no matter whether they lived by the Euphrates or the Nile or in the land of Jordan. The Persian Empire was based on cultural decentralization. It guaranteed its subjects complete cultural autonomy as long as they were loyal. Everyone was allowed to be happy in his own way. The theocracy in Judaea was an obvious sign of this not disinterested tolerance.

This change must have been a liberating force from every point of view. After Solomon's death (935) the united monarchy of Israel in the North and Judah in the South had collapsed. The Assyrians had incorporated the area ruled by the small state of Israel and ultimately Samaria itself in Assyrian provinces (733 and 722). Finally Judah and Jerusalem had been captured by the Babylonians and the upper classes compulsorily deported. Now the Great King of Persia at last put an end to fifty years of missed opportunities. Of course David's empire had not been resurrected, but David's city had.

All this meant a new beginning. New possibilities were waiting to be realized. Yet no one had the courage to take this step forward. The fault did not lie only or primarily with the poverty-stricken country of Judaea and its restricted circumstances, nor even with the obstacles and setbacks of everyday life, which certainly made people tired and disheartened. These extreme limitations could have been borne and overcome if a limited and limiting spirit had not also accompanied them: the spirit of legalism. A new understanding of the Law dominated thought and action. The Law, which was based on very ancient traditions going back even to Moses' time, had stood the test of crises down the years. In fact, it had proved itself a powerful force in great catastrophes. Now it was expected to create a new community—the religious state.

In ancient Israel God's law had not had this meaning. Jehovah, the Lord, alone was responsible for beginning anything. It was only through his gracious call that he had summoned the people of Israel, made the covenant and created the nation. God's covenant established the order of things. Only then—after the making of the covenant and in the context of the covenant—did God's laws and commandments apply. In every way God's law had always presupposed the community. But now in this late period the order was reversed. The Law assumed creative power, even the power to create a church. The worshipping community became a 'confessional church'.

After the exile the Sabbath and circumcision became confessional characteristics. The Law was now regarded as absolute and eternally valid. Historical events wrought by God ceased to be the foundation of the Law and the Law itself became the father of history. For instance, in order to maintain the purity of the community and absolve it from sin, all existing mixed marriages had to be rigorously annulled (Ezra 10.7–44). In a completely *a priori* manner, as if it had fallen from heaven, the Law became the foundation of the theocracy. A dangerous change took place; before, alongside and above God's election, the deeds of men—and indeed of the individual—assumed decisive importance. From now on, however much the movements within Judaism differed, there were two fixed points of reference binding on them all: Temple and Torah, God's House and the Law.

2. *Orthodoxy and Pietism*

Priestly orthodoxy saw in the theocratic state the complete fulfilment of the promises of the prophets. The eschatological hope had been achieved and was thus eventually disposed of. The theocratic state was 'the end of the Law' (cf. Rom. 10.4 for a different view); indeed it meant the last day had already arrived. The 'ecclesiastical history of Jerusalem' with the Law as its basis is described in the work of the Chronicler (I and II Chronicles).

The theocratic state on Zion is the goal of God's journey from creation itself. The Temple and the Law are the goal of history. The theocratic state was the child of legalism.

From the very beginning the establishment of the new relationship of church and state led to tension and conflict. The schismatic Samaritan community, which claimed to possess the older form of the Law, seceded from the very beginning (Ezra 4.1–5). Probably even before Alexander destroyed the Persian Empire, 'the fools who lived at Shechem' (Ecclus. 50.26), 'the sinners who hated the Lord' (II Chron. 19.2), had erected their rival shrine on Mount Gerizim (c. 350–330).

The internal conflicts within Judaism, however, were more important than this schism. The prophets who had directed their gaze to the future with great intensity and had declared God's intervention and judgement in the coming catastrophes, had disappeared (Ps. 74.9); but where to? They were busy once more, in the very centre of the theocratic state which no longer needed them. The history of the prophets had been a history of revivals. Revivals had constantly occurred throughout the country. Moses himself had promised that in time to come the Lord would raise up a prophet like him from among their brothers (Deut. 18.15). And God fulfilled his promise, even in the theocracy of the temple-state. As soon as priestly orthodoxy thought it could confine the prophetic spirit within sacred institutions, it broke free, as Samson did when he was bound. Pietism arose in opposition to orthodoxy. In small groups and larger movements the spirit constantly found expression in speech. At first it did not speak through famous names, but anonymously. Here and there one or two new chapters were added to an earlier prophetic writing as in Isaiah 24–27, Zechariah 12–14, Joel 3.

Isaiah 24–27, a small work of four chapters, was probably originally a small independent prayer-book of the 'Pious', who were dissatisfied with the solution of the theocrats at Jerusalem. The temple-state on Zion was by no means unimportant in their eyes; but it was certainly not everything. It was the prelude to the end, but not the end. It was only provisional, a temporary solution. Consequently they began to look forward to something more permanent, to 'that day' (Isa. 27). That day would see the reunion of the Northern and Southern kingdoms in a single Davidic Empire. But prior to this the world powers would be

c

destroyed. Later generations extended the scope of this expectation:
they saw the whole universe uprooted and involved in the coming
of 'the day'. The whole earth, the whole of mankind would be
summoned to judgement (Isa. 24.1–6). It would no longer be
possible to separate earthly and heavenly events (Isa. 24.23).

> Then the moon will be confounded
> and the sun ashamed.
> For the Lord of hosts will reign
> on Mount Zion and in Jerusalem
> and before his elders he will manifest his glory.

'This' world is no longer separated from 'that', the present
age is no longer separated from the age to come. That 'day' will
be the gateway to a final state of affairs within this world. Yet the
'everlasting covenant' (Isa. 24.5) that has been broken will be
renewed not only for Israel, but for all nations: the Lord will
prepare a feast on Zion, the scene of his royal advent. A new sound
never heard before will be heard (Isa. 25.7–8).

And he will destroy on this mountain the covering that is cast
over all peoples, the veil that is spread over all nations. He will
swallow up death forever, and the Lord God will wipe away
tears from all faces and the reproach of his people he will take
away from all the earth.

The universalistic view of the resurrection of the dead (Isa.
26.19) does not exclude a particularistic and exclusive judgement:
judgement will pass right through the temple-community like a
sharp sword and separate the righteous and the godless—between
those who are looking to the future with faith and those who are
content with material wealth in the present (Isa. 26.7–11).

3. *Early Revelations*

The theocratic state, representing the 'here and now', was
constantly being confronted by the pious and expectant Jews
with the question, 'What do you believe about the "beyond and
hereafter"?' These pious believers gave birth to the new futuristic
view, called 'apocalyptic'. It claimed knowledge of a mystery soon
to be 'revealed'. The origin of apocalyptic is rooted in the old
prophetic spirit. Its form, however, can hardly be understood

without the world of ideas it met through contact with Persian religion. Such borrowings are not infrequent in history; individuals and nations do not pass one another by dumbly. Even if, as often enough, they are divided by walls and hedges, they call out to one another in words which embody varying shades of opinion. Their views and ideas, their language and judgements, exercise a mutual influence. They reject a great deal, they accept a great deal. They learn from others how to express their own contribution better. As today, so then. In the towns and settlements, on the streets and markets of the Empire, it was not only wares that were compared and exchanged. Men of flesh and blood, who talked and thought and learned from one another, met there. Or is only the secular mind supposed to have the power to learn? It is a sign of the vitality of the prophetic tradition that it was able to reinterpret itself when confronted with foreign religions. It utilized Persian ideas particularly. Thus it not only preserved old traditions, but brought them up to date. The prophetic voice was rejuvenated in the words of those who waited for 'the day'.

But the rise of apocalyptic did not only extend men's vision. It also narrowed their vision. The little Isaiah-apocalypse (Isa. 24–27) separated the pious and the sinful. The apocalypse of 'Trito-Zechariah' (Zech. 12–14) makes deliverance and purification to commence over Jerusalem. In fact, 'the spirit of compassion and supplication' is to be poured out on the house of David and the citizens of Jerusalem. But the prophets of hairy mantle together with the unclean spirit are both to be removed from the land 'on that day' (Zech. 13.2–6). God himself will be present in person. Only a remnant, one-third, are to be purged in the judgement of fire. Two-thirds are to be utterly destroyed (Zech. 13.7–9). The faithful who wait for the day hold fast to the temple-cult and the Law. But in contrast to the princes and citizens of the theocratic state they look into the future and understand the present by what they see there.

Finally, the apocalypse (Joel 2.28ff.) added to the small book of Joel attaches a strict condition to the promise that the spirit shall be poured out on 'all Israel': namely, only those who call on the name of Yahweh through the spirit will be saved at the final judgement of the world (Joel 2.32). Restriction of the promise to the revival groups is foreshadowed here. Men were already on the look-out for possible signs of the coming separation which the

Spirit would bring. Can one tell already who belongs to the company of the redeemed? One can at least recognize those who will *not* be saved. Anyone who considers the theocratic state as ultimate is already marked for destruction. Only the person whose actions are determined by futuristic expectation will belong to the true Israel: in other words, only the person whose hopes extend beyond the theocratic state of Jerusalem.

The groups in which the three small 'revelatory' booklets were collected and read spoke of the coming judgement which God himself would execute on his own house (cf. Ezek. 9.6; 1 Peter 4.17). They set themselves in opposition to the theocrats, while remaining loyal to the Temple and Torah. They were able to see beyond the walls of cultic and legal requirements. Wonderful intuitions flashed upon them in these ecstatically stirring collections of oracles. All three apocalypses know that God will act through catastrophe. Two of them, Zechariah and Joel, announce the Spirit as a gift of the last days. But each of the small anonymous apocalypses reserves its special emphasis for expectation about the future which was growing everywhere. Isaiah (26.19) promises the resurrection of the dead. Joel (2.28) declares that the Spirit will be poured out 'on all flesh'. And Zechariah, in connection with the promise of the Spirit, speaks in puzzling language of an unnamed person who will be 'pierced': men will look on him and 'on that day' make great mourning in Jerusalem itself—as the Canaanites make a practice of doing for their dying vegetation-god in the fertile plain of Megiddo (Zech. 12.10–14). Obviously the mourners themselves are responsible for the death. Also they seem willing to repent. The figure of the slain person remains a complete mystery like his precise fate. Is he a martyr? All the evidence, and probability itself, is against this. Some scholars think it possible that the passage refers back to the theme of the suffering servant of God, who removes the sin of the many (Isa. 53). On the other hand, the apocalyptic writer sees new horizons and seems to be contemplating the figure of a coming One who will be the victim of a crime. By mentioning the god Hadad-Rimmon he even touches on the secret of the resurrection of the dead. But he does not state this explicitly; in fact, he actually passes over it.

Jewish apocalyptic is already in these first witnesses—fragmentary, anonymous bridges—pregnant with secrets. There is a flicker of lightning like that of the age to come over a dusky land.

One feels one can see Good Friday and Easter, Whitsun and the Day of Judgement on the distant horizon. But immediately everything is swallowed up in darkness again. Only a rumbling sound as of distant thunder lingers in the ear: 'on that day'.

4. *Exploitation and Despair*

UNDER THE PTOLEMIES: 323–199 BC.

The above glance at the small anonymous oracles of revelation brings us to the Hellenistic period of Judaism, or more precisely, to the period of the Ptolemies of Egypt. It lasts the whole of the third century. Alexander, the 'mighty king' (Dan. 11.3), had crossed Palestine on his path of conquest on two occasions, both close together. In 332 he came from Syria after his victory at Issus and went southward to Egypt along the Mediterranean coast. After a seven-month siege he took the old Phoenician island-fortress of Tyre (Zech. 9.2). By means of modern siege-technique he smashed their brave resistance without mercy. Gaza in the Philistine plain had to endure the same fate for two months. Then the way to Egypt was open. A year later the conqueror, who had been proclaimed God's son in the meantime, marched through Palestine again, this time north-eastwards into the heart of the Persian Empire. His stay in Jerusalem is a myth. There was nothing in the Temple on Zion to attract him. The temple-state lay at that time just off the path of the tornado, but it was quite near enough as it swept by.

At first the theocracy was outwardly unaffected. But the spirit of modernity was not to be halted and soon its pressure was felt. Jerusalem was subjected to chronic Hellenizing tendencies, from Phoenicia and even more so from Egypt. The new spirit of the times was one of cold, calculating reason, the spirit of rational planning. Palestine became the object of the Egyptian planned economy. Here, too, the Ptolemaic system of the revenue monopoly proved itself ideally suited for exploitation. Palestine, chiefly dependent on natural products, fell under the rule of profiteering businessmen. The tax collectors, who now began to practise their mischief, were not harmless revenue officials, who sometimes made their figure into the nearest higher round-number to the disadvantage of their customers, but large-scale gangsters.

The old crown-lands from Solomon's day were the kernel of

the royal domain which stretched from the coast to the Jordan valley and Transjordan. It often changed its political owner and always formed a profitable source of income for whatever treasury it was subject to. The rational business sense of landowners, sheep-breeders, contractors and money-lenders found its eldorado in these domains; the system of farming-out served to make them even more attractive. A certain Zeno united all the above callings in his own person. He was the right-hand man of the Alexandrian Minister of Finance. The prosperity of his flourishing business is still shown today by his voluminous correspondence which has been preserved.

The activity of this man and other managers naturally excited the imagination of writers. Today one would write a comedy or produce a film about them. At that time a fairy-tale-like 'novel', the Tobias-novel, not to be confused with the apocryphal Book of the godfearing Tobit, was composed. The story tells of the scattered sons of a certain Tobias who lived in East Jordan. More precisely, it tells of the son and uncle, and their respective adventures. The son outdoes all the other bidders at an auction of revenue rights in Alexandria. His men blackmail the former tenants by cunning and force. His armed gangs terrorize whole towns and districts. They are related to the High Priest in Jerusalem and they draw him into their cunning speculation. Shylock is a gentleman compared with them. Even if the narrative is often in the style of *The Arabian Nights* and the delight in fiction exaggerates historical traits, the book communicates the character of the period: something like this could have happened. Fragments of more reliable sources point to similar situations. Josephus, to whom we are indebted for the above account, was not simply using the amusing incident to fill in a period for which he had insufficient first-hand evidence.

In the course of the Hellenization of the world the hierarchy of Zion also gradually became more worldly. The unity of 'state' and 'church' already carried the seed of secularization within itself. Law and property, Temple and business were linked together. Soon even the office of the High Priest was a marketable commodity. An unknown voice made itself the spokesman of the silent (Eccles. 4.1; 3.16):

> I saw all the oppressions that are practised under the sun. And behold the tears of the oppressed and they had no one to comfort

them. On the side of their oppressors there was power, and there was no one to comfort them. . . . In the place of justice even there was wickedness, and in the place of righteousness even there was wickedness.

The author of Ecclesiastes, whose words were written at this time, suffered in an even deeper sense under the yoke of existence. The patriarchal world of the cult had been invaded by rational thought a long time before. Many of the ideas associated with the cult had been spiritualized and given a new meaning. Blood-sacrifices had lost sway (Ps. 50.8–15). Moreover a widespread mood of rationalism threatened to undermine faith and to cast doubts on its certainty. For a long time now the fate of the individual had been subjected to the questioning attitude of Job. Had history any meaning? Was it possible to trace the hand of God in what was originally his prime sphere of activity? It had no obvious purpose either 'for good or evil' (Zeph. 1.12).

These difficulties became increasingly more radical in the Hellenistic period. Doubt became more widely corrosive: not doubt in God's existence, but in his readiness to intervene with help in the history of the world and the life of the individual. The belief that God is hidden and incomprehensible brought many serious people to the brink of scepticism and cynicism. A feeling of general uncertainty about life was prevalent. Had God let his plan be wrenched out of his hands? Did it now rest with the all-embracing plans of men? Yet, those who had surrendered to their own reason were the very ones who were overcome by despair. 'All is vanity and a feeding on wind. Everything is full of trouble. Everything makes itself weary. There is nothing new under the sun. All is vanity.' But the man who says this knows that somehow another hand holds him safe, when the abyss of meaninglessness yawns beneath his feet. He is resigned, but he is resigned in the presence of God. Perhaps he is nevertheless seen by God, the God whom he himself can no longer see.

Man declares his own bankruptcy, but he knows he is not qualified to declare the bankruptcy of his God.

5. *Life in Society*

The weariness of the 'Preacher' is balanced by the will to succeed which infuses the Wisdom of Jesus, son of Sirach (Ecclesiasticus). It was not written till the end of the Ptolemaic period, which it sums up. Two generations later ben Sirach's grandson in Alexandria translated it from Hebrew into Greek. Anyone who wants to understand the pious Jew's attitude to the Law in the Hellenistic period ought to read this book. It is moulded by the cult and open to the world at the same time. Here speaks the spirit of those whose connections with the priestly aristocracy of Jerusalem remain unbroken and who are quite devoid of apocalyptic fantasies. We are close to the Zadokites, from whom the Sadducees of the Gospels are descended (Mark 12.18). Temple and Torah are the focal points of this ideal. Cult and ritual are the most important supports in life. The Law, however, is identical with wisdom. It is the source of the river of Paradise. Wisdom itself is eternal. It is like the fullness of the primal ocean (Ecclus. 24.1–29). The fear of God, therefore, is the fulfilment of the Law (19.20).

Consequently, the teacher of wisdom is henceforward the teacher of the Law, or, as he will soon be known, the scribe. Scribal wisdom entered into conversation with the Greek spirit. It began to welcome the idea of education. But it did not surrender the inheritance of the fathers in the process. On the contrary, it sang their praise in the seven chapters of Ecclesiasticus (44–50) which have been called a 'small national epic'. Since the beginning of time the Highest had distinguished them from all other nations by their wisdom. There was a splendid succession from Enoch to Nehemiah, and even to the High Priest of those days, Simon II (*c.* 190 BC).

This view of wisdom tried to establish and maintain a morality that was both illuminating and powerful. Its dominant, basic insight was rationalistic; fulfilment of the Law brings advantage, neglect brings hurt. Good works produce salvation, sin produces disaster. This manual of practical rules for living is, properly understood, something like a religio-moral treatise. It will educate for life in society. It seeks to dispense advice and warnings for every situation in life. It teaches one how to conduct oneself in the family and in public, in the presence of parents and older people, friends and women, men in authority and slaves. It inculcates a readiness to help the poor, hospitality to strangers and even considerateness to the public (7.7). In the spirit of rational orthodoxy and religious rationalism the art of the doctor and the mixtures of the apothecary are recommended along with prayer and sacrifice for times of illness (38.1–15).

All this was sometimes very homely but never monotonous. Lively refrains recur constantly throughout the book. Towards the end the basic theme of 'Now thank we all our God' rings out (50.22–24). But it is clear that reason never leaves piety to stand alone. In fact, the task of religious thought is simply to justify the rational activity of men retrospectively. It is not accidental that the great humanist Erasmus, when attacking Luther, used Ecclus. 15.11–20 to call upon the 'free' man to answer for himself. This is the way religious legalism thinks; it understands 'education' in a Greek way and no longer looks forward to a future. The logic of the hierocratic system has made it irresistible. Man creates and fashions his own future. He 'keeps fidelity and honour even to the grave'.

6. *The Greek Bible: the Septuagint*

The most important cultural event for Judaism of the Egyptian period was a literary one; namely, the translation of the Old Testament from Hebrew into Greek. The story preserved in the *Letter of Aristeas* tells how King Ptolemy II Philadelphus (285–247) had the Torah translated for the library in Alexandria at the request of its director. The High Priest in Jerusalem sent him seventy-two men learned in the Torah and the Torah-scroll for this purpose. These scholars worked in a palace on the island of Pharos—under the sign of the lighthouse—balancing work and leisure in a rational way according to a schedule planned in accordance with the requirements of physical culture. They completed the work seventy-two days from the beginning of their confinement together; hence the name 'Septuagint' ('the Seventy'), abbreviated to LXX (the Latin numeral for 70).

This legendary account was obviously intended to exalt the Jewish Law, the Jerusalem priesthood and Jewish culture. It does this by means of extravagant, vivid anecdotes, though it also gives us an insight into the historical factors of the time and place and result of the translation. It is true that the translation took place in the third century. It is true, moreover, that Alexandria was the birthplace of the Greek Bible; this Egyptian royal city had long sheltered a numerous and spiritually thriving Diaspora. Finally, it is true that the Pentateuch (Genesis to Deuteronomy) was translated first and that different hands participated in the

translation. The motive, however, was hardly the command of a
king but the requirement of the worshipping community, who no
longer understood Hebrew or Aramaic satisfactorily, but only
Greek, as was the case later with the great Alexandrian Jew, Philo,
who was a contemporary of Jesus. Similarly the Hebrew Bible
was as good as useless in missionary work. The admission of
proselytes (cf. Acts 2.11) from Greek-speaking areas, who had
become Jews after being circumcised, necessitated understandable
texts. The Septuagint, therefore, was from the very beginning
the book of the synagogue, which in contrast to the Temple and
its sacrificial worship was used chiefly for preaching and prayer.
It is not accidental that the oldest synagogues have been found
in Egypt, dating from the third century.

In the course of about a hundred years the remaining scriptures
of the Old Testament had all been translated, together with the
'Apocrypha' (literally 'hidden', i.e. unofficial). The order of the
Hebrew Bible—Law, Prophets and Writings (Job, Psalter,
Proverbs, Ecclesiastes, Song of Songs)—was altered in the
Greek Bible to Law, Writings and Prophets. This latter order
still affects the arrangement of modern Bibles.

The Septuagint is more than simply a translation. Quite apart
from the fact that the translation in different books is of very
different quality, it is often a loose translation or a paraphrase.
There are deliberate alterations and explanations. The extent to
which the Greek version made use of an older and better text than
the Hebrew version cannot be discussed here. The most important
fact for us to note is that the spiritual understanding of the Old
Testament message has been radically altered in parts by the
transition from the Hebrew-speaking to the Greek-speaking
world. This is true both of individual ideas and observations and
of the total impression. The climate of its piety seems remarkably
rationalistic and moralistic, in the sense of Jewish legalism. For
instance, the Hebrew expression for expiation means that God
creates and man receives it, but the Greek text permits man to
propitiate God by means of cultic acts. It was not only possible
for the New Testament to link up with these versions in form and
content; it was also necessary for the New Testament constantly
to go beyond them in both respects.

Nevertheless, the synagogue failed to retain this great gift which
was made expressly for it. The Septuagint became the basis of

the Christian Bible in the Christian Church, the source of Christian knowledge and the tool of the early Christian missionaries. As a result it fell into disrepute with the Jews, and Rabbinic Judaism tried to displace it by means of fresh Greek translations (Aquila, Theodotion, Symmachus). In the early Church, on the other hand, it became the mother of translations, particularly in eastern, non-Greek-speaking countries. The older translations into Latin ('Old Latin'), Coptic, Ethiopian, Armenian and Arabic, are its 'daughters'. Thus, the Septuagint became unintentionally the gift of the Hellenistic Diaspora of Judaism to Christianity. But it was the apocryphal writings bequeathed with it that became the piers of the bridge historically linking the 'thousand years' with the 'one day'.

7. *Acute Secularization*

UNDER THE SELEUCIDS: 198–129 BC.

In the year 198 BC the struggle between the Great Powers— the 'King of the North' and the 'King of the South' (Dan. 11)— to gain control of Palestine was resolved. The Syrian Antiochus III (the Great) besieged the army of Pharaoh in the region of the Jordan's source near the holy grotto of Pan—a place called Paneas, later known as Caesarea Philippi (Mark 8.27). Its relation to its new overlord turned out to be friendly at first. The Great King of Syria entered Jerusalem in triumph to the cheers of the masses. His own words in an edict to one of his ministers of state were: 'The Jews showed their zeal for us when we entered their land by giving us a magnificent reception when we rode into the city led by the Sanhedrin; they catered for the soldiers and elephants most royally and helped in the siege of the Egyptian garrison stationed in the citadel.' The victor's generosity was not slow to show itself in favours. The returning evacuees were exempted from taxes for three years and after that were entitled to a thirty-three per cent. reduction. Special privileges were to be granted the theocratic state: help in extending the Temple, constant supplies for sacrificial worship, permanent exemption from taxes for the clergy, the council of elders and the 'scribes,' who are mentioned here for the first time.

Disputes over the succession in the Syrian royal family and the divisions in the temple-state of Jerusalem prevented this dream from being realized. However, the period of goodwill was all too brief. The Hellenization of Jerusalem which had begun in the last century made rapid headway. When Hellenistic cities introduced the modern spirit of sophistication and disintegration here and there throughout the country, the capital could not stand out against chronic secularization any longer. A rationalistic, reformed Judaism arose, which liberalized the upper classes first, especially the priesthood. Whereas the average devout man was still emotionally attached to Egypt, the aristocracy leaned to Syria. The High Priest, Jason, suggested to the king that the right of every Antiochene to take part in Greek sports should be extended to the citizens of Jerusalem. He built a 'gymnasium' (sports stadium) at the foot of David's city.

The Greek spirit exercised a particular attraction upon young people from good families. The *jeunesse dorée* surrendered itself to the follies of fashion. With their broad-brimmed, Greek hats— the sign of 'the free'—they hurried to the sports stadia, where teenagers set the fashion. Even the members of the Temple staff were not impervious to the attraction of things foreign. Priests neglected their altar-service and went off to the arena to practise throwing the discus and to win Greek prizes (II Mac. 4.7–17). The spirit of emancipation must have seized the youth of Jerusalem at that time like a fit of ecstasy. They not only wanted the delights of physical recreation and the joy of participating naked in games and sports—the reason for their disguising the mark of circumcision so far as they could; they wanted to be rid of restriction forever. They wanted to share in the world-wide experience of mankind. 'Let us mix with the nations round about us! For since we have been separated from them we have been overtaken by great misfortune' (I Mac. 1.11–14). These words of the old were echoed by the young people.

This new style of life was accompanied by corruption, of course. The Jason just mentioned received the office of High Priest in 175 BC at a price of 360 talents of silver—perhaps about £120,000. His brother, who was in office at the time, was removed. The king's interference with the 'internal' circumstances of the temple-state was not held against him, however; it was put down to the account of the 'modern' priestly aristocracy, who not only surrendered the principle that the highest office was lifelong, but also encouraged the introduction of foreign blood. The precedent found many followers. No wonder that three years later another interested party, a certain Menelaus—yet another Greek name!—when commissioned by Jason to deliver the taxes to Antioch used the occasion to supplant his master. The king was so pleased with the profit of £100,000 that he deposed Jason and gave the office of High Priest to his clever messenger.

The king of Syria at this time was Antiochus IV, whose nickname was Epiphanes, that is 'the god who appears'. He was the son and second heir of Antiochus the Great, an energetic ruler, but a bad politician, who dug the grave of his own state. The offers of the wealthy Jewish candidates for the office of High Priest aroused the interest of the king in the treasures of the Jerusalem Temple. His wars were costing money. Hence one day in the year 170 he appeared in Jerusalem shortly after one Egyptian campaign and just before another and seized the costly inner fittings of the shrine (I Mac. 1.17–24). He provoked great unrest in the Jewish capital by his massacres and his entry into the Temple (II Mac. 5.11–16). Later writers described the grotesque scene: the king sacrificed a sow on the altar in the open air, sprinkled the sacred scriptures with its blood and compelled the Jews, including the High Priest, to eat its flesh.

At all events, there is no doubt that as a result of the changing world situation a decisive step was taken in 168 towards the liquidation of the Jewish cult. The fluctuating destiny of the Hellenistic monarchs had for a long time stood under the shadow of the growing great power of the West—Rome. With its hands tied by the Third Macedonian War (171–168) Rome at first watched the efforts of the ambitious Seleucids quietly. Antiochus had already occupied the whole of Egypt as far as the capital. Then in the summer of 168 the decisive action was fought at Pydna: Rome was victorious, Macedonia defeated. Rome recovered its freedom to act. The Roman Senate sent a special messenger in haste to Antiochus with an ultimatum that he should immediately and unconditionally evacuate the whole of Egyptian territory including Cyprus and relinquish all his claims to the land. The news of Rome's intervention spread like wildfire throughout the East. Antiochus had to retreat. His authority was dealt an almost fatal blow. Rumour wanted to know whether he was already dead. In Phoenicia and Palestine revolts flared up which threatened to destroy his lines of communication in the rear. This decided the

humiliated king to make a drastic example for all the world to
see. No one would oppose him lightly. The rebels were to be
given a terrifying punishment. Antiochus planned to eradicate
the theocratic state for ever. One sabbath his regiments marched
into Jerusalem murdering and plundering, burning and ravaging;
and the defenceless population was involved in a wild bloodbath.
Oriental savagery gave free rein to every brutality. The walls
were razed and David's palace was to be replaced by a Syrian
citadel.

The most decisive act, however, was the edict that the temple-
cult should be eradicated. Immediately the command rang out:
'One king, one kingdom, one cult'. On pain of death the Jews
were forbidden all that they had regarded sacred from time
immemorial. Innumerable demands were made of them to which
they could not agree under any circumstances unless they were
willing to cease being Jews. All religious services, all sacrifices,
the celebration of the Sabbath, the sign of circumcision, the
possession of the Holy Scriptures (the Old Testament) were
forbidden (I Mac. 1.41–64). The Temple was to honour the name
of Olympian Zeus (II Mac. 6.2).

Every month the birthday of the king was to be celebrated
with a festival and the Jews were to take part in the sacrificial
banquet. A reign of terror compelled the people to take part in
the Dionysian processions with ivy garlands round their heads
(II Mac. 6.7). The whole population had to demonstrate its
active loyalty by taking part in the new cult in town and country.
Every village had its altar at which everyone had to offer sacrifice.
Officials of the king superintended the execution of the decree.
The 'abomination of desolation' (Dan. 9.27; cf. Mark 13.14),
probably the altar of Zeus in Jerusalem, was erected in the Holy
of Holies (I Mac. 1.54). The king's plan seemed to have succeeded.
The new religion prospered, probably because of its appeal to
the people's natural instincts in which ancient Canaanite paganism
still slumbered. Jewish religion was extinguished at a single blow.

The king had miscalculated, however. Large parts of the city
undoubtedly apostatized. In high financial circles and among the
ecclesiastical aristocracy, men were capable of utter disloyalty.
The 'progressive' Antiochene party at Jerusalem had to capitulate;
that was what they had been paid for, long ago. Long before
the match was applied, they had piled up the gunpowder ready

to be lit. When chronic Hellenization was replaced by acute, the explosion took place.

8. *The Peasants' Revolt*

Here and there in country places, however, ancestral family piety was still practised and faith was undiminished. The 'Pious' still offered their apocalyptic prayers. They were conscious of their unity with all whose strength sprang from joy in the Lord (Neh. 8.10). In their country's hour of need, and still more in the hour of persecution for their faith, pious men of all tendencies must have become aware of their identity. Devotion to the Law and the Temple and faith in the eschatological hope made common cause.

It happened like this. In a village in the hills west of Jerusalem there lived a priestly family called, after their ancestor, 'Hasmonaean'. One day the Syrian tax collector appeared and demanded from the peasants the heathen sacrifice prescribed by law. The aged head of the family, Mattathias, refused. When another Jew complied, the old man struck him dead and proceeded to kill the royal official (I Mac. 2.15–28). This was the signal for open revolt.

The 'Pious' flocked to arms. Pietism prepared to give battle. At first, true to the Law, they let themselves be killed by the enemy on the sabbath without resistance. But soon, if a man was attacked, he defended himself, even on the Lord's day (I Mac. 2.29–48). In fact, they even took up weapons to attack if the situation required it. The leader of the revolt was Judas, the third son of Mattathias, who was now dead. He rushed on his prey with a roar like a young lion (I Mac. 3.4). He was given the name 'Maccabaeus'—'hard as a hammer'—and his brothers were called 'the Maccabaeans'. The Maccabaean peasant revolt erupted with elemental force; it was spontaneous and intense. The Syrian shrines throughout the country were destroyed and what began as an improvised local war gradually became a planned full-scale military action. Sudden attacks changed into set battles, partisan groups into armies. Finally, Jerusalem itself was captured. The Temple was ceremonially rededicated in December 165, exactly three years after its desecration by the heathen, and was restored to divine service as before. Both capital and province were securely garrisoned and fortified.

Although Antiochus IV met his death while campaigning against the Parthians in the year 164, the fight for freedom continued. It became a 'holy war', such as ancient Israel had waged a thousand years before against the native inhabitants of Canaan in the time of the Judges. In appearance it was very similar: it was fought without a king and was meant to support a particular form of government. It was a war fought not by professional soldiers, but by a voluntary army of Jewish peasants fighting for God and his Law against Canaanite forms of worship. The resurgence of Canaanite religion was encouraged to a certain extent by the Syrian conqueror, and was, in a sense, the gift made by the East to the Greek world in return for what it had received from Greece. But—a decisive difference—the 'hammerhard' brothers were not charismatic leaders like Gideon or Samson. They did not expect divine miracles, but human intervention. Battle-speeches are to be found in both, of course, but the Maccabaeans did not appeal to the Lord as their only help so much as to human bravery. God no longer stirred their hearts. That 'Jews should make a brave fight' before friend and foe is the primary aim (I Mac. 11.51). Was that the realization of the great watchword of Deuteronomy? It was said there, 'The Lord is one' (Deut. 6.4), and as the one true God he requires the undivided allegiance of the whole nation at one cult centre serving a united Israel. This allegiance was effected by a compulsory unification. Judas and his brothers pushed forward in the north to the Lebanon, and in the south to beyond Hebron; everything lying in between or to the east of Jordan was made a member of the temple-state, both politically and religiously. Gentiles and rebels were to be either exterminated or converted by force.

Thanks to the dynastic quarrels in the Syrian royal family not only religious freedom but also political independence was gained. Judas' brother, Simon (142–135), founded the dynasty of the Hasmonaeans. He was general, prince (ethnarch) and high-priest all in one. Jerusalem was now ruled by priest-kings. They were purely politicians, enlightened despots of Hellenistic stamp like the great sultans round about. They were surrounded with a false aura of divinity. Josephus said of John Hyrcanus (134–104) that God had bestowed on him the three highest gifts of grace: the honoured titles of king, high-priest, and prophet. He was the first man to hold the threefold office. In fact, the Hasmonaeans were ruthless politicians who believed might was right. Their foreign policy was one constant war. They assumed the crown and the title of king. The national coinage was used to glorify their reputation. They flirted, culturally speaking, with Hellenism. Their domestic policy made a reign of terror into a reason of state, and court politics throve on intrigue and the assassination of kith and kin.

The office of high-priest came to an end almost accidentally. On one occasion when 'King' Alexander Jannaeus (103–76), who was hated by the people, was pouring out the usual libation of water while officiating at the altar at the Feast of Booths, the crowd howled and hooted derisively and called him a 'bastard', after which they pelted him with the lemons which really belonged to another part of the ritual of the festival. His reply? At his command the soldiers from Asia Minor are said to have killed 6,000 people. The politico-religious opposition of legalistic piety was only subdued after a civil war lasting six years. And then he exacted terrible vengeance. While he himself feasted with his harem, he had the last 800 rebels who fell into his hands alive nailed to crosses in Jerusalem and their wives and children murdered before their eyes. This produced a mass-exodus in the circles of those who stood nearest to the rebels. It was not until 63 BC that the degenerate dynasty, which had meanwhile worn itself out by fraternal strife, was finally put down by the Roman general Pompey.

A great historical heritage was exhausted. An intellectual and spiritual offering of many generations seemed to have been ignominiously wasted. The sacrifices of those who had died for faith and the Law were in vain; the battle-camp, which had been 'the cradle of the nation' (Wellhausen) in ancient Israel, appeared to be the grave of Judaea. The religious war of the Maccabees had driven out the demons of heathen secularization in order to make room for the seven worse spirits of Jewish secularization. Yet in different ways the dreadful time had brought vigour and clarification. At least two movements which were to shape the future, because they both reckoned with the future, were formed at this time: the brotherhood of the Pharisees and the cell-movement of the apocalyptists.

Both had a vital effect on Jesus of Nazareth and even more so on Saul of Tarsus; and through them they both had an influence

D

on the early Christian Church. It is impossible to understand the New Testament fully without some knowledge of them. The apocalyptists, moreover, have stamped their influence on all succeeding views of history in the West, including the non-Christian West, right up to the present day.

9. *The Brotherhood*

The Jewish historian Josephus, looking back later (AD 75/79), related how ' there are three types of philosophical schools among the Jews: one formed by the Pharisees, another by the Sadducees, and the third by the so-called "Essenes", who live according to specially strict rules'. Of these three sects the Pharisees are the oldest. 'They are noted for their ability to expound the Law, they make everything depend on God and teach that for the most part man has the power to choose between good and evil, but that in every event there is an element of fate. In their view all souls are immortal, but at death only the souls of the righteous are given another body, while those of the wicked receive eternal punishment.' All this is seen through the spectacles of popular Hellenistic philosophy and copiously schematized. The Pharisees do not fit into any 'philosophical' category. Moreover, the three sects cannot be classified simply by asking what attitude they adopted towards 'fate': the Essenes being placed on one extreme as fatalists (believers in fate) and the Sadducees on the other extreme as nihilists (sceptics concerning fate), while the Pharisees, finally, come in between, holding a position which is neither fully deterministic nor yet completely libertarian.

But Josephus is right in saying that the Pharisees emerged in the religious war of the Maccabees and were the oldest group. And the focal points of their thinking and teaching are—if one dehellenizes the formula—the Law of God, the obedience of men and the future of the world. 'Whoever possesses the words of the Law, possesses life in the world to come,' says the 'Sayings of the Fathers' (Pirke Aboth). 'The world's foundations are three: the Law, worship and love in action.' In other words, man exists *between* the Law which has been given and the world which is to come. For the Pharisee piety means living between yesterday and tomorrow in a genuine fulfilled present. This 'interim' character gave them from the very beginning a special place within the

Jewish theocracy. They stood for the law of the fathers which linked them with the aristocratic, priestly orthodoxy of the Sadducees and separated them from all the enthusiasts who were at home in the apocalyptic groups. On the other hand, they talked of the world to come; this separated them from the hierarchy, for whom the future was already fully present and could be experienced in the worship of the Temple, and linked them with the apocalyptists' hope. This same interim character was responsible for the twofold judgement of outsiders. The priests inevitably regarded them as progressive, while apocalyptists thought they were reactionary.

The old temple-state, which began to disintegrate as the crisis gradually built up, was the home of the Pious long before the Syrian oppression. They were not a 'movement' or 'sect', but simply the people of God who were spiritually alive set in the midst of a civilization that was becoming worldly. They saw how modern views forced their way into the religious community and destroyed ancient beliefs. They were conscious of the gulf between the faithful and the ungodly, which expressed itself in the rift between God and the world. They were named quite simply 'the Pious': people who were really in earnest about God. Their name in Hebrew was *Hasidim*, in Greek *Hasidaioi*. This is the same word basically as that denoted by 'Hasidism', which refers to that movement of religious enthusiasts in the fiercely persecuted Eastern Judaism of the eighteenth century. Its author, Baal-Shem-Tob, was the exact contemporary of Zinzendorf (both 1700–1740). Martin Buber has given the modern world a very penetrating and sensitive interpretation of this Hasidism. But the *Hasidim* of the third century BC did not have their enthusiastic and almost mystical fervour. They were still undifferentiated inwardly and still stood, so to speak, on this side of the great decisions, by which history was going to mould their appearance. The related Aramaic word for 'Pious' leads, when translated into Greek, to the term 'Essene'. Thus, the one term conceals quite different groups at this early period. The one thing that unites them is opposition to the secular leader of the theocratic state and the expectation of intervention by God in the future. Indirectly, the early apocalyptists also belonged to them.

When the time came, the Pious supported the Maccabaean revolt (I Mac. 2.42). But some of them continued to oppose the priests (cf. I Mac. 7.13). These people were later called *Perushim* by their opponents (in Greek *Pharisaioi*—the 'separated'). The name probably does not refer to political separation. It is true that they supported the Hasmonaeans and other pious activists from an early period. They were resolutely opposed to every attempt to gain worldly power with all its consequent cunning and lying. They looked to God's intervention for liberation from the miseries of the time, not to the actions of politicians and statesmen. Their alliance with those in power fell to the ground, therefore, as soon as the ostensible object of the religious war was achieved. In fact, it turned into bitter enmity. Alexander Jannaeus persecuted the Pharisees. It was only on his deathbed that he advised his wife Alexandra to make a reconciliation with them— for reasons of political shrewdness: if one wanted the support of the masses one had to be on good terms with the Pharisees, for they were a powerful moral force in the community and at that time had a majority in the Sanhedrin. Nevertheless, it was not for the foregoing political reasons that they were called 'the separated', but because of their basic attitude to the 'world'. They rejected the Hellenistic collaborators of rank and education, for whom the Law retained its traditional validity, just as much as the *Am-ha-arez*, literally the 'people of the land', and so the masses (John 7.49), the people who, apart from their social position, were strangers to the Law and wanted to have nothing to do with it.

The Pharisees styled themselves *ḥabirim*, i.e. 'companions' or 'members of a fellowship'. Their alliance was not an order, still less a sect, but a brotherhood or association. Although it consisted of enrolled members who were subject to certain rules, it remained a 'movement' rather than 'a union'. Ecclesiastically it was a lay movement, like the German *Kirchentag*, predominantly middle-class, but with upper-class and well-to-do people also belonging to it (cf. Mark 12.40; Luke 16.14). Their religion cost them something and they were prepared to make sacrifices (Matt. 6.2). If we might adopt Zinzendorf's well-known dictum, 'they decreed there could be no Judaism without fellowship'.

We are accustomed to seeing the Pharisees as almost exclusively wicked figures. But not even the words of the Pharisee in the parable in Luke 18.11–12 were recorded with the insinuation that they were to be despised. The expression 'hypocrite', etymologically 'play-actor' (as in Matt. 6.2, 5, 16), does not refer to subjective experience, attempting to deceive, but to the objective fact that the life which men think they can live on the basis of tradition alone is constantly discordant and at loggerheads with itself. Before we listen to the 'Woes!' of Jesus concerning the 'hypocrites' (Matt. 23.13) we must take notice of the earnestness of these men.

The Pharisees' intention was to form a repentance-movement. They wanted to restore twice over in good works what God's people had withheld from him through their wickedness and ingratitude. The Pharisees interpreted their life as a permanent state of repentance. Their aim was not a liturgical, isolated, or sabbatical Judaism, but an active, workaday Judaism. They really intended to be 'Jews in earnest'. Their true home was not the Temple, but the synagogue. Moral decision rather than cultic sacrifice was the true manner of their service of God. What could not be expressed in action had no value for them.

Of course, their piety was based on the Law; but not the Law which was a pious survival—as in the case of the Sadducees— and which fostered a good conscience of apparent orthodoxy. In the face of both conservative custom and modern indifference the Pharisees appealed to existential reality. The Law was no past greatness for them. It was to be put into practice; it was to be realized in the present. It was to challenge men to decision here and now. It was to be obeyed and implemented. For the Pharisees it was a matter of disciplined 'exercises in Judaism'.

In order that the Law of a former period—the time of Moses— could be used at the present day, it had to be interpreted and brought up to date. In case of doubt the decisive factor was not the literal interpretation of the Law but its main trend or under- lying meaning. Tradition proved the greatest help in this. Originally oral, it sought to develop the significance of the written Law for the present, and to bring the life of modern man in to subjection to the ancient will of God. In course of time ex- planations of the Law were fixed in writing and then brought together in collections. These are the additions or 'traditions of the elders' of which Mark 7.13 speaks. They were concerned with the concrete expression of reverence for God and love of one's neighbour in life. At the same time they acted as a hedge to protect the garden of the Law. No Law, no code of behaviour. No code of behaviour meant the end of morality. Hence the strict enforcement of the Sabbath rest, praying, fasting, and almsgiving. Hence, too, ritual washings, for the world is evil and impure. The old ideal emerged again: 'a kingdom of priests, a holy nation', a people separated from the unclean world by God (Ex. 19.6). These words made strict demands. The vocation of the priest entailed daily ritual washings. Ritual purification and obedience to the Law went together.

This ideal was common to many movements within Judaism. Methods of realizing it, however, differed widely. The brotherhood of the Pharisees had given it a meaning which was serious, practical and popular at the same time. Their interpretation of the Law sought to make it possible for everyone of good will to fulfil it. Some of the limitations and weaknesses of this attempt are revealed for us by Jesus. Here it is sufficient to recognize the historical roots of this popular and homely moral teaching and to understand what caused it as well as its aims. The outstanding characteristic of Pharisaism should be clear. It lay in the conviction that God's will, as laid down in the Law, concerns the whole of Israel. Indeed it ultimately concerns the whole world. The whole world and all mankind rest on the hidden foundation of the Law. This was the reason for the Pharisees' desire to proselytize (Matt. 23.15). The Pharisees showed great concern over Judaism's public image. They proclaimed a 'century of Judaism'.

10. *Apocalyptic: the Meaning of History*

The Maccabaean period saw not only the formation of the Pharisees' brotherhood but also the emergence of apocalyptic circles from the darkness of anonymity. It should be added, of course, that they did not come right out into the open, but remained in the half-shadows of pseudonymity. Their first literary composition of any size was the Book of Daniel. It became an immediate classic, 'a book of world literature' both in style and content. It still vibrates with the fresh experience of the Syrian persecution under Antiochus. It makes use of older material and is written by an unknown figure under the pseudonym of a Jewish seer, 'Daniel', who was supposed to have lived at the court of the King of Babylon about 540. Probably the book was published shortly before the death of Antiochus IV, about the end of the year 165/4.

Daniel, a man—or a group?—possessed by the prophetic spirit, understands the meaning of this period of persecution as the meaning of all history. Individual facts and connections may be artificial, events pictured in the code of flashing images may be legendary and exaggerated, and the dream-vision may appear overburdened with mythology, but judged by later apocalypses the fantasy of Daniel is moderate, restrained and sober.

In fact it is an extremely important book in at least three respects. Firstly, the concept of world-history comes to birth in Daniel and for the first time is developed in a significant way. Nebuchadnezzar's dream (Dan. 2) and Daniel's vision (Dan. 7) are the clearest expressions of this theme which is touched on several times. With the help of the idea, borrowed from Persia, of four kingdoms succeeding one another it was stated that history is never an isolated, individual affair directed by men, but a unity in which God is at work. World-history is based on God's eternal plan. The aim of this plan is already determining the trend towards universal judgement.

Secondly, world-history is a conflict between the passing powers of this world and the eternal kingdoms of the Most High. The stone falls from above 'without any intervention by the hand of man', smashes the colossal statue which is made up of various materials and fills the whole earth like a great rock (Dan. 2.34)— God's heavenly kingdom. The eternal kingdom that appears on the clouds of heaven is represented by the Man. Its appearance is the signal for the judgement of the four beasts of prey (Dan. 7.13–27). The kingdom of God judges not only the empires of the world, but also supersedes the theocratic state.

Finally, the riddle of world-history is 'the Man' (often translated 'Son of Man'). Who is the Man? Is he an individual? The seer himself? Or a community of saints? The apocalyptists as a group? To whom is 'might, honour and power' (Dan. 7.14; cf. 7.27) given? The Man is, at any rate, no longer an earthly power, but a force from beyond. So much so, in fact, that it is stated more than once that he comes down from heaven. The whole drama is played out 'in heaven'.

It is impossible to understand world-history without paying attention to its three zones, 'beginning, middle and end'. Three motives are at work in it: God's eternal plan is its source; the temporal conflict between human and divine power extends over its course; and God's eternal kingdom is its destination.

The apocalypse of Daniel employs other media than those which stem from the thought and imagery of the people of God. It uses ideas that come from outside, from the religion of the Persian Zarathustra, and to some extent also from Babylonian religion. In this category comes the concept of the four ages of the world; likewise the idea of the resurrection of the dead which is linked with that of the Judgement, and the idea of the heavenly 'Man'. But the seer does not work in a Persian or Babylonian spirit; his is the old prophetic spirit. He does not view history mythically as a concatenation of supernatural events. He sees it historically. When he employs mythological pictures and ideas, he is referring to real, earthly, historical events. Persons, events, places, dates and contexts which today are the subject of historical confirmation can be traced in his book even down to individual details. But it is precisely as secular events that they are the expression of God's power.

This new view of history—for a 'view' is certainly involved—signifies a development of the prophetic appeal to history. Scholars have established three definite differences. Firstly, the prophets see God as Creator and Lord of history and as substantially involved in the world. The apocalyptists see God and the world not as partners but as rivals and opponents. The phrases 'monistic' and 'dualistic' express the difference in another way, but are not a precise description. Secondly, the prophets expect the consummation of history, whereas the apocalyptists reckon with its replacement by a totally new world. Thirdly, for the prophets judgement takes place within the coming history: it can be altered by those who repent, and in fact, those who are backsliders can be restored. According to the apocalyptists judgement takes place once and for all: it is unrepeatable, irrevocable and unalterable like death. Judgement, from the apocalyptic point of view, is linked with a definite terminus—the 'day', which can be calculated in calendar days.

11. *Apocalyptic: the Goal of History*

This brings us to a basic and decisive aspect of apocalyptic: history can be calculated and described. It can be realized and 'objectivized'. The wise man can make himself master of it. The understanding of history together with much else is aided by its division into periods. The knowledge and study of history are learned and practised in the circles of the initiated. Apocalyptic knowledge is secret knowledge. Only chosen ones like the seer in ecstasy may share in it. He may see now what is to happen 'in the near future' (cf. Luke 18.8; Rom. 16.20; Rev. 1.1). Now this basic knowledge—like everything of consequence—is an ambiguous gift to mankind. On the one hand it is a product of the general rationalism of 'modern man' in late antiquity. The fact that apocalyptic literature emerged from the study is a feature it shares with all literature. But it was also thought out in the study. Its *Sitz im Leben* is the scribal group. It is a typical product of pious reflection. To what extent a living experience lies behind it, we do not know. At any rate, we should not imagine the apocalyptists as drunken enthusiasts. They were thrilled and enraptured by their study of the scrolls of the Torah, no doubt. When they began to meditate on the Law, the Writings and the Prophets, spiritual illuminations may have been granted them. But these divine insights were then transformed into holy wisdom.

Thus its revelatory writings fully conform to the times, for this is the period of Hellenism and Judaism, the period of reason and the Law together. The dating of the end of time in the context of salvation-history is just as much a child of the times as the comprehensive catalogue of the state-library of Alexandria; or the globe of heaven and the map of the world which scholars had succeeded in producing for the first time; or the economic textbook with its statistics of revenues and the history book with its tables of chronology; or the land register of the Ptolemaic tax officials, the tax register of the auditors, the statement of accounts issued by credit and deposit banks, and not least the horoscope given by the court astrologer for the ruler and his courtiers. The dazzling growth of the 'Chaldaean art' was, however surprising, one of the characteristics of the Hellenistic age. Alexandria, Jerusalem and Rome were bound together by more than geographical proximity in an age of numbers and measurement.

On the other hand, apocalyptic enriched and deepened the prophets' understanding of history. It extended the horizon of history from that of a nation to that of the whole world and all peoples (universal history). It was concerned to bring the cosmos in all its dimensions, from heaven to hell, into its field of vision. In so doing it satisfied not only the interest of the spectator, but also challenged those who were involved to a decision of the utmost importance. Its reference to the secret of the 'Man' linked the problem of history closely with the problem of man. After Daniel world-history was specifically concerned with the 'Man'; humanity became its subject. Apocalyptic encouraged knowledge of human existence and sharpened the sense of historicity. To live historically was to live responsibly.

The Christian world has taken over this understanding of history which was given its distinctive content in the New Testament. The historical consciousness of the West, from Augustine to Hegel and beyond to our own day, has been largely due to the impulse of sublime apocalyptic. Recent historical knowledge bears the stamp of its thought-forms; it has preserved the outlines of what was at that time a new style of question, while subjecting it to a critical and methodical examination. The secularized world, even in the decisive rejection of the Christian 'canonized fable', which since Voltaire it has been customary to indulge in every few years, lives, though unwillingly and heedlessly, by the truth of that history which activates faith. Today we are in a better position than ever before to appreciate that the Jewish apocalyptists were the historians of late antiquity. And conversely, present-day historians are the modern apocalyptists.

Jesus himself and the circles from which he came most probably lived in the climate of apocalyptic piety. He himself shared many basic beliefs with them. But he also differed from them, no less and no less strongly than from the Pharisees. We must take a brief look, therefore, at other forms of apocalyptic.

12. *Apocalyptic: the Revival Group*

The Book of Daniel was only a beginning. It was the expression of a much more extensive and complicated world of apocalyptic piety. Amidst the oppression and persecutions of the Maccabaean and Hasmonaean period the question of what meaning could be attached to the suffering of the present time would not be silenced. When would a better future dawn? In answering this question they had recourse to many traditions, which were of very different origin and value. Babylonian and Persian wisdom, Egyptian and Greek knowledge were in turn combined and interwoven with the basic tradition of Jewish prophecy.

Even before the Romans entered Palestine (63 BC), a collection
of scrolls which had been composed at different times over the
last hundred years had been made and formed into a composite
whole. It was given out as the revelation of the seventh father of
the human race and named 'Enoch' after him. The number of
Enoch's years corresponded to the 365 days of the sun's year. It
was known from the first book of the Old Testament that Enoch
had secret communion with God during his lifetime. But the most
unusual thing about Enoch was his departure from the world:
'and then he was no more because God had taken him' (Gen.
5.18–24). Enoch had not died. He had not experienced death. He
ascended to God like a man going from a lower to a higher room
with the help of another. Later generations saw in Enoch 'a miracle
of the knowledge of God for all time' (Ecclus. 44.16); he was even
regarded as the discoverer of all knowledge, mathematics, astronomy, writing and other secret skills. The ancient ancestor became
the interpreter of the present and the seer of the future. Contemporary history and mythology are both reflected in the pages of
this strange 'book'. The Book of Enoch is neither a prayer-book
like Isaiah 24–27, nor a manifesto like Daniel, but a learned
text-book for pious souls who thirst after universal esoteric
knowledge. Its readers would not only be instructed intellectually,
of course. They would be warned, comforted and censured in
the midst of this wicked, sinful world. They would receive
guidance as to what they should do. Their ancestor who had been
carried off to God describes his experience in dream-visions and
fantastic pictures. He is able to reveal what he has seen in the hidden
world of God—the history of the theocratic state from Adam to
the Messiah which is the history of salvation and of the world
combined. History appears divided into four periods once more.
It is described in wild, chaotic allegories. The heroes of theocratic
history are like domestic animals, the ancestors like bulls, and
their descendants like sheep. The Gentiles are sometimes compared
to birds and beasts of prey, the heavenly 'genii' of their earthly
host are like shepherds, the fallen angels like stars, the faithful
angels like men. God, the 'God of the whole world', appears as
'Lord of the sheep'. Finally, the Messiah enters as a white
buffalo.

All these and other peculiarities would have nothing but anti-
quarian interest for us today if it were not for the fact that the

'Man' of the Book of Daniel reappears here and in view of the coming events plays a role of special importance. This apocalyptic figure appears in the context of the judgement of the world once more. God's wrath rests on the 'flesh of men'—till the 'Day' of the second Flood and Judgement. The Flood will come, but a remnant will be left. The nations will attack Jerusalem, but the crater of the kingdom of the dead will swallow them. The scattered citizens of the theocratic state will be brought home from every corner of the earth. Then the 'Man' will appear. The 'Man' already exists but is concealed in heaven. He is, in fact, pre-existent (i.e. older than the world); 'before the sun and the zodiac were created, before the stars of heaven were made, his name was known to the Lord of spirits'. This 'Man' is being kept in heaven at this moment as judge over the rulers of the world. On 'that day' he who is hidden will be revealed together with those who belong to him, who likewise are living with the 'Lord of spirits' at this moment.

There are three points to notice. Firstly, the 'Man' is here identified with the 'Messiah'; a man anointed king by God is at the same time a being of divine nature who shall judge the world. He is the world's judge.

Secondly, this judge, who is, incidentally, called 'the righteous', is the Chosen One who is not to be separated from the Chosen Ones. He and his own belong together: they are both pre-existent and both concealed in the heavenly world. They are both revealed together. According to God's command those who belong to the 'Man' are to share with him in all his sufferings.

Thirdly, and most strangely, the Messiah-Man is Enoch himself! He is carried off to heaven and installed as the 'Man'. He is born for righteousness, and peace is promised him by God in the name of the world to come.

When will all this take place? Or rather, when will all this be revealed? For in heaven it is all already 'there'. When, then, will it be 'here'? The answer is: 'On that day', the day of judgement and deliverance, the day of resurrection, the 'day of the Man' (see Luke 17.30). Apocalyptic thought is not static and its statements fluctuate. It is constantly changing, seeking to draw new ideas into its vortex and develop them. Even the way the figure of the deliverer is conceived varies within a single group of statements. But one thing remains unaltered: attention to 'the day of his coming'. It becomes increasingly clear this 'day' will be the day of God and the day of Man and the day of the world combined—otherwise it will not take place.

The world of Jewish piety has many facets. There are differences and tensions between the morality of the Pharisaic brotherhood and the mysticism of the apocalyptic group. Even within these groups there must have been schisms and sects. But all these tensions are based on one great unity. This unity is the source and essence of the principle that understanding leads to piety and piety to understanding. What has been said by one scholar about the Book of Daniel applies to both wisdom and piety, as well as to the movement of the 'Pious' from which they sprang; the Pious, Pharisees and apocalyptists alike, make preparations for 'ideological resistance', 'the moral revival of Israel'. Their refusal to take up arms is deliberate and on principle. For they expect everything from God. Only the intensity with which they wait for God's wonderful revelation varies.

3

ROME: THE WORLD-EMPIRE

1. *The Vassal State*

AT THE END of the sixth century BC the Jewish temple-state
was rebuilt with Persian permission (520–510). The event occurred
in the bright light of world-history. In central Italy—about the
same time according to tradition—the then insignificant city-state
of Rome broke away from Etruscan rule. Rome proceeded to assert
itself as a republic in a number of long-drawn-out crises, both
internal and external. As a result of unsparing exertion in the
Punic Wars it gained control of the western Mediterranean.
Hannibal, the Carthaginian, after making the West smart under
modern Hellenistic strategy and tactics, fled to Syria to Antiochus
the Great. The internal crisis of Hellenistic civilization prepared
the way for the might of Rome. Force fought and triumphed over
superior fighting technique.

Imperialism in the East and its virtual failure left Rome to
inherit an empire which it had not striven for and which it only
accepted with hesitation. Mommsen rightly believed that 'Rome's
dominion of the world does not at all appear as a great plan
conceived and executed because of an insatiable desire for land,
but as something which thrust itself upon Rome unasked for and
even against Rome's will'. Fortunately, one might add. For the
victory of Rome prevented the complete disappearance of
Hellenism in Orientalism.

As is well known the 'pacification' of the world took place
under the prudent, calculating Augustus. And at first the price
which those involved had to pay in advance for the future good
fortune of their grandchildren seemed terribly high. No nation
was exactly delighted with the *Pax Romana*.

The shadow of Rome had lain for a long time over international
events in the East, particularly over the victories and dynastic

changes of the Seleucids and finally over the downfall of the kingdom of Syria (129 BC). Now Rome set foot on the soil of 'the land of the Philistines'. After a bitter resistance of three months Pompey broke down the entrance to the fortress of Jerusalem with his siege-machines. He entered the Temple and even the Holy of Holies with his men. But he was no Seleucid, and on the next day worship and sacrifice were restored to normal as if nothing had happened. Palestine became part of the Roman province of Syria. The theocratic state of Israel was reduced to Judaea, East Jordan and Galilee. The state of the Hasmonaeans ceased to exist as a political entity. The last descendants of the ruling house officiated as high-priests in the Temple.

Only an adventurer by the name of Antipater, a former governor in Idumaea, the south of which was formerly known as Edom, outdid his high-priestly lord as vizier of the Temple by winning the favour of the Great Caesar. The protection had to be paid for; his sons were employed in the north and south as 'generals'. The younger of the two, Herod, 'the scion of heroes', purged the hill country of rebellious Galilee of armed insurgents. In spite of strong protests and action on the part of the Sanhedrin, which in normal times would have cost him his head, he carried out his policy of martial law in all its brutality. With one eye on a future successor he got engaged to the princess Mariamne from the Hasmonaean house. In due course he married her. In 40 BC through the mediation of Mark Antony he received the promise of the Roman Senate that he should be called King of the Jews. First of all, however, he had to fight for his kingdom with the help of the Romans; this took three long years. In the year 37 BC the last bastion, Jerusalem, fell. The troops of his Roman allies behaved so badly in the city that Herod had to beg them to leave with innumerable fair speeches and presents. By means of constant vigilance and adaptability Herod succeeded in fitting in with all the twists and turns of Rome's frequently changing domestic and foreign policy. After the battle of Actium (31 BC) he hastened to declare his loyalty to Octavian, the future Augustus, the deadly enemy of his former lord. Consequently he was confirmed afresh in his kingdom with the addition of the crown-lands which Antony had given Cleopatra and which the queen, who was as ambitious as she was business-like, had farmed out in conformity with the custom of the times. These crown-lands included the

profitable coastal cities, the fertile borders of Galilee and the
rich oasis of Jericho with its palm and balsam plantations and
salt and asphalt mining-rights. Apart from certain territory by
the Dead Sea and the Jordan valley that was under foreign rule
the new kingdom was as extensive as David's empire and stretched
right up to the gates of Damascus in the north-east.

It was towards the end of Herod's long reign (40/37–4 BC)
that Jesus was born (Matt. 2.1; Luke 1.5).

2. *The Despot*

There are three things to be said about Herod's rule.

Firstly, he was a despot who did not trust anyone. He established
his rule by brute force. Palace intrigues kept him almost constantly
on tenterhooks. Political and religious opponents were unscrupu-
lously liquidated. His brother-in-law, Aristobulus, whom he had
made high-priest at the age of seventeen, was the first to go, when
he threatened to become too popular with the people. After a
gay party in the castle at Jericho his comrades went diving with
him in the park; the game went on until he was drowned. He was
followed by the second and most loved of Herod's ten wives.
Herod was never able to forget her murder as long as he lived.
Her two sons and her mother were put to death soon afterwards.
Even as he lay on his death-bed Herod ordered the crown prince
Antipater to be executed. Even the Hasmonaeans had never gone
in for murder on such a scale. The demon of deep distrust poisoned
everything and prevented him seeing anything but ghosts.

The people, too, had to suffer under him. Josephus tells us:
'Herod kept the strictest watch over all his subjects and used all
possible means to prevent them expressing their dissatisfaction
with his regime. He forbade all gatherings of citizens, public as
well as private, and set his spies everywhere. If anyone was caught
infringing these orders he was severely punished. Many people
were taken, openly or secretly, to the fortress Hyrcania and
executed there. Everywhere, town and country alike, there were
men whose task it was to keep a check on all meetings. In fact,
it was said the king himself, dressed as an ordinary citizen, often
mixed with the crowd at night in order to acquaint himself with
what people thought about his rule. Most of his subjects submitted
to his commands, partly from real agreement, partly from fear.

But whoever persisted in resisting obstinately and could not put up with his crimes was ruthlessly set aside.'

But the same Josephus praises Herod as an outstanding soldier, general and politician, an expert archer and a skilled sportsman, a daring rider and an enthusiastic hunter, and above all a genial, pleasant companion. Like all great men his character had two sides to it—he was a child of fortune, who terrified and at the same time fascinated his contemporaries. Certainly he possessed a most interesting personality from many points of view; even when he was quite old he took lessons in rhetoric and philosophy.

It goes without saying that a Hellenistic prince in Roman times who made claims for himself had to be a patron of the arts and sciences. Accordingly he invited eminent men of Greek education to his court. The lawyer, Ptolemy, was his chancellor; his brother, Nicodemus of Damascus, philosopher and natural scientist, relied on extensively by Josephus, was his historian.

3. *The Patron of the Arts*

This brings us to the second point about Herod. He was very modern in his ways. At the same time he tried to be a benevolent father-figure in the Hellenistic-Roman style, not just to play at being one. His people ought to be able to live in peace and safety. They ought to lead good, happy lives. The citadel in the capital, called Antonia after Mark Antony, served to protect every citizen In the borderlands on the edge of the desert which were exposed to Arab invasions security was provided by forts. An army composed of Thracians, Gauls and Germans was permanently on the alert. By means of extensive building activity Herod altered the face of Jerusalem and of the whole country. The Temple and citadel were rebuilt and extended at lavish cost, the foundations were sunk nearly 150 feet deep and a new palace built. Not only buildings in the capital but whole cities were named after famous Romans. Samaria was rebuilt and called 'Sebaste'—the Greek word for Augusta. Strato's Tower on the coast was renamed Caesarea after Caesar. Both names necessitated the building of temples to Augustus for the celebration of Emperor-worship— a practice which began in the East and spread to Rome later. Jerusalem, Jericho and Caesarea each had their theatres, amphi- theatres and racecourses: Caesarea also had a harbour nearly

E

200 feet wide, with a mole nearly 120 feet deep. Its amphitheatre
was opened in the year 10 BC with gladiator shows and animal
contests. The oval arena, which measured about 100 by 65 yards,
exceeded even the Colosseum at Rome which was constructed
ninety years later. In memory of his mother Herod built a
luxurious country-seat with the advice of Italian architects.

His modern outlook and his international culture were impres-
sively attested in three continents. 'When he had completed
his great building works at home he showed royal generosity to a
number of cities abroad. He supplied Tripolis, Damascus and
Ptolemais (Acco) with gymnasia; Byblos (Gebal) with a city wall;
Berytus (Beirut) and Tyre with arcades, halls, temples and market
places; Sidon and Damascus with theatres; the port of Laodicea
(cf. Col. 2.1) with an aqueduct; Askalon (his birthplace) with
splendid baths and fountains, as well as colonnades of admirable
proportions and workmanship. To other cities he presented woods
and meadows' (Josephus).

Although he himself used to live a respectable life there were,
of course, attached to his court, following the fashion of the Roman
Orient, eunuchs and boy-prostitutes, libertines, and favourites who
had the resounding official title of 'friend' (cf. John 19.12).

4. *The Defender of World-Judaism*

Finally, Herod wanted to be a Jew in spite of his acceptance
of Greek civilization, He was not ashamed of his overtures
towards Greece and Rome, not even of the protection which he
afforded to the state-cult. Yet, at the same time, he was conscious
of being the defender of world-Judaism. It was part of his responsibility, he felt, as a modern Jewish king. Wherever fellow
countrymen or co-religionists suffered religious or legal oppression
for any reason at all, he espoused the cause of the oppressed. And
when he did so he knew how to use all his authority with skill
and energy. Under certain circumstances he did this even with
his superiors, but in this case without success.

His extensive building activity was meant to advance the welfare
of his people. It was one of his chief aims to raise the economic
and social conditions of the Jews. By his building programme the
king created employment for the labourer. It meant hard work,
of course—and Herod loved a cast-iron discipline where work

was concerned—but the labourers also had their reward. It is true that luxurious practices at court swallowed enormous sums of money, which had been raised for the most part in taxes. But taxes fluctuated within limits which on the whole were observed by other despots of that time. Planned colonization resulted in a prosperous civilization and stimulated trade and commerce.

The general political calm also favoured the Jews' internal economy. Temple and temple-state helped to restore each other to a certain extent. Jerusalem became a great place of pilgrimage once more. Its foreign trade, stimulated by the cult, stretched over the whole of the then known world, as can be proved. At the time of the great festivals the number of pilgrims vastly exceeded the number of inhabitants. The visitors brought money into the country. This was a considerable material advantage, added to which was the religious consideration that Jerusalem and its cult formed the religious tie which held world-Judaism together.

Herod had a deep concern for both these things—for the protection of Jews abroad and for the welfare of Jews in Palestine. The poor harvests of 24 and 23 BC had brought Palestine to the brink of famine. Herod was able to counter the catastrophe by decisive steps. His measures have been described as models of organizational and social concern. Nor was he afraid to make personal sacrifices. No one will blame him for granting tax relief to the discontented populace in order to guarantee the stability of his own rule. It was possible to trace his powerful hand everywhere. He even clamped down on the menace of the bandits, thus giving the citizen a feeling of personal and legal security.

Nevertheless, the energetic king found no real support for what he did either among the priestly hierarchy or the 'Pious' who maintained every religious observance. How was he to find it among the ordinary people, who hardly thought beyond the daily routine! It is doubtful whether he was an Edomite, as Josephus suggests. His father was governor of Idumaea, which makes it unlikely that he was a native of the country. In autocratic states it was the custom not to put natives of a country in positions of trust there, except in special circumstances. Herod's mother, on the other hand, was probably the daughter of an Arab sheik. If the Jews really did call him 'the Idumaean slave', they were probably referring less to his parentage than to the fact that he was not equal in birth to the Hasmonaeans. He was an upstart and behaved as such. He was hated not so much because he was not a pure-blooded Jew, as because he was a quisling of the highest order. He was a fellow conspirator of the oppressors against Jewish freedom. It was really Rome that guaranteed his political existence. It guarateed the vassal-state, which meant in practice his reign of terror and despotic ways, which were incompatible with the theocratic state. His almost demonic cunning and his incalculability were simply loathed by both the pious and the rational Jew.

Wellhausen has given us a memorable picture of Herod's character. 'He was one of those Orientals whose very instinct is to rule. His morality was politics. Every crime demanded by political interest he committed deliberately. He had no idea that he might be blamed for self-preservation; he was surprised at the hatred he incurred and was embittered by the ingratitude he encountered. If his crimes seemed necessary to him he had a perfectly clear conscience about them; he never thought himself wrong. One cannot accuse him of spiteful cruelty. He was not a cruel tyrant by nature but a man of deep feeling, passionate and desirous of affection. Love of family and friend constituted an outstanding feature of his nature; he showed this curiously enough by the way he esteemed his brothers and sisters more highly than his wife and child.

He has been compared with David. But David lived within a period and an environment that were suited to his ways. Herod was not born to rule the Jews in the age of Augustus, to be an ape of civilization and at the same time to accommodate himself to the Pharisees. He was a boar in the vineyard of the Lord, but had to act as its guardian. He himself made his unusually difficult position worse by his marriage alliance with the Hasmonaeans. This was the greatest folly of his life; on this he foundered.

His kingdom had nothing durable about it, but the picture of his personality, which stands out so decisively against the background, sticks in the memory because of its dazzling colours. He has become the typical tyrant, the exact opposite of the child born at Bethlehem.'

5. *Jesus*

Jesus was not—as the poet Schiller says of himself—'born in Arcady', but in Palestine, the Palestine of Herod the Great. At his birth Nature made no promises of joy. No music of pastoral pipes for him. The shepherds mentioned by Luke were not musicians but men with a call in their hearts and a prayer on their lips, men with ears ready to listen. It is true that according to the third Gospel a company of the heavenly host sang praises to God at his birth (Luke 2.13):

> Glory belongs to God in the highest
> And on earth grace is given to his people.

But the song was sung in heaven while the noise of weapons still clashed on earth. And 'peace', that is, the 'health of the world', was promised to the chosen, not to the sick king in Jericho trying to cure his intestinal cancer. The world of Jesus is not romantic but highly realistic. Matthias Claudius captures the reality of that hour:

> God views events divinely,
> And worldly pomp's rejected.
> Herod and all his host
> Are robbed of all their boast,
> And shepherds on the hillside
> Are His elected.

We note here a very simple fact: Jesus was a historical person, like Herod and Augustus. He lived at a definite time and in a definite place, and is not to be confused with other men.

Jesus really lived. Whether one welcomes the fact or regrets it, his existence is one of the indubitable facts of history.

The historicity of Jesus, however, has been repeatedly contested since the end of the eighteenth century. In October 1808 Napoleon stayed in Weimar on a visit. The Emperor held a conversation with Wieland about Christianity. In the course of this conversation the high-ranking guest whispered in the Privy Councellor's ear that it was really a big question whether Jesus ever lived. The aged satirist smiled: 'I am well aware, your Majesty, that there are fools who doubt it, but it seems to me as foolish as doubting whether Julius Caesar lived or whether your Majesty is alive.' The Emperor was probably referring to the works of the Frenchmen, Dupuis (d. 1809) and Volney (d. 1820). Dupuis propounded in detail in three bulky volumes the theory that Jesus was a mythical figure, the product of astral speculation, in other words the personification of the sun. The course of the sun through the

constellations of the zodiac, brought down from heaven to earth
as it were, has been remodelled as the life of an ostensibly
'historical man' in this world. Volney advocated the same thesis
in three pages, in the form of a fantastic vision which he experienced
in the ruins of Palmyra. In the account of his journey which
contains this vision he attributes a decisive role to the 'Virgin'—
the constellation Virgo—and ingenuously exposes all Christian
doctrine as a clerical fraud.

Later (1844), the theologian Bruno Bauer, especially in his book
Christ and the Caesars (1877), saw in Jesus a personification of
Stoic ideas. At the beginning of the present century the Bremer
pastor, Albrecht Kalthoff, tried to understand Christianity from
a 'social-theological point of view' and to explain Jesus as the
product of a communistic Christian 'people's movement'. This
economic theory was carried over into the study of the primitive
Church: apocalyptic Judaism, a proletarian movement, furnished
growing Christianity with its thought-forms and drive. 'Thus
the Christian faith took the Messianic hope for the future to the
organized masses; its emphasis on the future captivated the hearts
of all who were sick of the past or perplexed about the present.'
About the same time the English writer, J. M. Robertson, and
the American mathematician and philosopher, Smith, tried to derive
the Gospels, partly mythologically, partly symbolically, from a
pre-Christian Jesus-cult going back to the patriarchs. The
Marburg Semitist, Jensen, wanted to understand Paul as well as
Jesus—not to mention the men of the Old Testament—as figures
of saga pure and simple, derived from the early Babylonian epic
of Gilgamesh. The culmination of all these efforts is to be found
in the writings of Arthur Drews, who for twenty years resolutely
preached a monistic pantheism. In the name of 'reason' his
'philosophy' rejected history in general and the historicity of
Jesus in particular. He ended where the French had begun with
their fantasies over a hundred years before: with astral mythology.

Absurd though all these hypotheses are, and undeserving of a
rational refutation, yet they express a genuine and original discovery in a bizarre form. The actual question which moved him
to write is put most clearly by Smith: 'Is it conceivable that a
single individual could have been the cause of such a large and
rapidly spreading religious movement?' Purely rationalistic
religion is unwilling to recognize that the person of Jesus of

Nazareth, is, historically at least, incontestable, because this would disrupt, it is said, the means we have at our disposal for understanding history. At the bottom of this dispute concerning the historicity of Jesus is the question of faith, concealed in the garb of historical scepticism. Worldliness recognizes, to adapt a word of Nietzsche, that 'if Jesus existed, how can I bear to exist? Therefore, Jesus did not exist'. The Christian believer will not be content, it is true, simply to affirm the historical existence of Jesus. Even if the denial of the historicity of Jesus is the sign of false belief, yet its affirmation as such is no proof of true faith.

In the course of our discussion it will become increasingly clear why this is so. For the moment it must be sufficient to vary the well-known words of James (2.19): 'You believe that Jesus of Nazareth lived. You do well; but even the devils believe it— and tremble.' The Reformed confessions of faith say quite plainly that 'historical belief *alone* does not save'. Saving faith perceives a conversation in history and becomes involved in it. Presently we shall have to consider the whole of the New Testament and ask whether it reveals a history which involves us in a conversation. And if it does, what is it saying to us? What do we perceive in this conversation? What do we understand from the history of Jesus which the New Testament transmits?

6. *Non-Christian Sources*

Before we consult the New Testament we must ask once more whether the historicity of Jesus is attested outside the New Testament, in non-Christian sources in other words. The answer is yes *and* no!

Firstly, then, affirmative evidence. The historicity of Jesus is nowhere doubted, either among ancient historians or Jewish writers. The Roman historian, Tacitus, makes the following remarks in his *Annals*, Book XV (written after AD 110), in connection with the persecution of Christians instigated by Nero in Rome in AD 64: in order to divert the suspicion of fire-raising from himself the Emperor placed the blame on others and subjected them to special torture. 'These people were hated for their abominations and given the name of "Christians" by the populace. Christus, from whom their name derived, was executed at the hands of the procurator Pontius Pilate in the reign of

Tiberius. Checked for the moment, this pernicious superstition broke out again, not only in Judaea, the source of the evil, but even in Rome, that receptacle for everything that is sordid and degrading from every quarter of the globe.'

A little later Suetonius in his biography of the Emperor Claudius (ch. 25.4) wrote as follows: 'He (Claudius) expelled the Jews from Rome because they were continually making disturbances at the instigation of Chrestus (*sic*).' Neither of these Roman writers knows very much about Jesus. They obviously considered 'Christ' a proper name. Suetonius either misheard or copied down a word already misheard and saw in 'Chrestus' a Jew living in Rome. The actual expulsion, which took place in AD 49–50, is also referred to in Acts 18.2: the Jewish Christian tentmaker, Aquila, with his wife, Priscilla (= Prisca), came from Rome to Corinth at this time, where they met Paul who was also a tentmaker (cf. Rom. 16.3–4). Tacitus seems to play on the word 'Christian': in view of their crimes the populace called them 'the honoured ones' (*Chrēstiani*). But these very facts give unmistakable historical colouring to the reports of these two historians. To know how reports stemming from fantasy or serving a particular bias appear, one must compare the above with the insertion in the text of Josephus (see below). Neither Tacitus nor Suetonius speaks of 'Jesus', but simply of 'Christ'. What else should a Roman who looked down on the Jews know about the Jewish 'sect'! The educated Roman's lack of interest in what was going on in an obscure corner of the province of Syria is a sign of the authenticity of the recorded incident. The events are still so near that they are only registered; their historical significance cannot be evaluated till later. Yet the nearness is more obvious than real; there is no remoteness—but there is no close involvement. It so happened, a religious enthusiast was put to death. Even the name of the Roman official who conducted the trial is known. But history on the grand scale passes over it—at least for the time being—and proceeds with the chronicle of events.

The Jewish historian, Flavius Josephus, also knows of the historical existence of Jesus. He mentions Jesus in his *Antiquities* XX 9.1 (written about AD 90): it is only an incidental reference, it is true, but he gives Jesus his correct name. The high-priest 'called together the Sanhedrin and brought before them the brother of Jesus, the so-called Christ, James by name, together with some others, and accused them of violating the law, and condemned them to be stoned.' This execution of James the brother of Jesus in AD 62 is not to be confused with that of James the son of Zebedee, the disciple of Jesus, by Herod Agrippa in AD 44 (cf. Acts 12.2). Josephus separates himself from Jesus and the early Church by the phrase 'the so-called Christ': for him Jesus is not the Messiah.

The authenticity of this passage is proved by other passages in the same work. 'About this time arose Jesus, a man of great wisdom, if one may call him a man. He performed quite unbelievable deeds and was the teacher of those who willingly received the truth. In this way he drew to himself many both of the Jews and of the Gentiles. He was the Christ, and when Pilate, on the indictment of our leading men, had condemned him to death on the cross, those who had loved him at the first still remained faithful to him, for he appeared to them alive again on the third day, as the prophets sent by God had foretold along with thousands of other wonderful things about him. And even to this day the race of Christians, who are named after him, has not died out' (XVIII 3.3). It does not need too attentive an ear to perceive that the syncretistic Jew, Josephus, cannot possibly have written all that. It comes from a Christian pen and is a later addition, much later in fact. It is all somewhat florid, as in late legend. Both form and content betray it. It is a clumsy insertion and represents poor apologetic.

Finally, we have a reference to Jesus of Nazareth, 'Jeshu-ha-Nozri', in the Talmud, the official source of orthodox Judaism after Christ. The most important passage reads as follows: 'On the eve of the Passover Jeshu-ha-Nozri was hanged, and a herald went before him (?) 40 days crying, "He is to be taken away and stoned because he has practised magic and treachery and has seduced Israel. If any one knows any justification for him let him come and declare it." But none was found and so he was hanged on the eve of the Passover.' The passage as it stands is obviously very late. Fantasy has contributed a great deal towards obscuring accurate recollection. But through the haze of exuberant tradition the outlines of a historical figure can be traced.

Jewish legend has also added other features, which pass over into fiction, to the picture of Jesus. Jesus is supposed to have been the son of a certain Panthera (originally a nickname of his father Joseph? or his grandfather?). But for polemical reasons the Babylonian Talmud makes Panthera a Roman soldier and the lover of Mary. In popular German religion of the Nazi period the slanderous reference to Mary's adultery had to help to maintain the fiction of Jesus' Aryan lineage! According to other passages in the Talmud Jesus is supposed to have had five disciples.

All this is poor tradition. It assumes that the name of the arch-heretic was avoided if possible. Because people did not want to know anything about Jesus, they finally knew only absurd things or—absolutely nothing. But the comparatively small value of this tradition which aimed to bury Jesus in absolute silence shows how impossible it was for Talmudic Judaism to dispute his existence. In fact, it forms a powerful piece of non-Christian evidence for his historical existence. Incidentally, does not our present incompetence to deal with the historical Jesus point the same way?

The last piece of Jewish evidence to be cited for the historicity of Jesus is a passage of the chief Jewish prayer. In the twelfth of the Eighteen Benedictions (at least in additions to the Palestinian text) Christians as well as Rome are cursed on account of Jesus. The following is the petition addressed to God: 'For the renegades let there be no hope, and may the arrogant kingdom (= Rome) soon be rooted out in our days, and the Nazarenes and *minim* (=false teachers) perish as in a moment. May they be blotted out from the book of life and not inscribed with the righteous. Blessed art thou, O Lord, who humblest the arrogant!' This prayer was prayed three times each day by the faithful. We may hope that these times are long past, but even today orthodox Judaism preserves an awareness of this knowledge of the historicity of Jesus.

7. *Faith and History*

Judaism's knowledge of Jesus is, in fact, greater than all that can be gleaned from disinterested historical enquiry: more than Tacitus, and Suetonius and even Jesus' fellow countryman Josephus. For all these writers who display nothing more than a historical knowledge of Jesus fail as witnesses to the real historicity of Jesus, primarily because they know little or nothing about the actual history of Jesus. They are content to state the fact 'that' he lived, and nothing more. They know nothing of the 'what' and the 'how'. But even if this historical knowledge had been far more extensive they would probably not have perceived in this history the conversation which takes place in all history.

This history can, indeed, only be understood from the standpoint of faith as the first Christians understood it, or from the standpoint of unbelief as with the Jews and those who made the decision to contest its historicity. To understand it one must accept or reject it. No third way—to postpone a decision, for instance—is possible.

The question of the historical Jesus, therefore, brings us back ultimately to the New Testament. Even from a historical point of view the writings of the New Testament are the only 'sources' worth serious consideration. This is especially true of Paul's letters; their source-value in the whole field of ancient literature is outstanding. It is also true, however, of the Gospels, although they were not written by eye-witnesses in every respect and most certainly not by Jesus. The reliability of these documents is not lessened but strengthened by the fact that they were written by believers, for in this case love and hate open the eyes, while the indifference of the neutral observer produces blindness. The value of the sources and the degree of their reliability in individual items has to be proved case by case, of course. But critical scholarship has confirmed the long-standing and well-founded judgement that 'no other tradition in the whole history of the world has been examined with such care and been tested from so many sides as that of Jesus; how quickly the figure of Socrates could be removed from history by the method of Drews!' and 'no book of the ancient world has come down to us in manuscripts so old, so numerous and so relatively harmonious as the Gospels and the Epistles of Paul!' The fact that both scholars—Heinrich Weinel and Martin Dibelius—conclude their statements with exclamation-marks, which are only inserted on rare occasions in scholarly treatises, denotes the absolutely fundamental character of their verdict and the facts which support it.

8. *Gospel and Legend*

We shall try to make clear the limits of historical reporting in the New Testament by means of one example, which is representative of many others and which we shall discuss briefly. The example chosen is the tradition of Jesus' birthplace.

Jesus was not born in Jerusalem or Nazareth but in Bethlehem. So much at least we are told by the Gospels according to Matthew and Luke. These reports have been doubted for some years by modern scholars. The birth stories come from a relatively late period. They show strong traces of legendary embellishment. They stand in contrast to the statements of the rest of the Gospels, to which they were later attached as a sort of introduction. They are not only at variance with each other, but are also internally inconsistent. None of this can be honestly disputed. Moreover, what is true of all the Gospels is true of the birth stories also. They do not set out to be historical reports or precise records, but rather to invoke faith, not faith in a place, of course, but faith in a person.

The birthplace as such cannot be the basis of Christian faith: at most it is a sign. Neither Mark nor Paul gives even the name of Jesus' birthplace, let alone makes it a condition of faith. According to John 7.40–44 the Jews argue about the place of Jesus' origin. 'Some said, "This is the Messiah." But others said, "Is the Messiah to come from Galilee? Has not the scripture said that the Messiah is descended from David, and comes from Bethlehem, the village where David was?" So there was a division among the people over him.' This dispute was obviously not geographical, however, but theological. The Galilaean origin conflicts with the Messianic prophecy in Micah 5. This is how the problem appeared in the period after Christ. The original Hebrew text did not have the name of Bethlehem at all. It spoke of the small 'house of Ephraim', the tribe from which the second David was to come. The prophet Micah is not interested in any birthplace. In mysterious, oracular tones he declares that the origins of the Messiah lie in primaeval time. As 'Primordial Man' he will unite creation and redemption and bring the beginning of time to completion in the end of time in accordance with God's plan of salvation. Nor does Bethlehem seem to have played a decisive role otherwise in pre-Christian teaching about the Messiah within Judaism; if it played any part at all it was purely symbolic. The fourth Gospel perhaps desires to criticize a one-sided Jewish-Christian view of the Messiah, which regarded Jesus simply as the Davidic King. Exponents of such a group would be people like Nathanael, who is represented as asking the question: 'Can anything good come out of Nazareth?' (John 1.46).

Matthew 2 and Luke 2 reply in unison that Jesus was born in Bethlehem, the city 'of David', five miles south of Jerusalem, in the hill country of Judaea. But they immediately contradict each other over the question of where his parents lived. According to Matthew his parents lived originally in Bethlehem. As a result of changes in the political situation they were driven to Galilee after a detour via Egypt. There is no mention of a Roman census. They settled in Nazareth by God's guidance, because they were afraid of Archelaus, the successor of Herod the Great (Matt. 2.22). According to Luke, on the other hand, his parents already lived in Nazareth. They only came to Bethlehem temporarily as a result of the imperial edict about registration when Quirinius was governor in Syria.

If the narratives are understood as historical reports, they are mutually exclusive. Historically, only one can be right: Either—Or. Any attempt at harmonization would clash with the wording and the sense of each passage. But they do not set out to be understood as precise historical references. They aim to state something about *the person* of Jesus by means of the reference to place and circumstances. Again they differ. Matthew is saying that Jesus is the king who brings salvation, appointed by God for Israel. His birthplace is his herald; he comes as David's son for David's people from David's city. Luke, on the other hand, wants to convey that Jesus is the Saviour of the world. He comes from Galilee. But he does not come from the circle of the Galilaean patriots, who were driven to revolt against Rome by the Roman edict about registration. At the time of the edict a Galilaean by the name of Judas raised the standard of revolt and set in motion a mass-movement, but was killed in battle (Acts 5.37). The underground-movement against the Romans had formed itself into the Zealot-party, as we learn from Josephus. Jesus' parents, however, obeyed the edict of the Emperor, who was politically the ruler of the world in which the gospel was to make its way. The child of Bethlehem does not separate himself from the world. This is God's will.

The legendary character of the two traditions inevitably raises the question of the historical kernel, without which no legend usually begins. This kernel consists in the fact that the birthplace is called Bethlehem. The different reasons given for the event and the incompatible statements about where Jesus' parents lived heighten the probability of this. That the question of Jesus' birthplace—a secondary question for us—should only be discussed after his birth, also tells in favour of Bethlehem. Not one of the innumerable Messianic pretenders claimed to come from Bethlehem. The wilderness or the Mount of Olives or the Jordan or a miracle or simply the demands of the hour were frequently used to authenticate a man's mission, but never a birth certificate from Bethlehem.

9. *Chronology*

If a man rejects the conclusion of the above discussion, this does not mean he is an unbeliever, any more than he becomes a believer by holding the view that Bethlehem is Jesus' birthplace. In fact, even the devils can accept these verdicts (James 2.19). But there is no reason to draw the wrong conclusion and think that, because the Gospels do not set out to be historical sources, therefore they cannot be. It is true that the narratives of the New Testament have no interest in enriching our knowledge of the past. They seek to awaken faith, not to mediate historical knowledge. Nevertheless, in spite of their strict purpose, they do provide plenty of valuable historical knowledge. They are historical sources as well as documents of faith.

That they have this character only in a very limited sense, as far as details go, supports their overall reliability. Once again let us take the account of Jesus' birth as a typical example. To ask when Jesus was born sounds natural enough. The answer sounds equally natural: in the year 0. For it is from this year that we reckon dates both backwards and forwards: 'Before Christ' and 'In the year of our Lord'. Herod the Great, however died in 4 BC. If the report that Jesus was born in Herod's reign is historically correct, then at the latest Jesus must have been born four years before he was born! But this would be more than paradoxical; it would be absolute nonsense. Of course the New Testament is not responsible for the oddity; it is the work of a learned chronologist who lived five hundred years after Jesus. This was the Roman abbot, Dionysius Exiguus. About AD 525 he fixed the birth of Jesus on 25 December, 753 years after the founding of the city of Rome. The 754th year then became year 1 of the new era. But in doing this he was five full years out in his calculation. For Herod died in the year 749, reckoning from the foundation of Rome. Jesus, therefore, was born in the last years of the tyrant's life, probably between 7 and 4 BC according to our reckoning.

The date of the registration, which according to Luke 2.2 took place while Quirinius was governor, is less easy to dispose of. It could not have taken place while Herod was alive and the country was independent; furthermore, Quirinius was not in charge of Syria while Herod was alive. Even if it stretched over a period of 14 years (from 7 BC to AD 7) it could not have taken place in Judaea before 4 BC. Luke is probably thinking of the action of AD 6/7 mentioned by Josephus, because in that year the Galilaean revolt broke out (cf. Acts 5.37).

With regard to the story of the Magi and the star of Bethlehem (Matt. 2.2), it is probably wisest not to become involved in calculations based on astronomy, even if eminent astronomers from the days of Kepler (1606) to the present day have calculated that the constellations of Jupiter, Venus and Saturn were in the sign of the Fish for the year 7 BC. Matt. 2.9 has nothing to do with stars converging, it describes the emergence of a single hitherto unknown and miraculous star. The point of the legend is lost if it is later turned into history or astronomy for 'pious' reasons. If one does this, the story loses its point; it can no longer affirm that the event of the child's birth was totally incalculable. Only if the event was impossible to calculate can the message of the gospel be heard: the laws of heaven have lost their spell to bind. The heavenly child is born. The stars surrender their rights to another.

10. *Genealogy and Ancestry*

The different emphases in the message of Matthew and Luke can be seen particularly clearly in the two genealogical tables in Matt. 1.1–17 and Luke 3.23–38, where Jesus is linked with a series of ancestors. The differences are as clear as noonday in every respect. Matthew opens his Gospel and thereby the whole life-story of Jesus that he wishes to relate with a genealogical tree; Luke attaches his list of ancestors to the story of the baptism and thus places it at the beginning of the public ministry of Jesus. Matthew begins the genealogy with Abraham and proceeds in three epochs of 14 generations each to the child Jesus; a total

of 42 generations. Luke begins with Jesus at the age of 30 and
works backward to Adam and God. 77 individuals are named
and they are divided into 4 periods; 21 from Jesus to the exile,
21 from the exile to Nathan, 14 from David to Isaac, and 21 from
Abraham to Adam. In both outlines the number 7 (2×7 and
3×7)—the key to apocalyptic thought about a world-week—
figures prominently.

In content the two tables are completely different. They cannot
be compared or connected genealogically, not even if one proposes
—as Luther did, for instance—to find Joseph's genealogy in
Matthew and Mary's ancestry in Luke.

One thing is clear: they both aim in their different ways to
link the thousand years with the one day. They have no historical
purpose, however; their aim is to declare a message. Yet the
emphasis of their message is different, too. Each evangelist wishes
to stress and say something different.

Matthew declares that Israel's Anointed comes from Israel
and for Israel. But Israel's need is for victory over sin. It is
not Sarah, Rebekah and Rachel, the ancestral mothers of Israel
honoured by the Rabbis, who are typical of Israel, but the great
sinners, adulteresses and whores like Tamar (Gen. 38), Rahab
(Josh. 2), Bathsheba (II Sam. 11 and 12) and the foreigner, Ruth
from Moab. It is not the merits but the sins of the royal ancestral
mothers that weigh upon the child who is born to the immaculate
mother. From the beginning, therefore, by the question of origin
alone God declared Jesus' solidarity with sinners. The genealogical
tree of Matthew is like the key of a melody. To leave it out of
account results in wrong notes being played and heard. The story
of Jesus cannot be understood without the Old Testament. Anyone
who tries to do so must fail. Matthew protests loudly against every
tendency to isolate Jesus from the history of Israel. His 'proof from
prophecy', now heard distinctly for the first time, has a profound
theological and historical significance: namely, to show that God
always rules by electing. In the war against the faithlessness and
obstinacy of one particular nation God brings the history of the
nations to its intended conclusion.

In contrast to Matthew's particularism Luke speaks the language
of universalism from the beginning: David's and Abraham's son
is also Adam's child. Not only the patriarchs of Israel but the
very first fathers of all mankind are included in Jesus' history.

Noah, the restorer of civilization after the flood; Enoch, who was taken up by God; Seth, the 'offspring' replacing Abel whom Cain murdered; and finally, or rather originally, Adam, through whose sins death became king in the world. Adam is the archetype of the Fall, but he is also the archetype of mankind's oneness. Jesus, therefore, is Adam's son who by his obedience overthrows the regime of death (Rom. 5.12–17); he is the 'last Adam' who gives life to all, the 'second man from heaven' who overcomes the degeneration of the world with immortality (I Cor. 15.45–57). In him dawns the kingdom of the 'Man' (Dan. 7), the man who is 'the son of God' (Luke 3.38). The theme of Luke is 'Jesus, the Saviour of the world'. The great joy will be shared by all people (Luke 2.10). The whole world will be taken into his service.

11. *The Great Silence*

The New Testament has a different interest in Jesus from ours. We are interested in every possible detail of his life: his birth, his youth, his education—in short, how he became what he was. The Gospels are less interested in the questions of where, when and how he was born. Their primary interest is to convey the news that he has been born and that he has been born for men. A man of flesh and blood, a man belonging to a definite time and place, appeared; no disembodied phantom, as Gnostics in late antiquity thought; no idea enshrined in human form, as speculative philosophy imagined; no personified myth, as some modern theologians have suggested. 'The word became flesh' (John 1.14). A man appeared, 'born of a woman and subject to the Law' (Gal. 4.4). How this worked out in concrete terms is described by Luke (2.21): he was circumcised on the eighth day, like every other Jewish child, and given a name which was as common in those days as any name popular today. He was called Jesus. In the light of the birth-narratives the whole of Jesus' youth seems wrapped in darkness. Only Luke tells how he once went up to the Feast of the Passover in Jerusalem with his parents (Luke 2.41–52). He was twelve years old at the time, in accordance with the practice of those days, which considered a boy of thirteen ready to undertake the obligations of the Law and the cult. In the confusion caused by so many troops of pilgrims Jesus got separated from his parents. This well-known story is difficult to reconcile

F

more fully. It ought not to be filled out by means of unreal medita-
tions on what was possibly happening *to* him and *in* him at this
time. He who spoke when his hour had come will not permit
himself to be interrogated about everything that happened within
him at this time of silence. When the lightning strikes, it is
irrelevant to ask how it grew into such a concentrated ball of
energy. It is enough simply to know Jesus is alive and already
in the world.

12. *Divide and Rule*

While Jesus was silent the Roman and Jewish world, the modern
world, was at work. With the death of Herod the Great the Jewish
kingdom was dissolved permanently. Augustus showed no desire
to promise the crown and title to Herod's successor. In any case,
the father's heritage was divided, in accordance with his will, into
three unequal parts. The principle *divide et impera*—divide and
rule—scarcely needed to be used by Rome in this case. Things
arranged themselves automatically.

Archelaus resided in Jerusalem as 'ruling prince'—ethnarch—
over Judaea and Idumaea and Samaria. His brother, Herod
Antipas, was in charge of Galilee and Peraea (East Jordan), while
his brother Philip ruled over the northern and north-eastern
regions beyond Lake Gennesaret, towards the borders of Damascus
and the Lebanon. Both were styled 'minor princes' (tetrarchs).
Philip died in AD 34, after thirty years of tolerant rule.

Herod Antipas, who is called simply Herod in the New Testament, was Jesus' provincial governor. He lived by the Lake in
the newly built Hellenistic capital of Tiberias, named in honour
of the second Emperor. He was described by Jesus on one
occasion as a fox—or jackal (Luke 13.32). He seduced the wife
of his half-brother and had John the Baptist, who told him to
repent for what he had done, put to death (Mark 6.17–29). His
first father-in-law, an Arabian king from Damascus, took revenge
for the insult to his daughter by initiating a successful war of
revenge. The Emperor Caligula finally removed the ambitious
prince in AD 39 and banished him to Lyons.

Archelaus' rule was the shortest of all. He had the whole
Herodian family and all the people against him. Many people
felt the hour had come to restore the theocratic state. The Pharisees
scented Messianism in the air. There were frequently armed

tumults in the Temple. Meanwhile guerilla forces came to life again in the country. Fanatical armed insurgents and their leaders made a great stir. Everything was topsy-turvy everywhere. Finally, Rome stepped in. The Syrian governor Publius Quintilius Varus (6-4 BC)—the same officer who was heavily defeated and lost his life thirteen years later in the Teutoburger Forest—remembered that as the Imperial legate he did not embody the military force of Rome in his sword and general's insignia for nothing. He returned from Antioch with two legions by forced marches. He was joined by Arabian auxiliaries, whose chiefs did not want to let the opportunity for booty pass. Galilee was thoroughly purged of partisans, Samaria was overrun, and Jerusalem captured. Varus ordered the pursuit of the survivors who had not yet capitulated or had fled into the country districts. Eight thousand who were caught were crucified alive. All this, which took place in 4 BC, was not calculated to make either the Romans or their puppet Archelaus more popular. Jewish delegations, among them some who belonged to his own family, went to Rome and demanded the removal of the 'ruling Prince'. Finally in AD 6 the aging Augustus yielded to pressure and banished him to Vienne on the Rhone.

The pretence at monarchy was finally brought to an end. A special garrison-statute was issued for Judaea and Samaria. The district was given a Roman military administration and relegated to a procuratorship. Procurators, i.e. specially authorized men, were installed in provinces whose cultural peculiarities required an elastic, unbureaucratic but at the same time vigorous treatment. The most important task of these special governors was financial administration. It was for these reasons that the Emperor, to whom these districts were directly responsible, chose his procurators from the equestrian order, i.e. from the moneyed class. Naturally they possessed supreme judicial power and presided over the penal court of justice; they were also in command of the armed forces. The headquarters were situated in Caesarea. The new imperial city became the garrison of the legion whose cohorts were spread throughout the country. One of these cohorts formed the occupying force of the citadel of Jerusalem. The procurator only came to the Jewish capital on the occasions of the festivals in order to preserve the public peace with a strengthened military force. One of this line of procurators was the notoriously greedy and brutal equestrian, Pontius Pilate (Luke 13.1). He exploited the country for ten whole years (AD 26–36). That his name was linked with the death of Jesus was known even by Greek and Roman historians; in fact, they only mention his name in connection with the name of Jesus.

13. *The Caste*

While there is still nothing to be heard of Jesus, the leaders of the theocracy and the Pious were active in every direction. Their groups assumed an increasingly sharper profile. We shall set them in juxtaposition on this occasion.

Firstly, then, there are the Sadducees. They take their name from Zadok (LXX Saddōk), the leading priest at the court of David (II Sam. 15) and after Solomon's victory the chief priest in Jerusalem (I Kings 1.32). He evidently became the founder of a priestly dynasty—the Zadokites. It is from these that the later Sadducees were descended. Another tradition connected them with a former Pharisee, Sadok, who founded the Zealot party in AD 6/7 along with Judas, the Galilaean rebel leader.

Their historical lineage is thus very complicated. But, at any rate, they seem to have been closely connected with the priestly aristocracy, without losing their link with eschatologically-orientated messianic circles. During part of the reign of the Hasmonaeans they fell into disrepute because, 'clerically' minded, they pressed for a theocracy. The opposition of the Hasmonaeans to the Pharisees, however, brought them into alliance once more with the priest-princes. In this way the Sadducees became an aristocratic caste, which indirectly influenced the course of history.

Their religious position is a peculiar one. They were conservative and followed the temple-tradition, even if they were not quite orthodox. They firmly rejected all non-biblical and post-biblical innovations. They recognized only the written Law as binding, and were strictly opposed to the further development of the Law by custom and precedent, as in the 'oral law' of the Pharisees. But, in contrast to these views, they affirmed the freedom of the will, which rendered enthusiastic devotion and belief in miracles superfluous. They denied the immortality of the soul, the continued existence of the individual after death and a future judgement. They found no sufficient scriptural proof for a doctrine of the resurrection of the dead. There were for them not two ages, but just one age in which all men live. And they recognized no angels or other intermediary beings such as demons.

Socially, they represented the well-to-do, somewhat complacent upper middle class. Culturally they were broad-minded and open to Hellenism; in short, 'modern'. Liberals in social ethics they had a flair for *real-politik*. Religion and culture, common-sense and traditional worship were neatly harmonized—as in the Book of Sirach.

In the New Testament they are met with more on the periphery. Their question to Jesus, as to which husband the woman who had married seven brothers in turn would belong to in the resurrection (Mark 12.18–27), shows how they challenged Jesus to come to terms with those who represented the official theology of the theocratic state.

14. *The Order*

One of the results of the pietistic movement, which we met in the Maccabaean period, was the formation of the monastic order of the Essenes. Essenes is the Greek transcription for *Hasidim*, the Pious. Since the discovery of the Dead Sea Scrolls (1947 onwards) not only can the outlines of this movement be sketched with greater precision, but also a number of questions as yet unanswered arise. The Essenes were obviously not a philosophical school, as Josephus suggested. They were not even a single, sharply defined group. Rather, they formed a broad movement which gave rise to different branches and various forms of association simultaneously in various places. Each of these in turn probably experienced further external and internal changes in the changing course of history.

One of these Essene foundations could have been the monastic community of Qumran. This was obviously the site of the mother-house; it was marked by stricter religious observances and narrower, tighter forms of community. The daughter communities, such as the lay-brotherhood of the 'Community of the New Covenant at Damascus', do not seem to have submitted to the demands for celibacy and poverty in the same way. On the whole, the individual settlements seem to have been presided over by a hierarchic order under an overseer. Entrance was granted only after a twofold probationary period of several years. Josephus tells of a 'terrible oath' which the postulant brother had to swear while he bound himself to preserve the secrecy of the doctrines.

An extremely exact discipline governed daily life. It consisted of study of the scriptures, prayer and work. Infringements of the rule, especially during common assemblies, were graded but all were punished fairly severely. Peculiar features of the community included daily washings and immersions together with daily cult-mealtimes in common. Novices were never allowed to take part in these.

The water ritual and the doctrine of the two Messiahs points to the fact that there was a planned attempt by the movement to realize 'the kingdom of priests' (Ex. 19.6). Old Zadokite, i.e. priestly, patterns of thought seem to be present in the background. As we know from the documents, a split had, in fact, occurred within the priesthood of the Temple, probably during the Hasmonaean period. Increasing secularization as a result of Hellenism had led to the departure or the secession of an extremist priestly group, who were influenced by the idea of the wilderness, in which the people of God were to meet their Lord. Henceforth no blood sacrifices were to be offered to God. This group wanted to be 'a covenant not to go into the shrine any more'. These Essenes, then, were not simply opponents of the idea of the theocracy and the Law; they were their most enthusiastic champions. They did not reject the cult; rather, they prepared for the eschatological cult, in place of the corrupt cult, and made ready to celebrate this at some future date in the purified shrine. But, for the present, secularized Jerusalem no longer afforded them, or rather did not yet afford them, a spiritual home. The time was not yet ripe for them there. Hence they went out into the wilderness—a radical, messianic repentance-movement.

As their teaching has often been compared in recent years with that of Jesus and the first Christian community, we shall examine their message and the way they thought about themselves.

Briefly, they considered themselves to be the 'remnant' of God's people which was to be purged by judgement. Their members were the elect of the eternal covenant, the new covenant promised by Jeremiah (ch. 31). In fact, they were themselves the 'New Covenant' in the land of Damascus (cf. Amos 5.27). The period was an affluent one, but they deliberately (i.e. freely) chose the charismatic ideal of poverty. They accepted it with inward joy as a gift of grace. They saw 'the last times' breaking in, the time when God would kindle his war of vengeance throughout the world. And they would fight on his side.

For the position is this. Two spirits—God and Belial, light and darkness, the spirit of truth and the spirit of iniquity (i.e. falsehood)—are locked in conflict according to the eternal predestination of God. The monastic brethren have already made their decision. When they were admitted into the army of salvation they swore 'to love everything that he has chosen; but to hate everything that he has rejected'. With the two spirits are associated two armies; the 'sons of light' wage war against the 'sons of darkness'.

When does this war begin? 'When the exiled sons of light return home from the desert of the nations to camp on the slopes of Jerusalem.' This war heralds the end of time (i.e. the eschatological period). This eschatological war will last forty years. This way and that the fortune of war will oscillate. The sons of light will win three rounds and the sons of darkness will win three rounds. Finally, however, 'in the seventh contest the strong hand of God subjects Belial and all his angels to his rule, and eternal destruction is the fate of all such men'. Judgement brings reward and punishment. Whether the body continues or a new one is given is unclear. A holy battle array, battle regulations with precise tactical instructions, prepare the soldiers of the holy army for the mortal combat.

Special problems are raised by the three holy figures who are peculiar to the community of Qumran: the teacher of righteousness, the priest-Messiah, and the lay-Messiah.

The 'teacher of righteousness' is obviously the founder of the 'Community of the New Covenant'. In a commentary-like exposition of Habakkuk (1 and 2) a fragment of the history of this man comes to light. He (the teacher of righteousness) stands in a special relationship to God. He proclaims what will happen to the last generation. For it is the time of disobedience. Inspired by God he knows how to explain all the words of the prophets, all the secrets of God. He is also called the priest whom God has given to the house of Judah. The fate of his followers depends on their relation to himself. God will deliver all who prove loyal to the teacher and hold fast to the Law. He is persecuted by a godless, sinful priest, a man of lies, the prophet of lies.

We do not know who is meant by the teacher nor who is meant by the lying prophet. There is no clear indication, let alone agreement, concerning the time or the more intimate circumstances of the events mentioned. One passage referring to the wicked priest is particularly puzzling; he 'appeared to them on the occasion of the rest-day of Atonement in full splendour in order to confuse them and trip them up on the day of the fast, the day of their sabbatical rest'. Whether this is a reference to the teacher's death as a martyr is doubtful. The 'removal' of the teacher is presupposed in another passage: this could refer either to his death or his ascension. At all events, it was hoped that he would return.

There is a mysterious connection between his death and the emergence of two other figures, namely the two 'Anointed ones' (Messiahs). One is the priestly Messiah 'from Aaron', who occupies the first place at the cult-meal. The other is the royal Messiah 'from Israel', who is subordinate to the former in rank. The royal Messiah, or the warrior-prince, stands at the head of the generals who are in command of the 'thousands of Israel' in the holy, eschatological war.

15. 'Church' and 'State'

This appears to be the revival of an old tradition: the tradition of the division of powers, spiritual and worldly, religious and political. A real difference, expressed in the closeness and opposition of two institutions, lies behind this. The difference of priest and king reaches far back into Israel's history, to the time when the people of Israel settled in Canaan and became a state. This difference, a source of tension and conflict, made Israel's history dynamic; in fact, it unsettled it and made it, from the point of view of secular history, so tragic: Israel's history is 'not the soil of good fortune'.

The foundation of the temple-state with Persian support seemed to offer a compensatory solution. The prophet Zechariah (c. 520–518 BC) saw in a night vision a lampstand with seven lamps, and on the right and left of it two olive trees. The seven lamps are the eyes of the all-seeing Lord, the olive trees are the two 'sons of oil', i.e. the Anointed. The vision is concerned with actual contemporary figures (Hag. 1.14; Ezra 5.2)—the governor

Zerubbabel, who carried through the repatriation of the Jewish community from Babylon and who was a descendant of David, and the high-priest, Joshua (Zech. 4.1–14). The prophet is commissioned through the vision to crown Zerubbabel, the royal Messiah. The day when the Messiah ascends the throne is to be the day when the Temple is completed; for this Messiah will build the Temple. Next to him Joshua will hold office as high-priest. There will be no disputes between the highest political and highest religious authority in the temple-state over their respective spheres of influence (Zech. 6.9–15). This is the first time a prophet relates the expectation of a future Messiah to a contemporary historical figure. It is also the first time that a priest is called 'high-priest' as the head of a priestly hierarchy.

When the expectation of the Messiah-King was disappointed the text was later emended so that the crown was placed not on the head of Zerubbabel, the political leader, but of Joshua the priest. Later still the text was altered so that not two but only one Messiah sat on the throne; namely the Anointed, who is king and priest in one (Zech. 6.11). The priestly Messiah has supplanted the royal Messiah.

This was also the view of the Qumran community, although both royal and priestly powers re-emerged and appeared as two different persons. The basic trend was the same. The political leadership became a priestly affair; the Messiah from Aaron was the leader. But this did not mean the highest lay official had risen above the priesthood to the position of leader; the Messiah from Israel was subordinate.

The doctrine of the two Messiahs was not limited to a particular circle, but was widely diffused in the Judaism of the time. In the caves near the Dead Sea, fragments of an apocryphal book, first published centuries ago, the so-called 'Testament of the Twelve Patriarchs', have been found along with other things among the manuscripts preserved in the clay vessels. (It is significant that fragments of the Testament of Levi and another work previously unknown are discussed at Qumran.) 'Judah' speaks as follows to his successor in the Testament of his name which has long been famous: 'Children, love Levi, that you may live, and do not raise yourselves against him, that you be not destroyed! For to me (i.e. Judah) God has given *kingship*, to him (Levi) the *priesthood*; and he has subordinated the kingship to the priesthood. I have been entrusted with power on earth, he has been entrusted with power in heaven. As the heaven is higher than the earth, so is the priesthood of God higher than kingship on earth. For the Lord has also chosen him before you to draw near to him and to eat at his table together with the first-fruits of what the children of Israel eat.'

This passage gives us a bird's-eye view which illuminates not only the salvation-history of Israel but is also deeply rooted in large parts of other religions. It occupies a position of basic importance for the understanding of the New Testament and the person of Jesus of Nazareth. The challenging question of Jesus to the Pharisees about the interpretation of the reference to the Messiah in Ps. 110—is he David's son or David's lord?—probably presupposes the doctrine of the two Messiahs (Mark 12.35–37). Moreover, the idea of the two Anointed ones created the basic presuppositions of Western society. The Middle Ages thought of themselves as united and all-embracing, a Christian theocracy. This united Christendom was ruled by two powers, the spiritual head and the secular head. Priesthood and kingship, allied together, directed the destiny of the one 'Christian body'. It is true their spheres of authority, concerning religious and secular matters, were to be distinguished, but they were related as a unity to the common task—the earthly and spiritual goal, the welfare and salvation of those who were united in the theocracy. But the subordination of worldly to spiritual power from the outset remained decisive.

The origin of this clearly lies in the Jewish view of the division of powers within the indivisible theocracy. The opposition between Pope and king in the Middle Ages was occasioned by the way the relationship of the two powers was based on force and by trends of rulership at that time. Its deeper cause, however, lay in the social system as such: namely, in the way parity and co-ordination of offices was combined with the simultaneous subordination of one office to another. The pre-Christian theocratic state of Israel is the seed-bed of this view.

In modern times the tensions which existed in the Middle Ages between the highest authorities of Christendom have assumed a new form in the rivalries between Church and State. The modern totalitarian states are ultimately a reaction against the clerical-priestly solution of a former age. The spiritualization of worldly affairs was followed by the secularization of spiritual concerns, a trend already noticeable in the late Middle Ages. The Church was to disappear in the state or the community—absolutely and without remainder. But even this solution, however much it represented a counter-movement, was only mooted within the context it had previously been given by the Jewish doctrine of the two Messiahs. It had a historical precedent in the system of government followed by the Hasmonaeans, who wanted to be prophets, priests and kings all at the same time and thus fell victims to the demon of power.

16. *Qumran*

As is well known, Qumran is situated near the north-western corner of the Dead Sea on a steeply rising marl terrace admirably suited for defence purposes. The settlement was both a monastery and a barracks. The brothers of the order prepared themselves by prayer and a study of the Law for the last conflict. Every one of them was a soldier in the holy army of the Lord. The levy of ancient Israel was resurrected in the new militia. The place of the ancient mountain of God, Sinai, was taken by Mount Nebo where Moses had died. It looked out from Moab's shimmering blue mountains over the Dead Sea and the valley which concealed the grave of God's servant so that no one knows where he is buried 'to this day' (Deut. 34.6).

Qumran considered itself the vanguard of the last things. It was both a holy institution and a civil state. Hierarchy and ritual, fervent mysticism and stringent morality held an assured place here. Though does one build so firmly if one knows the heavenly world is advancing upon one? Apparently only this-worldly revolutions were reckoned with. Whatever the future might bring, it would not bring anything new beyond what was already known or possessed: namely the unalterable will of God in the Law and the New Covenant, the 'union' of the predestined and the faithful.

At Qumran something that had been part of the ancient glory of the Jewish priesthood arose in a new form. God was enthroned upon songs of praise, based on the psalms but freshly composed and set to new music. Their doctrines, which expounded and developed the contrast between light and darkness, elaborated

Persian ideas, as the apocalyptists had. Yet the Hellenistic spirit also exercised a formative influence; their allegorical exegesis of Old Testament texts was similar to, even if more original than, that of the Diaspora-synagogue in Egypt, for example. The Alexandrians, like the Jewish Philo, who could only read Greek and who read the Septuagint, gave a spiritual interpretation to the literal words and related the mythology of the past to the reality of the present. They understood the divine in such a way that they could apprehend from it the possibilities of human existence.

Moreover, the esoteric knowledge of the monks and especially the deliberate secrecy about doctrine and usage were indications of foreign influence stemming from the spirit of the times. The witnesses of Yahweh, the Lord of destiny, were not the only ones who had 'a golden key on the tongue' (Sophocles) in important religious matters. One need only cite the Pythagoreans. The composition of the order was similar, in fact, to the structure of this ancient Greek cultic association of five hundred years ago. Philo was certainly wrong if he made the Essenes sun-worshippers and grouped them philosophically as exponents of the contemplative life. The later freemasons of the eighteenth century, who were builders of 'the Solomonic temple', had not much more in common with them than the small hatchet, the loin apron and the white garment mentioned by Josephus. Nevertheless, is there not an air of modernity about this flight to the wilderness—this piece of Judaism in Hellenistic dress in the Roman province of Syria?

17. *The Scribes*

Although the Sadducees represent the orthodox who are tending to become a clique, and the Pharisees the pietistic brotherhoods, and the apocalyptists the moral revival groups, and the Essenes a covenant for a distinctive Judaism in the form of an order, dwelling in monastic or half-monastic settlements—yet all these movements belong together, in spite of all their differences and oppositions. Law and cult are fixed points of reference for all— though valued differently by the respective groups. They sprang from the same native soil, namely, the movement of the 'Pious', among whom the ancient prophetic and priestly heritage was

held in readiness for the new world-crisis, the conflict with the
Hellenistic spirit.

The scribes cannot be included in these groups and movements.
The fact that in the Gospels according to Luke and Matthew
(especially Matt. 23) 'scribes and Pharisees' are joined in one
formula soon led to the misunderstanding that both descriptions
are identical or that the scribes belonged only to the Pharisees.
In fact, the expression 'scribe' means 'one who is skilled in the
Law', it describes a vocation. Corresponding to their subject-
matter—the Law—the scribes are both theologians and jurists.
As teachers, called rabbis, they formed the learned fraternity.

After they had completed their education and been schooled
in the Law the young new members were formally received into
the guild. At a public ordination with the laying on of hands the
spirit to fulfil his office of teacher was poured out on each candidate;
this was the same spirit that had been active since the time of Moses
(Deut. 34.9) in what was thought to be an unbroken succession
of teachers of the Law. The ordination gave the one who was
ordained the right to officiate henceforward as judge in disciplinary
trials and to decide questions of doctrine. He could also now use
the title of 'Rabbi', which corresponds to something like our
'Doctor'. This ordination had nothing to do with a sacramental,
priestly ordination. It was more like a degree-ceremony at a
university. An entrance—or probationary—dissertation was usually
required.

Everywhere where the Law was taken seriously there were
scribes, or at any rate could be—among the Sadducees as well
as the Pharisees. The regard for the Law felt by the Pharisees
gave the scribes a place of special esteem among them, assured
them of a following and qualified them—particularly as experts
in the Law—for positions of authority in the Sanhedrin. Thus
they helped to form the public image of the lay-movement of the
Pharisees at the time of Jesus. They could, however, also belong
to other circles such as those of the apocalyptists who cultivated a
pious, esoteric existence. They too preserved an esoteric knowledge
of God, Man and the Future. Finally, they came to be included
among the 'wise', as in Philo and Josephus. Alongside the nobility
of birth they formed the aristocracy of learning at that time.

Yet, in a certain sense, the formula 'scribes and Pharisees'
does describe the historical facts. For the Pharisees, with the

help of the scribes, brought about that formalization of piety which we know so much about from the New Testament. We shall have to guard against seeing this contrast in terms of black and white. The Law was to dominate life in every detail. Hence the rise of Jewish casuistry, the attempt to make the stipulations of the Law applicable to the individual case, on work days and holy days. The Law was meant to be a great source of help in life, by means of which life was strengthened. Consequently its effect was both burdensome and liberating. Both aspects should be noted.

The burden consisted in the fact that the Torah was understood as a collection of individual stipulations. In an age of numbers this was fragmented by the ancient synagogue into 613 separate commands, 248 positive ('thou shalt') and 365 negative ('thou shalt not'). Yet this was by no means the end of the distinctions; there were difficult and easy commands. There were endless discussions between the rabbis and their pupils about them. Men knew they were under the constant surveillance of the Law, whose gaze penetrated every nook and cranny of life.

Human activity, however, was also fragmented. The whole of life disintegrated into purely separate and unconnected events. The numerous paragraphs within the corpus of the Law which demanded definite actions by men were distinguished more and more finely. The discussions of the specialists became increasingly subtle. Ingenuity tumbled over itself. This is especially true of the questions relating to the sacredness of the sabbath. Thirty-nine major activities were forbidden on the sabbath. They were enumerated in detail. Their number was given a theological explanation. Every major activity was divided into several minor activities, six minor for every one of the 39 major activities. This number, too, was given a theological explanation. Everything was then systematized; for the partition of the Law increased the desire for synopsis. We are now in the period after Christ's death. But the transition to the Talmud can be traced even while Jesus is alive. The 'traditions of the elders' (Mark 7.13) demanded additional validity on top of that of the Law.

Conflicts flared up, especially between the rigorous school of the Rabbi Shammai and the liberal school of the Rabbi Hillel. Both were active in the period from 20 BC to AD 15. Shammai was considered irascible, Hillel gentle. A Gentile once wanted to become a Jew. He had little time for the teaching given to

converts. As a condition of his acceptance of Judaism he required
that he should be taught the Jewish law while standing on one leg.
Shammai rejected the candidate; Hillel accepted him and taught
him 'the golden rule'—'Do not do to anyone what you yourself
would not like. That is the whole law. All the rest is commentary.'
(Cf. Matt. 7.12; Luke 6.31.)

The subject matter of these disputes was often very sophistical:
At what time in the morning should the creed be recited? First
answer: when there is sufficient light to distinguish between
purple and white. Second answer: no, when one can distinguish
between purple and leek-green. Other questions were as follows:
Does one recite it lying or standing? how does one say it during
a journey? or at work? how much of the body must be covered?
how long must one's devotions last? what gestures must one
avoid? Answer after answer. And still more questions. Is it lawful
to eat an egg laid by a hen on the sabbath? for instance. Shammai
said no, Hillel yes. According to Shammai the fact that the hen
did not know the Law is no excuse, for by eating the egg a person
is partly responsible: he is to a certain extent giving retrospective
approval to the lawless activity of the animal.

Nevertheless, it would be untrue to say that the teachers of
the Law wanted to make the Law more severe in a one-sided
way. Even without the example of Hillel's generosity it is clear
that the general aim was to make the Law really fit for use.
According to general opinion, of course, the Law was God's
greatest gift. It was eternal like God himself. It was pre-existent
like him. The Law was God's favourite book, the Lord himself
studied it on the sabbath. In the first hours of each day he would
read it for his devotions and his improvement. The Law was the
bodily form of everything good and divine. For the man who
follows it, it alleviates the hardship of life in this evil world. It
makes difficult decisions easier. In short, it can be fulfilled—
perfectly, in fact.

The Jews who strove to live according to the Law felt it was
the source of joy, the source of earthly and heavenly pleasure,
the elixir of life. For the Jewish Rabbi Paul, who was himself a
Pharisee (Phil. 3.5), the Law was obviously not simply a torment
(not torment in the sense that Luther experienced it through the
law of his Order), but Israel's patent of nobility in the sight of all
the nations (Rom. 9.4). For Jesus' contemporaries the Law did

not have the relentless sternness of the categorical imperatives which religions and philosophies usually enjoin. It was said of God, 'the lover of all life', by the Wisdom of Solomon (11.26), 'Thou sparest everything, because it is thine, Lord, who dost rejoice in what has life.' The God who gave the Law laughs when life goes well. Should he be angry with the man who relaxes the literal precepts with the help of this written Law, especially if the learned authorities give him a good conscience to do so? The Law can be conversed with. It teaches one how to choose the lesser of two evils. It is flexible when dealing with human weakness. Thus, through the Law, for instance, God gave Israel the privilege of divorce—before all other nations.

18. *The Day of the World*

All this, with its increasing tendency to become a caricature of morality—especially in the period after Christ—is the degeneration of a great inheritance. But one cannot deny the intensity of the movement which permitted this degeneration. Its intensity glowed in the inner reaches of prayers and hopes which were kept alive in Judaism by precisely such legalistic piety. The Psalms of Solomon, written in Greek, make this clear. The great needs of the time are audible in these psalms: the victory of Pompey over the Hasmonaeans (63 BC), his death in the following year and the establishment of the new regime of Herod. The opposition between the 'Pious' and the 'godless' becomes visible; hence, too, the opposition between those who were faithful to the Law, represented by Pharisaism, and those who conformed to the world, who are to be looked for in the circles of the Sadducees. These prayers and hopes are not those of a single group. They are the words of the temple-community confessing its faith. In them men trust the power of their own free will, which is free to choose between good and evil, and the work of their own hands. But at the same time reliance is placed on the future resurrection of the dead and on the Messiah of God. These prayers reflect the expectation of the Anointed, whose king is the Lord himself. He will destroy the heathen, not with power but simply by the word of his mouth (cf. Thess. 2.8). He will purify Jerusalem and make it holy. He will bring together a holy nation. For God has made him strong in the Holy Spirit:

G

He does not rely on horse and chariot and bow,
Nor does he gather himself gold and silver for war
Or set his hope on numbers
For the day of the battle.

Everything is realistically thought out, yet everything is in God's hands—completely earthly and completely heavenly, both at the same time. A royal hero intervenes, 'the proper Man whom God himself hath bidden'. And of the 'ancient prince of hell' it can truly be said that he is already judged. 'A word shall quickly slay him.'

The 'day' is before one's very eyes. So sings ardent desire in the Psalms of Solomon shortly before the crisis. It is the day of pity—day of mercy—day of judgement—day of election—the day of the Anointed.

But about the time of the collapse of the vassal-state of Herod the Great (4 BC) and Archelaus' banishment to Gaul by Augustus (AD 6), an apocalypse bearing the title of The Ascension of Moses was circulating among the various pietistic groups, probably including that at Qumran. It contains precise instructions as to what is to happen to the 'books': 'Thou shalt arrange them, anoint them with cedar-oil and place them in earthen vessels in the place which he has appointed from the beginning of the creation of the world, that his name might be invoked there until the day of repentance when the Lord visits them at the end of time and all is consummated.' In this passage both external event and inner meaning are found in close association. The storing of the clay vessels with the scrolls, known to us from the discoveries in the caves near the Dead Sea, is linked with the day of repentance. Then follows a brief sketch of Israel's history from the entrance into Canaan up to the eschatological present. There is a reference to 'the shameless king, not of priestly descent, a daring, godless fellow', who ruled for thirty-four years—obviously Herod. Then come 'the cohorts and the powerful king of the West' who has the Jews crucified in large numbers—obviously P. Quintilius Varus. This is the moment for the last things to come to pass. Taxo, 'a man from the tribe of Levi', enters with his seven sons. They are ready to die rather than transgress the commandments of the Lord. And then comes 'the messenger, who holds the highest place'. He will overthrow the devil. In the cosmic catastrophe the Gentile nations will be judged. Israel, however, will be exalted to heaven.

Who is Taxo? A historical person? A heavenly figure? Who is the messenger? Moses returned? Riddle after riddle. We do not know. The name Taxo, which is derived from Greek, means 'one who orders'. A figure is promised who is to set right the times which are out of joint.

19. *The New Age*

Behind Taxo stands the question, '*When is the "day of the world" coming?*'

How did Rome stand in relation to this question? As far as Rome was concerned it had already been answered before Jesus was born. When the little Jewish apocalypse announced the coming of Taxo and 'the messenger', the day of the world had already dawned for Rome.

In Rome, too, the question had once been a very live issue. Classical antiquity of both East and West was always full of oracles. The wisdom of the Greek Sibyl had made its way to Rome via South Italy at an early date. Tradition had it that the last king of Rome from Etruscan stock had acquired the Sibylline books in the sixth century BC. Since then they had been in the care of a special college of priests in the temple on the Capitol. At critical hours of decision for the Republic they replied to solemn questions with divine advice. Ancient oriental wisdom, newly revived by Hellenism, breathed through the sayings of the Sibyl.

Centuries of almost incessant warfare in the western and eastern Mediterranean, but especially decades of bloody civil wars, raised the question, 'What is the meaning of it all? Where does it all lead to?' An apocalyptic climate encouraged messianic hopes. The poet Virgil in his epic, the Aeneid, justified the Roman Empire in terms of world history and gave its first ruling house a mythological salvation-history. In his *Fourth Eclogue*, on the basis of a Sibylline oracle, he prophesied the birth of a saviour of the world and the onset of the 'new age'.

The ages of the world revolve, and primaeval time is now returning. From high heaven a new generation descends. A child is born. The weapon-bearing 'iron age' must yield to the 'golden age'. In this way every trace of wanton folly and horror is effaced. The

nations breathe again in relief. Gods and heroes greet the child
who will bring peace to the world. The world will enjoy a paradisical existence. A world-wide springtime blooms in the kingdoms
of plants and animals. The sheep no longer fears the lion. The
serpent dies. The poisonous plant becomes a medicine. Grapes
grow on thorns. The oak-tree drips honey. Vestiges of former
corruption which still remain on land and sea will be removed by
a second Achilles. When the child grows up the world will no
longer have need of dangerous merchant shipping. The farmer
produces crops without hoeing, the vineyard bears grapes without
pruning—spontaneously. The steer wears no yoke. The ewe
grows purple wool on its back, so that dyeing becomes unnecessary.
The child comes.

> 'Run, run, ye spindles! On to this fulfilment
> Speed the world's fortune, draw the living thread.'
> So heaven's unshaken ordinance declaring,
> The Sister Fates enthroned together sang.

> Come, then, dear child of gods, Jove's mighty heir.
> Begin thy high career; the hour is sounding.
> See how it shakes the vaulted firmament,
> Earth, and the spreading seas and depth of sky!
> See, in the dawning of a new creation
> The heart of all things living throbs with joy!

> . . . Come, little child . . .

In the very year when Virgil announced the birth of the little
boy the person to whom the song was referred later, both in Rome
and by the Christian Church, was already twenty-three years old.
Blood was already sticking to his hands. He had already appeared
on the stage of history amidst the terrorism which accompanied
every change in the days of civil war. That same year he reduced
the Umbrian mountain fortress of Perugia to ashes and was responsible for a terrible blood-bath. His adoptive father, the great Julius
Caesar, had been murdered by a conspiracy of nobles four years
previously, when, in an attempt on the crown, he tried to change
the military dictatorship into an hereditary monarchy. Ten years
later the youth had ripened into manhood and after a number of
hard battles became the sole ruler of the world (31 BC). The
Roman 'Messiah', Octavian, who styled himself 'son of the

deified Caesar', received from the legions the title of 'Commander' (*Imperator*) and from the Senate the name Augustus, which means both 'Augmenter' of the state and 'Highness' or 'Majesty'.

20. *The High Mass on the Capitol*

Even if the trees did not drip honey and the sheep did not grow purple wool, yet mankind in those days considered the peace and prosperity which Augustus brought a divine miracle. The new ruler did not want to be 'Emperor' like Caesar, but only 'First Citizen', first minister in the Senate and first citizen within the world-democracy. As the son and grandson of bankers he was an outstanding financier and a gifted administrator, but on the whole more a scholar by nature than a statesman. His emphasis on civilian plainness, his rejection of all courtly pomp, made him still more worthy of the love of his fellow citizens. His democratic disguise surrounded him with an even greater aura of untouchability. He forbade any cultic worship of himself, but the populace saw in him 'the Saviour', which many a Hellenistic monarch had pretended to be. At least, sacrifices were made to his 'Genius', the creative spirit which ruled his life, and to the 'Goddess Rome', whom he represented.

By virtue of his office of 'Highest Priest' (*Pontifex Maximus*)— a title which the Roman papacy took over—he celebrated, for the 'secular games', the centenary celebrations in 17 BC, the Mass of Thanksgiving which took place on the Capitoline Hill at Rome before all the people. The account of the festival records the following facts.

On four nights—from May 31 to June 3—Caesar Augustus, following the formula laid down by the Sibylline oracle, made prayers and sacrifices to the gods according to the Greek rites. Nocturnal dramas followed on each occasion.

One small point is significant. By special decree widows were instructed to shorten their period of mourning. Mourning would have excluded them from the festival. Only if the people had atoned for their sins and had thus begun a new period in their normal life could the period of mourning be counted as over. This moment—extraordinarily enough—had now arrived for the people and indeed for the Empire.

The turn of the century became the turning point of the whole world. At imperial command Horace composed his *Carmen Saeculare* expressly for this purpose. On the last day, the high point of the Jubilee, a choir of selected youths and maidens, twenty-seven of each, sang the great hymn of praise and intercession on the Capitol. A massive doxology formed the conclusion: powerful is Rome and world-wide her rule.

> Now Media dreads our Alban steel,
> Our victories land and ocean o'er;
> Scythia and Ind in suppliance kneel,
>   So proud before.

> Faith, Honour, ancient Modesty,
> And Peace, and Virtue, spite of scorn,
> Come back to earth; and Plenty, see,
>   With teeming horn.

> Augur and lord of silver bow,
> Apollo, darling of the Nine,
> Who heal'st our frame when languors slow
>   Have made it pine;

> Lov'st thou thine own Palatial hill,
> Prolong the glorious life of Rome
> To other cycles, brightening still
>   Through time to come.

The ritual dramas were followed by a week of dramatic performances 'in honour of the festival'.

The new era had made its entry both visibly and audibly. The world stood under the star of its advent, its 'day'.

21. *The New Gospels*

If Rome spoke, the East could not keep silent. It, too, sounded forth its faith in the Roman Lord in fulsome tones of joy and thanksgiving. Not only the new century, but every year within this 'more glorious age', was to commemorate the name of the 'Illustrious One'. The sixth month was given the name 'August', and so it has remained to this day (even if the shift of New Year's Day now makes August the eighth month). But how significant it would be if the beginning of the year were decided by His Majesty's birthday! In the province of Asia—the modern Asia Minor—this calendar-reckoning was adopted in 9 BC. In Priene and three other cities of the province two important Greek documents have been found on inscriptions, the one written by the proconsul there to the provincial parliament concerning the new beginning for the year and the other recording the decision of this parliament. The motivation and tone of the two inscriptions are even more interesting than their contents. The proconsul refers to the matter as follows: It would be difficult to say

'. . . whether the birthday of the Most High Emperor has brought more joy or advantage. We could justifiably regard it as the beginning of a new creation, as least as far as the use of things is concerned, even if not in respect of their origin. For everything had disintegrated and taken on a most calamitous appearance, until he restored the situation. He gave the whole world a new look. The world's one wish for itself was death, if it had not been for the birth of a good fortune shared by all—the birth of the Emperor. One could, therefore, with good reason consider him the beginning of existence and life. Regret for having been born was terminated and confined at last. One could not begin with a more propitious day than this both for public and private welfare; this day brought good fortune to all. Moreover, this was the time when magistrates in the cities of Asia Minor entered on office—an arragement obviously fitted by divine decree to be an instrument for honouring Augustus. Since, then, it would be difficult to give adequate expression of our thanks for what he has done unless we were to invent a new form of thanksgiving, and since people would prefer to celebrate this common birthday if there were the added pleasure of entering upon office on the same day, for all these reasons I am of the opinion that the birthday of the All-Divine Emperor, that is 23 September, should be reckoned as the beginning of the New Year for all cities.'

The provincial parliament held exactly the same opinion; they decided in accordance with the proconsul's suggestion and explained their decision as follows:

'The providence which orders all our life, in its loving care and zeal, adorned our existence with the most perfect of all jewels, when it produced Augustus. For the benefit of mankind it has filled him with virtue. It has sent him to us and our contemporaries to be our Saviour; he has ended the war and set everything in good order. The Emperor's appearance has surpassed the hopes of previous ages. He has not only excelled the benefactors who lived before him (cf. Luke 22.25), but he has left those who follow no chance of excelling him.

Throughout the world the birthday of the divine Augustus inaugurated the gospel of good news which he brought.'

Both inscriptions are supposed to have been erected along with others in the temple of the Goddess Rome and of Augustus at Pergamum, as in other chief cities of the area.

What seems to us like subservient flattery was at that time simply an exalted style of writing. The excesses conceal a genuinely human feeling and the desire to trust the reality of a great moment. For Rome in East and West, in the whole Empire in fact, the 'day of the world' had arrived with Augustus. Whoever understood the new 'gospels' no longer needed to wait for it. We hear it clearly; every coming day is overtaken in advance. It is outrun by Caesar's day.

THE EVE OF HIS COMING:
JESUS OF NAZARETH

FROM THE very earliest days in Israel the day always began with the evening; this was true, at all events, of the cultic day, the holy day and the Sabbath. 'From evening to evening shall you keep your holy day'—prescribed the Levitical law of festivals (Lev. 23.32). Commemoration of Israel's Exodus from Egypt began with rites which re-enacted the events of that night of death and deliverance. The Passover festival and the festival of unleavened bread which was fused with it were 'fixed for eternity'; 'on the fourteenth day of the first month in the evening you shall eat your unleavened bread, and so until the evening of the twenty-first day of the month' (Ex. 12.18). The 'first month' was later given the Babylonian name Nisan, and corresponded approximately to our April. The day of deliverance began with evening and morning. The days of the great week in which God created heaven and earth began with evening and morning. The seventh day on which God rested from all his work, from all that he had made, began in the evening (Gen. 1.5–2.3). Even today, Israel's Sabbath begins as soon as the first three stars begin to twinkle in the evening sky.

The 'day of his coming' begins in the evening, when day is drawing to a close in the rest of the world. It begins with the *eve* of his coming.

4

THE EVE OF GOD

1. *The Arrival of Elijah*

On 19 August, AD 14, the divine Augustus closed his eyes for the last time. With a Greek word on his lips he breathed his last at Nola, near Naples. He had ruled the Roman Empire for forty-five years; he had lived for seventy-seven. His ashes were intererd at Rome. As the flames of the funeral pyre closed round his remains, one of the senators wished he had seen how Augustus' body had sped to heaven from the fire and smoke. Gods return whence they came.

The unforgettable Emperor was followed by his stepson Tiberius, who was already fifty-six years old. Wise rule was dissolved in unmitigated tyranny. The power and authority of the Senate were limited and popular elections abolished. The Praetorian Guard, which had been stationed in Rome by Augustus to act as the imperial bodyguard, were given large barracks there and their Prefect became the most powerful person next to the Emperor. Treason-trials abounded. A state based on law and order became a state where might was right.

In the fifteenth year of the Emperor Tiberius' rule, between October, AD 27 and September, AD 28 according to Syrian reckoning, a strange revival-movement broke out in the eastern edges of Judaea, near the lower Jordan. It was kindled by the appearance and message of a man called John, who was given the name of 'Baptist' because of the new style of baptism by immersion which he practised. All the four Gospels make the day of Jesus begin with the appearance of this John.

We know very little about the origin of John the Baptist. The story that he was descended on both his mother's and his father's side from a priestly family, and that his father was called Zechariah, his mother Elizabeth, is probably historically true. The garland of legends describing the annunciation of his birth (Luke 1.5–25), the meeting of his mother with the mother of Jesus (Luke 1.39–45) and his birth (Luke 1.57–66), weave his destiny with that of Jesus of Nazareth from the beginning. Two hymns extol God's greatness and mercy, as revealed in the birth of this child, and the steadfastness of the promises God once swore to his people and the patriarchs—Mary's hymn of praise, the *Magnificat* (Luke 1.46–55), and Zechariah's hymn of praise, the *Benedictus* (Luke 1.68–79). These, too, are linked with the 'pre-history' of Jesus.

Suddenly, the man is standing in front of our very eyes: a hermit. What he eats and wears establish his mission and his call. Although he is a Jew from a country with an ancient civilization, he appears like a Bedouin wearing a camel skin and a leather girdle—like the prophet Elijah (II Kings 1.8). He lives on what he finds in the steppe-country, on locusts (perhaps herbs?) and the honey of wild bees. Both in prospect (Luke 1.15) and retrospect (Matt. 11.18) it is recorded that he did not drink wine or intoxicants. He lived, like the Nazirites, men dedicated to God under the Old Covenant, a vegetarian and abstemious existence. Thus, he embodies in his person the protest of the prophets against the civilization of the Greco-Roman world which dazzled high and low with its luxury and its false glitter (cf. Matt. 11.8). But equally he also embodies the protest against the world of the theocracy and its religious complacency.

The place of John's appearance, like his figure and his bearing, had something frightening about it for every one of his contemporaries. He sojourned in the 'wilderness': more exactly, in the uninhabited, uncultivated strip of land near the Jordan, where the wind whistles through the shrubs and the reeds (Matt. 11.7). The fourth Gospel (John 1.28; 3.23) gives the place as Bethany (or Bethabara) and Aenon near Salim, neither of which has been identified by archaeologists as yet. The important point is that for the apocalyptic expectations of the period the wilderness is a geographical symbol, it is the place from which the 'last things' are to take their course. Israel's beginnings lie in the wilderness. Its end, too, is to commence there. The wilderness tradition goes back to the early canonical prophets.

'On that day' the living God will reveal a new future to the faithless people. He will entice Israel into the wilderness, like a bridegroom alluring his beloved. By the miraculous power of

God the valley on which the curse of sin lies heavy is to become the gateway of hope. Israel will relive the days of her youth in vineyards. God will make a new covenant, the peace of which will be shared by men and beast, heaven and earth. The central point of the new order of the cosmos, however, is to be the betrothal of the Lord to his people in an engagement never to be ended, 'in righteousness and justice, in love and mercy, in trust and knowledge of God'. In the wilderness Israel will be elected afresh, to become a new people. But rebirth in the wilderness is preceded by judgement (Hos. 2.14–23; 1.10–2.1).

The wilderness is concerned with obedience to God, not with sacrifices and offerings, says Amos (5.25). In the wilderness Israel is free from the foreign influences of Canaan; she is not yet laid low by the pleasures of earthly fertility, and has not yet succumbed to the Baalim, the gods of blood and soil. Jeremiah sees the wilderness as the place where Israel is faithful in obedience (2.2) and God is faithful in leading her (2.6):

> Thus says the Lord.
> I remember the devotion of your youth,
> your love as a bride,
> how you followed me in the wilderness,
> in a land not sown. . . .
> It is the Lord
> who brought us up from the land of Egypt,
> who led us in the wilderness,
> in a land of deserts and pits,
> in a land of drought and deep darkness,
> ina land that none passes through,
> where no man dwells.

Hundreds of years ago the brotherhood of the Rechabites lived in the wilderness in nomadic style, true to their vow to drink no wine, build no houses, and sow no crops (Jer. 35).

The old word of the wilderness resounds through the New Testament. In the wilderness Israel was tested and rebelled against God (I Cor. 10.5; Heb. 3.8–11, 17). In the wilderness Israel experienced God's mercy in signs and wonders: the erection of the brazen serpent and the descent of bread from heaven (John 3.14; 6.31). God repeatedly spoke in a special way in the wilderness (Acts 7.30–44).

The Jews of Jesus' day knew that the angel of death had no power in the wilderness. No wonder that the wilderness, this mysterious no man's land, was the place to which they constantly looked back and which they constantly watched for, to see whether the new world would not make itself felt from there. The Messiah was to appear in the wilderness, and destroy his enemies with his miraculous power. Without weapons, and aided only by the intervention of heavenly help, as the Psalms of Solomon declared, he would accomplish the 'miracle of liberation'. In a different way Josephus reports that the period when Jesus lived was constantly being disturbed by messianic movements which had their *point de départ* or source in the wilderness. Between AD 44 and 46 the wonder-worker Theudas, mentioned also in Acts (5.36), led his 400 men dry-footed through the Jordan from the wilderness. He sought to repeat the miracle of early times (Jos. 3). After AD 52 another wonder-worker called men to his standard in the wilderness. In Cyrene in North Africa, the modern Libya, a Jewish weaver by the name of Jonathan led 'many poor people' into the wilderness. The Acts of the Apostles (21.38) mentions an Egyptian Jew, who led a revolt and marched into the wilderness with 4,000 'men of the Dagger'. These men— called *sicarii*—were nationalistic extremists, who killed their opponents in the midst of a crowd, especially during religious festivals, with the short *sica* (Latin for dagger). Josephus knew of one Egyptian who led 30,000(!) men from the wilderness to the Mount of Olives, in order to capture Jerusalem by a strong, sudden attack. Another 'prophet' is said to have attracted the populace to the Mount of Olives: the Messiah would appear there, and they would see with their own eyes how the walls of Jerusalem would collapse. His followers were wiped out by the procurator, Felix (AD 53–55). He himself disappeared without trace. The waves of messianic movements were surging forth out of the wilderness.

Not all came from the wilderness, of course. Galilee had been a seat of unrest for some time. We have already referred to Judas the Galilaean; he was a scribe and co-founder of the Zealot party from the days of the census in AD 6 (Acts 5.37). Probably Barabbas, also, who is well known through the trial of Jesus, and is variously described as a notorious criminal (Matt. 27.16), a robber (John 18.40) and murderer (Acts 3.14), was the leader of a group within an anti-Roman underground movement (Luke 23.19).

John appears in the 'wilderness'. But his appearance stands in the strongest possible contrast to the messianic movements of the time. The religious and secular activists, who want to overthrow the present order of society or at least hope for its overthrow, find in him neither a companion nor a rival, but one in complete opposition. John does not preach the overthrow of society but the overthrow of man. He preaches 'the baptism of repentance for the forgiveness of sins' (Mark 1.4; Luke 3.3). Matthew has added the word 'kingdom of heaven' to this theme (Matt. 3.2). *Man* must become new!

The preacher of repentance initiated a repentance movement. 'All Judaea and all Jerusalem' go out to him at the Jordan. Men flock after him. They confess their sins to him and receive the eschatological sacrament, which can only be taken once, in order to be saved in the imminent judgement: they are immersed in running water (Mark 1.5). Many members both of the Pharisaic brotherhood and the Sadducees' caste (Matt. 3.7) come to him to seek baptism. But the Baptist says to them imperiously, 'You brood of vipers! Who warned you to flee from the wrath to come? Bear fruit that befits repentance, and do not presume to say to yourselves, "We have Abraham for our father"; for I tell you, God is able from these stones to raise up children to Abraham. Even now the axe is laid to the root of the trees; every tree therefore that does not bear good fruit is cut down and thrown into the fire' (Matt. 3.7–10). The God whose coming John announces is no respecter of persons. The high lords of the temple-state and the leaders of the 'Pious' must face judgement. The old opposition of 'Pious' and sinners breaks down. This basic presupposition, on which all Jews were united—the brotherhood and the caste, the priests and the scribes, the apocalyptic groups and the holy army of the 'new covenant'—and which was accepted without discussion, is overthrown in the same way—without discussion.

It is impossible to describe the message of the Baptist in terms sufficiently revolutionary. If 'radical', a word which is frequently used today, a word in fact which is very much overdone, ought ever to be used it is for his message. Whether, and if so to what extent, it is also true of Jesus' message, we shall see later. Here it is true in the deepest sense of the word. John attacks the roots of human existence. He attacks the foundations on which the Jewish theocracy rests as a religious structure. By baptism sinners, if they repent, are made fireproof against the blaze of God's judgement. The 'Pious' are at its mercy. The assurances which Abraham's covenant seems to afford are worthless if a person relies on them. With his word of judgement John cuts down all false, pious security.

Luke, apparently, could not bear this brusqueness against the ruling class and referred the words of judgement to the mass of the people (Luke 3.7). But he tried to apply the words of the Baptist to the various strata of society. The common people, the tax-gatherers and the soldiers come to him with the concrete question, what should *they* do; and each group receives an equally concrete answer. One can summarize the concrete demand of John in one sentence: Do what is normal, what the tax regulations, what the terms of service, prescribe! God is a God of the ordinary, everyday routine. The glamour of the extraordinary is contrary to his nature. He is not the God of the sensational.

The Baptist's words about judgement are given special point by the fact that in one obscure passage he announces the coming of someone 'mightier'. So mighty is the one who is to come that John does not consider himself worthy to perform the smallest menial task for him. He is an absolute nonentity compared with his greatness. 'I baptize you with water, but he will baptize you with holy spirit' (Mark 1.7-9). Matthew and Luke have added 'and with fire' and compare the one who is to come with the farmer at harvest-time: with his winnowing shovel he throws the corn which has been thrashed high into the air against the wind, so that grain and chaff are separated (Matt. 3.11-12). The Baptist expects God himself or his representative, who is both judge and king. Will the one who is to come set fire to the world? Will he make the water-baptized into spirit-baptized? However one answers these questions, the world drives relentlessly towards the final decision. Even if John's picture of the Messiah is not that of Jesus, the day is certainly imminent.

Recently John has been occasionally linked with the community at Qumran, just as previous scholars linked him with the Essenes. Both internal and external evidence—the nearness of the place, priestly tradition, the connection of repentance and baptism, messianic expectations and ascetic practices—make such a relationship probable. From Luke 1.80 it has been concluded that up to his call by God John was 'in the desert'; it had already been assumed that he was handed over to the monastery at Qumran as a boy to be brought up by them. If he suddenly appeared on the banks of the Jordan as a hermit, this presupposes he must have broken with the brotherhood of the monastery. But neither of these suggestions is supported by much evidence in the New Testament. Moreover, the Baptist's preaching about judgement is basically different from the mentality of the order. He shares the wilderness-typology of the 'wilderness colony', it is true, especially in the interpretation of Isa. 40.3, which not only makes the 'way of the Lord' be built in the wilderness but also locates there the 'one who calls' and lifts up his voice; this is contrary to the Hebrew text but in accordance with the Greek of the Septuagint. But this view of the wilderness was also shared by innumerable messianic politicians and their followers, with whom John, at least, has nothing in common.

John the Baptist's importance is threefold. First, his announcement of judgement unquestionably goes back to the great prophets of the Old Testament. Even if apocalyptic has sharpened his observations and ideas, as it did those of all his expectant contemporaries, nevertheless he was no apocalyptist. His call to repent is direct and radical like that of an Amos (9.7–10) or a Micah (3.12) or a Jeremiah (7 ; 26.1–6). Moreover, it is not at all political.

Secondly, his baptism had the extraordinary character of an eschatological sacrament (Ezek. 36.25; Zech. 13.1). It took place not in basins or tanks as at Qumran, but in running river water. It is—for the first time—not a lustration performed by the penitent person himself, but an immersion of the penitent executed by someone else. The distinction of baptizer and baptized proves that the baptized person is not an active agent but a passive recipient, and that he has a gift to receive. This gift is made once and for all, and never again. Whoever is baptized is not only cleansed but he takes upon himself voluntarily and by anticipation the sentence of death which God will soon pass on the whole world.

Finally, John's mission is universal. He seeks to gather together God's people of the last days immediately before the impending judgement. For him this is a priestly people; but he does not seek to establish a sect formed by sorting and separation like the community at Qumran. Of course, he had disciples who fasted regularly and possessed set forms of prayer (Mark 2.18: Luke 5.33). According to Luke 11.1—in contrast to Matt. 6.9—we are indebted to this circumstance for the request which resulted in the Lord's Prayer. Yet the circle of John's disciples does not seem to have been primarily an end in itself. Their existence points rather to the fact that John, in contrast to the Qumran community, deliberately involved himself in the world and used his messengers for this (cf. Matt. 11.2). At any rate, he turns to all and invites all to make up their minds.

His fate is well known. The pretty prince Herod Antipas, who possessed the southern part of the country east of Jordan together with Galilee, had him imprisoned because he had censured his marriage to his sister-in-law, Herodias, 'and all the evil Herod had done'. When he was in prison John sent word to Jesus, whom he had baptized, to ask if he was 'the one who should come' or not (Matt. 11.2–6). Josephus sees in the imprisonment and execution of the Baptist the foresight of the prince at work seeking to prevent threatening rebellion. Mark (6.17–29) makes him the victim of the intriguing princess who uses the banquet on the birthday of her husband for her own ends. John's disciples are supposed to have buried his beheaded body quietly. We are not told where.

The fourth Gospel preserves a word of the Baptist about Jesus which comes near to being an invitation to his disciples to follow the man from Nazareth (John 1.29–37). The other three Gospels, by contrast, only know of words of Jesus about the Baptist. In them Jesus is emphatic in recognizing John as the greatest man who ever lived. He was no courtier but a character, a prophet, in fact more than a prophet (Matt. 11.7–11). His ministry is the turning-point for men and their destinies: 'When they heard this all the people and the tax collectors justified God, having been baptized with the baptism of John; but the Pharisees and the lawyers rejected the purpose of God for themselves, not having been baptized by him' (Luke 7.29–30). Even in the last days of his ministry, when High Priest, scribes and elders ask him by what authority he had cleansed the Temple forecourt, Jesus answers with a counter-question, 'Was the baptism of John from heaven or from men?' Jesus does not judge any further reply to

H

their startled silence necessary. Both Jesus and John belong
together. A person's attitude to John is a decision about Jesus.
John was the returned Elijah. But he was handed over to the
caprice of men; so 'they did to him as they wished' (Mark 9.11–13).

This judgement is all the more important because there is a
basic, twofold difference between Jesus and the Baptist. In the
first place, no miracles are recorded of John. And, secondly, John
does not seem to have been a spirit-filled person: his circle did
not claim to possess the spirit as a gift of the last days, as the
Qumran community did.

Jesus obviously received the call which came to him from God
through John the Baptist. It was not a special word of John's,
but John himself that constituted God's call to Jesus. More
exactly, there were two occasions when the existence of the great
solitary God became direct, living addresses to him: the appearance
of John the Baptist and his martyrdom. Probably Jesus was not
only baptized by him but was also his disciple for a time. But
our Gospels are silent on this point. Only the fourth Gospel
knows that two disciples of Jesus were originally disciples of
John (John 1.35–40). We have no certain knowledge of further
connections: we can only hazard conjectures.

It was only after Jesus' death that differences and conflicts
between the disciples of the Christ and of John developed. At
any rate, there seems to have been a Baptist sect which maintained
the water-baptism of John as the original sacrament (cf. Acts
19.1–7). Whether the group of legends and hymns in Luke 1
stems from their circle or not cannot be decided with absolute
certainty. Reading between the lines of John's Gospel at many
points one may detect echoes of what was once a violent dispute.
At any rate, there was a Baptist-cult which even in the second
century regarded John as the Messiah and expected his return.
About AD 200 the Baptist-worshippers seem to have merged
with the Syrian baptismal-sects, such as the Mandaeans, who
called themselves Nazoraeans of John and still exist in South Iraq
and Iran as a separate sect numbering 3,000 to 4,000 members.

2. *Between Baptism and Death*

Historically, Jesus' baptism by John in the Jordan is one of
the best attested facts of his life-story. All four Gospels attest it.

There is no doubt about it, just as there is no doubt about their report that Jesus was crucified under the procurator Pontius Pilate. The part of his life which is visible to us stretches between baptism and death.

Yet, on the basis of our present knowledge of the sources we cannot offer any biography of Jesus of Nazareth. Albert Schweitzer in his classical work has described the 'history of the study of Jesus' life' from the 'Fragment of an anonymous citizen of Wolfenbüttel' (H. S. Reimarus, d. 1768), published by Lessing in 1778, up to 1912. Two conclusions emerge, one positive, one negative. His positive judgement on one and a half centuries of historical work was: 'It is impossible to value too highly the achievement of historical study of the life of Jesus. It signifies a uniquely great pursuit of truth, one of the most important events in the whole spiritual life of mankind.' The negative conclusion was this: it is impossible to write a 'life of Jesus'. Any attempt to do so must be the work of historical or poetic fantasy.

The negative conclusion is the result of the character of the sources. It is true the Gospels are by no means bad as texts of late antiquity. Schweitzer granted that if we were satisfied with simply describing the public activity of Jesus, then 'there are few personalities in antiquity of whom we possess so many undoubtedly historical records and speeches as of Jesus'. But the Gospels do not set out to be biographies or to supply material for a biography. The Gospels are documents of faith. They are written down and put together in order that by means of a selection of narratives and sayings of Jesus they might awaken faith in men. The words with which the fourth Gospel originally ended also stand invisibly over the first three Gospels: 'Now Jesus did many other signs in the presence of his disciples, which are not written in this book: but these are written that you may believe that Jesus is the Christ, the Son of God, and that believing you may have life in his name' (John 20.30–31).

The evangelists are not biographers but collectors of traditional material. Unconnected narratives, conversations, parables and words of Jesus originally circulated as independent units. They had been repeated on different occasions: during worship, in preaching and in instructing believers in the mission to the Gentiles and in discussion with them. Later, these independent, smaller units were collected and arranged and set in a fuller

context. Indications of time and place linked the individual
pericopae with the structure of the Gospel as a whole. Unknown
individuals and groups with no literary pretensions created books
of instruction out of these *pericopae*, i.e. small sections of reading
and teaching material. As they were still close to the oral tradition
and were indebted to popular thought, they have been regarded
as 'minor literature'.

For these reasons it is impossible to trace any development
within either the public or private life of Jesus. The Gospels do
not supply the sequence of a life-story even of public actions.
We know as little about the length of Jesus' ministry as we know
of John the Baptist's, whose active ministry—after 27/28—is of
unknown duration. The fourth Gospel mentions three Passover
festivals (John 2.13; 6.4; 11.55), thus allowing for a period of
two to three years. The first three Gospels, called the 'Synoptics'
because of their common point of view, mention only one Passover,
that of Jesus' death, and allow for the possibility of including
everything that is recorded in less than a single year.

A special problem is posed by the date of Jesus' death. All four
Gospels agree that Jesus was crucified on a Friday at the time
of the Passover and that he rose again on the following Sunday.
They give different answers, however, to the question of how
that particular Friday—our Good Friday—was related to the
first day of the Passover, which was a moveable feast. The first
day of the Passover was Nisan 15, beginning with the previous
evening, Nisan 14, when the Passover-meal was usually held.
According to the fourth Gospel (John 18.28) Jesus died on Friday,
Nisan 14, at the hour when the Passover lamb was slain. According
to the synoptics he died on Friday, Nisan 15, on the first day
of the Passover, a time when executions were not normally undertaken, as Mark 14.2 reminds us. Both chronologies are theologically, or rather kerygmatically, motivated. The Johannine
chronology implies that Jesus is the true Passover-lamb (cf. John
1.29; 19.36), for he died on the eve of the feast when the Passover-
lamb was slain and eaten. In contrast to John, who is silent about
the celebration of the Last Supper, the synoptic chronology
implies that Jesus' last meal was a Passover-meal. If it is assumed
that the synoptic account, which admittedly many factors are
against, is basic, then one obtains a fairly probable date—for
two reasons. First, calculations based on astronomy have shown

that for AD 30 Nisan 15 fell on a Fri 'ay (7 April). Secondly, the next possible date—Friday, 3 April, A) 33 (Nisan 14, however)— is less probable, as it would conflict with the date of Paul's conversion as fixed by the Gallio inscription found at Delphi. Earlier dates—such as 11 April, AD 27 (= 15 Nisan)—need not be considered because of the date given by Luke 3.1.

Jesus began his ministry, therefore, between AD 27/28 and AD 29 and was probably crucified on 7 April, AD 30. This agrees with the date in John 2.20, where the forty-sixth year of the building of Herod's Temple is referred to: this was AD 27/28. According to John 8.57 Jesus was 'not yet fifty years old', according to Luke 3.23 'about thirty years old'.

The beginning and end, therefore, of Jesus' ministry can be fixed fairly accurately for the purpose of the historian; but this can hardly be said of the course of his ministry. The geographical references, which outline the wanderings and travels of Jesus, must be attributed to the composition of the respective evangelists. Their arrangement is not arbitrary, however. It has a deeper significance; it serves the purpose of the message. This is especially true of Luke's references to the places and journeys of Jesus, and is particularly so of his great 'travel-narrative' (Luke 9.51–19.27): Jesus' path from Galilee to Jerusalem is the path to suffering, which as the Christ he takes upon himself in accordance with God's plan of salvation. The oldest Gospel, Mark, has also arranged the material handed down to it in accordance with the great themes of its message: Jesus worked in Galilee (action: Mark 1–9), suffered and died in Jerusalem (passion: Mark 11–16). The journey forms the bridge between the two (Mark 10).

Jesus' own personal and inner development is even more inaccessible than the sequence of public events. The Gospels do not set out to give us a picture of his character but to proclaim his saving work. Today we can no longer do as Albert Schweitzer tried to do and give a dramatically moving picture of Jesus' inner motives, decisions and tendencies. A full-scale biography of Jesus has been out of the question for a long time; but even the comparatively brief period of his public ministry cannot be described satisfactorily in psychological terms. Any attempt to do so means retouching the picture; this does not make it either more convincing or more true.

The large majority of scholars have explained this fact for a long time not only by means of the general character of the Gospels which we have referred to but also by particular reference to the fact that an originally human existence has been reinterpreted and refashioned as a result of the Easter experience of the disciples and the early Church. The non-messianic life of a prophet has been later transformed into the messianic life of the Master who was exalted to be the Christ. This hypothesis reflects what is, in fact, an important observation: namely, our Gospels are the product of a community which did not fully know who Jesus of Nazareth really was until Easter and then only because of Easter. It was only as a result of the Easter experiences that they understood the meaning of his life, suffering and death. It was only the appearances of the risen Lord that opened the eyes of the first witnesses and set their hearts on fire (Luke 24.31–32). No wonder that they were unable to comprehend or arrange the words and actions of Jesus that they had seen and heard in the period before Easter, except in terms of the new existence granted them in faith. The light of Easter, therefore, is shed on every part of the Gospels, in which message and narrative are interwoven. Old Bengel once said that the Gospels 'breathe resurrection'. Indeed, many commentators think that whole narratives—such as the call of Peter, for instance (Luke 5.1–11)—originally described Easter experiences and were only backdated into the life of the earthly Jesus later. Many of the words which the evangelists ascribe to the historical Jesus were also, it is probable, originally words which the post-Easter community received from the ascended Lord through revelation. They had a vital experience of the presence of the living Lord in the direct movement of the spirit and of prayer. But this powerful presence not only aroused the will to recover the past. Its shining light also allowed many a historical contour to merge in the story of Jesus' life. The Christ-community had no ambition to draw up a general statement of what had actually happened based on exact minutes and complete documentation.

Yet although all these reflections are correct and although they have proved themselves so fruitful in advancing the study of the Gospels, they fail to allow sufficiently for one important, historical possibility. We saw earlier that a history of Jesus' development is not possible because the sources do not *intend* to provide such a history. There is, however, another possibility which is equally illuminating: they *could not* provide such a history. It is not only their point of view which is against providing such a history. The 'subject-matter' itself prevents them: namely, Jesus. The chief reason why the Gospels are not in a position to depict Jesus' development is that Jesus did not experience any development in the period under discussion. When he began his ministry his development was already complete. From the first day he is described for us he already *is* the person he is to be. What we take to be growth in him is, in fact, only the unfolding of his original being.

What we might like to identify as the later illumination of Easter in the Gospels proves to be a light indwelling this life from the beginning. Psychologically, it is true, the disciples were stirred into Easter-faith in the living Christ by the shattering experiences of Easter. But that they actually met *him* in the events of Easter was due to the fact that they had previously met him as the earthly one. His earthly life was of such irresistible force, seen purely as a human life, that it moulded the form of their future experience. The historical Jesus, Jesus before Easter, with whom they had journeyed through Galilee, sailed across the lake, and gone as pilgrims to Jerusalem, had already infected them with his power while they were with him. *He had possessed them.* The question seems out of place historically, and religiously almost blasphemous. For the sake of clarity, however, it ought to be asked at least provisionally—in order for it immediately to be forgotten again: what would have happened if the first witnesses had not participated in any Easter experiences? These experiences of the disciples certainly owe their content solely to the powerful intervention of God. But they owe the degree of their involvement and the colour of their vision to the disciples' past experience of the Man of Nazareth before Easter. Easter signifies God's call to return to the historical Jesus. The lost son returned to his father's house because in a far country the picture of the father regained control of him (cf. Luke 15). Similarly, the first company of believers was brought home out of the far country of fear and dismay through the picture of the historical Jesus. For the power of the earthly Jesus is the exalted Lord. But the criterion of the exalted Lord is the earthly Jesus.

3. *Home and Origin*

In the Gospels Jesus is called the Nazarene, or the Nazorite, both of which mean 'the man from Nazareth'. Nazareth is mentioned only in the New Testament, never in the Old Testament. Although Matthew and Luke describe it as a 'town' it may at that time have been a modest village with an Israelite population in the hill country of Lower Galilee, probably a relatively recent settlement, in fact. Josephus, who comes from Jerusalem, can never do enough to extol the fertility and beauty of Galilee. He emphasizes its abundance of flocks and vegetation of all types, and especially the mild climate round Lake Gennesaret, where almost the whole year round a 'noble contest of the seasons' takes place.

The parables of Jesus are redolent with the scent of his native land. From days of old Galilee had been a farming area. For centuries its surrounding fertile plains, at any rate, had been 'the King's land', i.e. demesne territory managed by bailiffs. Its old, perhaps even pre-Israelite, name of 'Galilee', which means 'circle of nations', was probably the result of the partly foreign feudal lords, the great lords of the manor, who maintained their own sovereignty and jurisdiction, surrounding the kernel of free hill-country with their possessions. This description, 'circle of nations' (Isa. 9.1; Matt. 4.15), was mistaken to mean 'Galilee of the Gentiles' in the sense that Galilee was a half-Gentile country. It was felt among the people, however, that the opposite was the case; the Judaism of Galilee, both racially and religiously, was always particularly pure. Galilee was the homeland of the Zealots, the religio-social fanatics, the patriotic activists. How far from ideal the economic and social situation was and how hated the absentee landlords were among the Galilaean farmers and agricultural workers can also be heard clearly in the parables of Jesus (cf. Mark 12.1–11).

Nazareth is Jesus' ancestral village (Mark 6.1). Here he grew up in the company of at least six other brothers and sisters. Apart from several sisters, whom we should probably think of as married, we know the names of four brothers: James, who later became the leader of the early Church in Jerusalem (I Cor. 15.7; Gal. 1.19; Acts 12.17); Joses, a diminutive of Joseph; Judas, claimed by the Epistle of Jude as its author, and whose descendants, small farmers in Palestine, are supposed to have been brought before the Emperor Domitian (d. AD 96) in Rome and to have still been alive in the reign of Trajan (98–117); and finally Simon, of whom nothing is recorded. Several of the brothers' names are names of the patriarchs, which shows that the old ancestral faith was kept alive in the family. The names Joses and Jesus are diminutives. 'Jesus' is the Greek form of the Hebrew name Jehoschua = Joshua, the name of Moses' successor. The father's name, Joseph, appears only in the birth stories of Matthew and Luke, apart from John 1.45; 6.42, where Jesus is called 'the son of Joseph'. He was by profession not just a manual worker but a carpenter and woodworker (Matt. 13.55). Justin Martyr (d. 165) claims to know he made farming equipment such as ploughs and yokes out of wood. At the time when Jesus began his ministry his father appears to be already dead. Jesus would learn his father's trade and he is called not only 'the carpenter's son' (Matt. 13.55) but 'the carpenter' (Mark 6.3).

Apart from the birth stories (Matt. 1–2; Luke 1–2) Mary, the mother of Jesus, plays only a subordinate role. She is referred to by name (Mark 6.3; Matt. 13.55) only occasionally. During Jesus' lifetime she did not belong to his followers (Mark 3.31–32), though Luke numbers her and her sons among the early Christians in Jerusalem (Acts 1.14). The fourth Gospel does not even mention her by name. According to John Jesus banishes her from his immediate presence with a harsh word (John 2.4), but by means of a word to her from the cross (John 19.26) appoints her a place in the Church where she can know herself safe yet also called to show love to others. The fourth Gospel presented an obvious obstacle to all future Mariolatry, which clearly began to spring up at an early date. Luke preserves a similar utterance in which Jesus points away from the blessedness of his mother to the blessedness of those who hear the word of God and keep it (Luke 11.27–28).

We know even less of Jesus' appearance than of John the Baptist's. Apparently it was quite normal. But even obvious things have to be left to the imagination. Jesus could read; he knew the Law and the Prophets and was able to read the lesson from them in the synagogue. Jesus could certainly write, since this was normally learnt along with reading. But he never passed on a single written word to his followers, nor is it ever recorded that he wrote anything. The exception to this, recorded in the fourth

Gospel's well-told story of the adulteress (John 8.6–8), only con-
firms this significant fact. As a Galilaean versed in the scriptures
Jesus probably spoke three languages: he knew Hebrew, the
language of the Old Testament and the liturgy; and Aramaic, of
course, the language of daily life, probably in the dialect peculiar
to Galilee, which the city-dweller found indistinct and rustic (cf.
Matt. 26.73) and the subject of wit. In view of the fact that Galilee
was surrounded by Hellenistic areas and colonized with Hellenistic
cities and that Greek had found wide acceptance as the language
of trade, it is possible that Jesus and his disciples knew Greek
also, at least to understand it and perhaps even to speak it. To
know two or three languages was by no means a sign of great
education. It was an inevitable result of the economic and social
conditions of the time.

4. *Divine Possession*

Suddenly, without warning, like John the Baptist before him,
Jesus appears on the banks of the Jordan. The oldest account
pictures his first appearance with almost telegraphic brevity: 'In
those days Jesus came from Nazareth of Galilee and was baptized
by John in the Jordan. And when he came up out of the water,
immediately he saw the heavens opened and the Spirit descending
upon him like a dove; and a voice came from heaven, "Thou art
my beloved son; with thee I am well pleased" ' (Mark 1.9–11).

This brief passage affirms an extraordinary event. Its importance
can hardly be overestimated. In some respects it is the most
important event in the whole destiny of Jesus of Nazareth. It is
taken up and developed in all the coming events which the Gospels
relate. It contains the future within it; more precisely, the future
of Jesus openly announces itself in this event. The baptism of
Jesus is, on any view, a fundamental event.

The earliest account of this scene was taken over by Mark as
it stood. It is still surrounded with an air of secrecy in his Gospel.
God himself speaks to Jesus. God addresses him as 'thou'. It all
happens in a direct manner, as if no one else was watching or
listening—not even the Baptist. God speaks to Jesus. Jesus hears
God's call. A threefold revelation follows.

First, God pronounces Jesus his son. He adopts him. The view
that God installs Jesus as his adoptive son fell into disrepute

through certain teachers in the early Church. Even today it is objected to by many Christians because it seems to exclude the eternal sonship and divinity of Jesus Christ. Is not Jesus God's son 'by nature'? In fact, it was thought in the old Canaanite Baal-religion that the king was 'God's son'. The Old Testament rejected this pagan view. It transformed the idea of the physical divine sonship of the Anointed into a solemn declaration by which God installs him with the rights of a son. This is expressed in Psalm 2, which embodies a hymn that was recited when the Jewish king was crowned in Jerusalem: 'You are my son; today I have begotten you' (Ps. 2.7). It is this 'divine decree' from the old royal ceremonial that Jesus hears. The words about being 'begotten today' are omitted by all the evangelists.

Secondly, the declaration contains a peculiar fulfilment of the first servant passage in Deutero-Isaiah (Isa. 42.1–4): 'Thou art my beloved son; with thee I am well pleased.' Isa. 42.1 says:

> Behold my servant, whom I uphold,
> my chosen, in whom my soul delights.

This decree of God may have applied to the whole nation of Israel. Now it applies to the carpenter from Galilee. God no longer bears it entirely in his own heart. God no longer converses with himself; he addresses Jesus. Jesus is the Chosen One of whom the apocalyptists dream. Soon dreams will become reality. The Chosen One will gather the chosen: in the Book of Enoch it was stated, in fact, that the Chosen One would be revealed with the chosen. Jesus will gather his own, even if he has understood the call to be the Chosen One differently. The moment when Jesus was baptized was the moment when the Church was conceived: soon it will be born. But the election of the Son as 'servant', i.e. God's representative, means service. Jesus is appointed his task: he is to proclaim truth or—the same thing—righteousness to the nations. We shall see how he performs this service (Matt. 12.18–21). Will he, too, the bringer of righteousness, have to suffer like the servant of God (Isa. 53) and the righteous (Ps. 34.19)? Such questions certainly would strain the narrative of Jesus' baptism too far. But the fundamental experience of Jesus at his baptism is open to all these interpretations.

Finally, adoption and election invest Jesus with the Spirit. The Spirit is the gift of the last days. It is promised to the Church

of the last days. We have already heard how it is to be poured
out on 'all flesh' (Joel 2.28–32), like water on a thirsty land
(Isa. 44.3). The Spirit is the moving force of ecstasy, dreams and
visions, as well as being the power behind the miraculous sign
which is to occur in heaven and on earth (Joel 2.28–32). It is the
freedom of grace and the freedom of supplication for God's
grace on the house of David and all inhabitants of Jerusalem
(Zech. 12.10). Such were the reflections of the apocalyptists in
their prayer books. The Spirit transforms men, individuals and
communities alike; in fact, it transforms mankind—the whole
world. God listens to the request of those who belong to him
(Isa. 64.1):

> O that thou wouldst rend the heavens and come down!

God comes down. But not on the many; only on the One. Jesus
becomes the one who is filled by the Spirit, the bearer of the
Spirit *par excellence*. Like a visionary he sees everything happening
above him and to him; he sees the Spirit 'descending like a dove'.
Is the dove—as in fairy tales—the royal bird which alights on the
head of the new ruler who is to be appointed? Is it the personified
power of God which fills the king, as they imagined in Persia? Is
it a reference to Noah's dove (Gen. 8.8–12) which announces
the end of the judgement of the Flood? Or does it symbolize the
moving of the Spirit on the waters of chaos (Gen. 1.2)? We cannot
be certain. Luke makes the Spirit descend 'in bodily form' like
a dove. Wherever the symbolic features come from, their fundamental meaning is clear: where Jesus appears, there God is present.
'Spirit' means, ultimately, God's manifestation of himself on
earth; it means God who is present here and now.

It is not surprising that this important event in the life of Jesus
should be embellished in legend and by pious fantasy. Justin
makes flames burst forth out of the Jordan. At an early date there
was speculation outside of the New Testament whether Jesus
by his baptism consecrated the baptismal waters for Christians.
The most beautiful rewriting of the event is in a Gnostic hymn
(Odes of Solomon 24):

> The dove flew down on Christ
> because he was its prince.
> She sang above him
> and her voice rang out.

Then all men and all creation began to fear. But the 'void' was 'sealed', i.e. the demonic powers were destroyed.

Matthew has made the baptism, in which only God and Jesus were involved, into an epiphany, a revelation visible by all the world. God's address *to* Jesus becomes a declaration of God *about* Jesus: 'This is my beloved Son.' Moreover, it is preceded in Matthew by a conversation between John and Jesus. John the Baptist expects Jesus to be the Baptizer who is to baptize him and all the world with the fire of judgement. He knows the time of his baptizing is running out and the time of the messianic baptism is breaking in. But Jesus replies, 'Let it be so now; for thus it is fitting for us to fulfil all righteousness' (Matt. 3.14–15). The new day, the evening of the day of his coming, begins with the one who will baptize with fire being baptized first of all, with Jesus identifying himself with sinners, and with his fulfilling that 'righteousness' which he desires to bring to the world. For thus it 'befitted' God's decree.

Jesus comes without winnowing fan. His coming is quite different from what John expected and proclaimed. The person of Jesus must have been a disappointment to the Baptist (cf. Matt. 11.2–3). But Jesus, too, must have expected something different from his baptism by John. Certainly he interpreted the phenomena provoked by John as a live call of God to go to the Jordan. Certainly he regarded the baptismal movement as a signal that God's rule would break in. But that God should address him and choose him as his Son, his Servant, the Bearer of the Spirit—that must have amazed him with elemental force.

In the experience of his baptism Pentecost was fulfilled for him alone. The earliest Christian community was able to explain the words and actions of Jesus in the light of Easter simply because they breathed the Spirit-event of his baptism from the beginning. Bengel's remark about the Gospels 'breathing resurrection' can be extended: from the time of Jesus' baptism they 'breath spirit'.

The demons in Capernaum ask, 'What have you to do with us, Jesus of Nazareth? Have you come to destroy us? I know who you are, the Holy One of God' (Mark 1.24). Believers, too, ground their decision to stay to the end with Jesus on the confession, 'We have believed and known that you are the Holy One of God' (John 6.69). The 'Holy One of God' is the man who is possessed by God and who freely and joyfully desires to obey him absolutely. Every word of Jesus and every account of his activity in the Gospels show him as a man who is so possessed by God that he forgets himself because of God. His self-forgetfulness is so deep that the question, for whom he spends himself, finds no proper answer at first. We shall see even more clearly how in some christological predicates of sovereignty absolutely nothing is appropriate to him. We cannot see into his so-called 'self-consciousness' except very indirectly. He is only interested in God and his demands and his promise. Because he knows that only God is 'good', and God alone, he rejects the description 'Good Master' (Mark 10.17–18).

If we want to know who Jesus really was and who he could be for us today, we must first of all suspend discussion of his titles. Thoughtless repetition of these titles will help us very little. Whoever calls Jesus 'the Christ', 'the Son of God', or 'the Lord', by no means proves himself a Christian; rather, he puts himself under the judgement of Jesus' word in Matt. 7.21–23. Whoever seeks to make quite clear to himself or someone else who Jesus was, may say with the New Testament that Jesus was a man of faith. The conversation about the withered fig-tree (Mark 11.20–25) implies this; certain sayings peculiar to Mark declare it expressly. 'All things are possible to him who believes' (Mark 9.23), and, 'all things are possible with God' (Mark 10.27). But it is also true that whoever wants to know what a man of faith is must read the Gospels. There he sees the man of faith active in speech and deed: the man who really let God be God. That is why the Epistle to the Hebrews calls him 'the pioneer and perfecter of our faith' (Heb. 12.2). It was because Jesus forgot himself in faith for God's sake that he was able to usher in the eve of God.

5. *The Impossible Possibility*

The baptism releases a whole chain-reaction of experiences and actions of Jesus, which can be grouped together as 'events of the Spirit'. Even the time when these fragments of tradition were collected and arranged in the early Christian communities was probably too far removed from the original events for the events to be fully understood. There was no denial that Jesus was a spirit-filled person, of course. But the awareness that Jesus accomplished and experienced the remarkable things he did as the archetypal charismatic person in the power of the Spirit of God is only partially preserved in our Gospels.

But this awareness that Jesus was the Spirit-bearer still receives forcible expression in Mark. Directly following the story of the Baptism it is recorded briefly: 'And immediately the Spirit drove him out into the wilderness. And he was in the wilderness forty days, tempted by Satan: and he was with the wild beasts; and the angels ministered to him' (Mark 1.12–13). Like Moses and Elijah, Jesus is alone in the wilderness before his public activity. Paradise returns: there is peace between man and beast. The angels minister to man. These are ancient apocalyptic views. But the return of paradise rests on the assumption that Adam must withstand the temptation of Satan. Because Jesus overcame the tempter, wild animals and angelic powers are at his service, for he is the new Adam.

Does this brief account conceal an intelligible event? The answer to this question depends on what one understands by Satan. In the Old Testament the idea of Satan does not emerge until very late, in the Persian period. Even then Satan is a subordinate figure. The term is derived from Israel's judicial life, and refers to the prosecutor in court. In Zechariah (3.1–2) he acts as a heavenly messenger of God. He has to charge and accuse the high-priest, Joshua. In the Book of Job he has the office of a general public prosecutor within the court of God, he has to trace every crime committed on earth and notify God (Job 1.6–2.7). Possibly this task is not limited to a definite person but can be allotted to various 'sons of God' for a fixed period. Side by side with this he can embody the demonic-destructive principle which seems to be anchored in God's plan of salvation (I Chron. 21.1; cf. II Sam. 24.1). It was only Judaism that treated Satan dogmatically and saw in him the evil spirit which seeks to destroy the relationship between God and man, especially between God and Israel. Whereas 'Satan' is a proper name, however, the word 'devil', i.e. slanderer, is more descriptive of vocation. 'Death came into the world through the envy of the devil' (Wisd. 2.23–24). The New Testament presupposes this Jewish idea of the devil, on the whole.

Later periods, especially the Middle Ages, grotesquely materialized the idea of Satan. Popular fantasy, in particular, converted the originally mythical figure into that monster which we are all so familiar with. The prince of hell, smelling of brimstone and possessing horns, tail and horses' hooves, who was meant to inculcate fear in men of a bygone age, today elicits only a smile at the most. But even if this caricature does not stand the test of the New Testament, the Evangelists, and indeed Jesus himself and Paul, shared the mythological ideas of their time. The fact that we can no longer share these compels us to ask whether the termination of the idea means the disappearance also of the reality contained in the idea. We cannot answer this on the basis of our religious experience, but only by examining the text of the Gospels for this reality.

The situation presupposed by all three Synoptics is the same. Jesus is the man chosen by God as Son, Servant and Spirit-bearer. He is in possession of the highest divine powers. The world stretches before him with its inexhaustible possibilities— the Hellenistic, Jewish and Roman world—in short, the 'modern' world of late antiquity. From a material point of view all positions in this world are occupied. Culturally, religiously, politically, there is not a vacant place which Jesus could occupy, let alone a place reserved for him. Life in those days possessed an uncanny compactness. Historically there is no means of proving that the time was exactly 'ripe' for the Gospel or that the call of Jesus 'had to' occur just at that particular time. Historically it would be easier to prove the opposite. There were experienced, competent authorities, powers and persons, readily available to satisfy cultural, religious, and political needs. Jesus and his gospel were not seriously in demand.

And yet, from God's point of view, 'the critical moment' (Greek: *kairos*) had arrived; 'the time' was fulfilled (Mark 1.15); the eschatological moment when the last things would actually take place had come. Paul expresses it by saying 'the fullness of time was here' (Gal. 4.4). The world was on the eve of its last day, the evening of God. With the evening of God it received its last, its only chance.

But what was this chance? It is certainly correct to say: Jesus of Nazareth. But who was Jesus? No ordinary person. Jesus was the man endowed with the highest powers of God. Above him and behind him stood God, the Lord and Creator of the world. But before him lay this world, with its innumerable possibilities. Jesus, the one possessed by the Spirit of God, saw himself confronted by this world of endless possibilities. He saw himself face to face with unconditional, abstract possibility. Who or what could hinder him from creating out of the womb of abstract possibility, out of pure nothing, a world which would be entirely his own world? This was the context of Jesus' temptation. We are not practising psychology or trying to insinuate our way into the inner life of Jesus by means of speculation. The Gospels reveal nothing about the inner life of Jesus at this point. But they do show us the unique situation in which Jesus stood— God behind him and the Tempter in front of him. For Jesus the tempter (Matt. 4.3), whether he be called Satan (Mark 1.13) or devil (Luke 4.3: *diabolos*), is nothing other than the epitome of unconditional, abstract possibility.

Matthew and Luke have extended the story of the one temptation of Jesus and converted it into a threefold temptation (Matt. 4.1–11; Luke 4.1–13). In doing so they have given it the form of a dispute between two scribes, following three avenues of conversation. They have also ventured to transpose the time sequence in a similar manner; what was essentially a point in time has become a period divided into three. What was quite literally invisible has been painted in three dramatically moving episodes. Explicitly (Matt. 4.3, 6) or implicitly (Matt. 4.8–9), all three temptations assume the view that Jesus is 'God's Son'. In appealing to this title the Tempter suggests that Jesus should remove three obstacles by three sorts of miracle.

First, Jesus is given the possibility of assuaging his hunger by a miracle of self-help. At his word the stones of the wilderness would turn into bread. Could he also satisfy the hunger of all men permanently? (This question is not framed in so many words, but is implied.) Jesus replies that man does not live by bread alone but by every word that proceeds from the mouth of God (Deut. 8.3). This does not mean that man lives by adding God's word to his diet, but that by reaching for God's bread a dialogue is initiated. God's active word is what gives substance to the earthly process of nutrition.

Secondly, Jesus is given the possibility of throwing himself down from the pinnacle of the Temple. This is supported by words of scripture (Ps. 91.11–12). He could remove the secret prejudices of the theocratic state by an impressive miracle, which would prove in the eyes of both hierarchy and populace that he was God's ambassador. Jesus replies that God may not be used for religious experiments (Deut. 6.16).

Thirdly, Jesus is given the possibility of obtaining world-dominion. Obeisance to the devil, the ruler of the world (Luke 4.5–6; cf. II Cor. 4.4), would qualify him for this. Jesus replies, 'Begone, Satan! God alone is to be obeyed and served' (Deut. 6.13).

It is not difficult to perceive that the point of the three temptations corresponds to the three spheres which made up the world of Jesus and of every other Jew at that time. The first temptation is to be a certain extent the 'Hellenistic' temptation; it takes the question of the material welfare of man as its theme. The second, the 'Jewish' temptation, would like to guarantee the heavenly salvation of man by means of the theocratic state. The third, the 'Roman' temptation, deals with the might and glory of the firmly established empire.

Jesus resists the three temptations by putting into practice the First Commandment. He rejects abstract possibility, which makes God, man and the world the plaything of his own will. He does not surrender to alien necessity. But he affirms the will of God to be the foundation of all reality. He finds sustenance in the fact that he can do the Father's will (John 4.34).

Luke makes the devil leave Jesus only 'for a season' (Luke 4.13). This permits recognition of the fact that temptation was his constant companion on life's journey and that it appeared with renewed force at the end of his life in Gethsemane (Luke 22.40–46; cf. 22.28).

6. *The Work*

The historical occasion of the first call Jesus received from God, in time at any rate, was the appearance of John the Baptist. The call led him to the Jordan. According to Mark it was the news of the Baptist's imprisonment which brought him back to Galilee (Mark 1.14). Where this news came to him is not said. At all events he could not have been nearby. But where was he then? And what was he doing meanwhile? These questions find no answer in the text. According to the fourth Gospel John and Jesus were active together for a period (John 3.22–26; 4.1–3). But these references are to some extent contradictory: on one occasion Jesus himself is baptizing (John 3.22), and on another this is denied and the work of baptizing is limited to his disciples

(John 4.2). Neither statement is very probable, since baptism plays no part at all during Jesus' lifetime according to the Synoptics. The so-called 'baptismal Gospel' (Mark 10.13–16) makes no mention of baptism.

Even if we give up all claim to determine the historical sequence of events, however, one thing is clear: for Jesus the arrest of John meant God's summons to return home. Now it is Jesus who preaches—but not judgement, as the Baptist had thought, but the nearness of the kingly rule of God as a source of great joy. It is not because of the seriousness of divine catastrophe, but in joy that at last 'the time is fulfilled', that he summons his hearers to repent (Mark 1.14–15). The words are similar to those of the Baptist; but there is a quite different ring about them. Jesus' call is, as the evangelist writes, a gospel, a message of good news, a report of a victory which has been won. No longer does Jesus preach of someone else, though he does not preach himself; he preaches only the nearness of God. And, most important of all, this God is not a God of judgement but of mercy. Mark sets this announcement at the head of his whole work like the title of a programme.

Jesus immediately sets to work. He calls complete strangers into his service, and—even more strange—they follow him without question. Two pairs of brothers are his first fellow workers. He finds them on the shore of Lake Galilee—whereabouts, exactly, is not said. All four are fishermen. The first two, who have Greek names, Simon and Andrew, are wading in the water and are on the point of throwing out their round cast-net. Then, in the midst of their work, they hear his call, 'Come, follow me! I will make you fishers of men.' No more intimate reason, no more concrete aim, is given. But they cannot resist the call and, though the work is unfinished, for his sake they leave all—immediately. A little further on the small fishing partnership of Zebedee is at work. Obviously they operate on a somewhat larger scale than the first two; along with the older man are his two sons James and John and his employees. Moreover they possess a boat and a sledge-net which they are just in process of repairing. Though the work is unfinished, they too, leave everything at Jesus' call (Mark 1.16–20).

All this must have happened near Capernaum, which was situated on the north side of the lake, not far from where the

upper Jordan flowed into it. The great trade-route to Damascus
ran through the town. Hence there was a tax office there (Mark
2.14). Capernaum was also a garrison-town (Matt. 8.5–13). Jesus,
coming from Nazareth, chose to live here for a time, or rather,
to make it a base for his travels (Matt. 4.13).

Almost everything that Mark records of Jesus in his first
chapter is fitted within the framework of a single day, and, what
is more, a Sabbath (Mark 1.21–39). They go to the synagogue
together. Jesus teaches there. What he teaches, we are not told.
But the response is described. They are filled with amazement.
For although Jesus is no scribe and has not studied (Mark 6.2),
his teaching possesses authority. It springs from an original
freedom. It makes a direct appeal. It grips the hearers. It 'gets
across'. The reflection of the professional theologian is alien to
it. And, above all, something happens in and through and beneath
this teaching. A man possessed shrieks out in protest at Jesus'
presence and almost betrays the secret of Jesus in the midst of
the excited assembly: 'You are the Holy One of God.' Jesus
rebukes the unclean spirit and reduces it to silence. Finally, after
convulsing the man and making a loud noise the spirit comes out.
Is Jesus an exorcist, who expels demons? Certainly such a view
would contain more truth and more historical accuracy than many
a modern description of Jesus, which erases from its picture
anything that is disturbing or not in good taste, on the ground
that it conflicts with the standards of a sound theology. But, in
this sense, Jesus was no 'theologian', but a man!—a man of the
Spirit. Wherever he appeared the power of God was mobilized
against the condescending world of the theocracy. Wherever he
opened his mouth, there was a commotion. But this was not
because something sensational in the modern sense had occurred,
but because in a world of oppressive restrictions normality had
suddenly arrived. What Jesus did was not 'the latest fashion',
but the exact opposite; it was old-fashioned, fundamental and
original—the wholeness of God in a sick age.

His contemporaries described this activity as 'new' teaching,
a teaching 'with authority'. In doing so they expressed something
very distinctive about it, something which was characteristic of
Jesus' work from the very beginning, something which was
unique in the sense that it constituted a unity of *word and deed*.
Things which usually fall apart and conflict with us formed a

unity and a wholeness in Jesus. Everyone who met him experienced this; what he said proved an action and conversely what he did proved to be a word of encouragement or demand. Anyone who has met Jesus, the complete, 'whole' man, can never forget the experience.

From the synagogue (Mark 1.21–28) he goes straight to Simon's home and cures his mother-in-law's fever (Mark 1.29–31). At the end of the day—the Sabbath!—we are given a picture of Capernaum, which Rembrandt's master-hand has preserved in his Hundred Guilder Print. 'That evening, at sundown, they brought to him all who were sick or possessed with demons. And the whole city was gathered together about the door. And he healed many who were sick with various diseases and cast out many demons; and he would not permit the demons to speak because they knew him' (Mark 1.32–34).

Is this the end of the day's work for Jesus? Not at all. 'And in the morning, a great while before day, he rose and went out to a lonely place, and there he prayed. And Simon and those who were with him followed him, and they found him and said to him, "Everyone is searching for you." And he said to them, "Let us go on to the next towns, that I may preach there also; for that is why I came out." And he went throughout all Galilee, preaching in their synagogues and casting out demons' (Mark 1.35–39). Luke makes Jesus' ministry begin with a sermon (Luke 4.14–30). This takes place in Nazareth 'where he had been brought up' (4.16). In the power of the Spirit he returns to Galilee (4.14) and goes to the synagogue on the Sabbath. The order of service provided for two readings of scripture, one from the Law, the other from the Prophets. To read the lesson was not the prerogative of any particular class such as the priests or scribes, but was open to all. Jesus indicates his readiness to read a lesson by standing up. The roll of the prophet Isaiah (61.1–2) is handed to him:

> The Spirit of the Lord is upon me,
> because he has anointed me to preach good news to the poor.
> He has sent me to proclaim release to the captives
> and recovery of sight to the blind,
> to set at liberty those who are oppressed,
> to proclaim the acceptable year of the Lord.

Up to this point everything has run its normal course. Jesus rewinds the roll and gives it back again into the custody of its keeper. He sits down. People wait for him to comment on the text. But, instead of speaking *about* the text, he lets the text determine the hour: '*Today* this scripture has been fulfilled in your hearing.' He himself is the bearer of the Spirit, whom the text proclaims. The prophetic word, subordinate to the word of the Law in many respects, creates a vital reality: it designates him as the archetypal charismatic person in the present moment of God's day. God's decision to challenge men to decide is taken. But amazement is followed by opposition, not faith. He is expelled from the place amidst fierce anger. As if by a miracle Jesus escapes being stoned.

The Spirit cannot be quenched. Jesus confronts men—both those who oppose him and those who believe in him—with the power by which he withstood the Tempter. We do not know anything about Jesus' frame of mind, nor are we meant to. But the fragments which are scattered throughout the Gospels point to a manner of life such as we meet with everywhere in the world of religions. This Jesus lives in an atmosphere in which something extraordinary can happen any time, and does, in fact, constantly do so. Inaudible voices echo round about him. Invisible lights shine upon him. Unforeseen things happen to him. Unattainable insights overtake him. What the Spirit has revealed to believers, to the elect, according to Paul (I Cor. 2.9), has already been made known to Jesus, the First Chosen One:

> What no eye has seen nor ear heard,
> nor the human heart conceived,
> what God has prepared for those who love him.

The power of the Spirit must have been infectious. It took hold of those who stood next to him. It shook them and kindled a similar experience of God in them. Perhaps many of the narratives which scholars have called 'epiphanies' (appearances) and which have usually been interpreted as due to the later illumination of Easter experiences should be re-interpreted in the light of these pentecostal events. This would include narratives such as that of the Transfiguration of Jesus (Mark 9.2–8), which draws the disciples away from the blessed contemplation of his bright figure and points them to his prophetic word.

It was one such pentecostal experience that led to Jesus' cry of joy, which Luke (10.21–22) and Matthew (11.25–27) preserve in quite different contexts. The strophes of this hymn are very distinctive. Jesus 'rejoiced in the Holy Spirit that same hour' and said:

> I thank thee, Father, Lord of heaven and earth,
> that thou hast hidden these things from the wise and under-
>   standing,
> and revealed them to babes;
> yea, Father, for such was thy gracious will.
> All things have been delivered to me by my Father;
> and no one knows who the Son is
> except the Father,
> or who the Father is
> except the Son,
> and anyone to whom the Son chooses to reveal him.

Even at the first hearing one can perceive the unusual tone of this hymn of revelation. Does the synoptic Jesus talk like that? Is it not much more like the Johannine Christ? At any rate, the exalted Lord speaks like this, as the end of Matthew's Gospel, for instance (Matt. 28.18–20), shows. The diction is metrical, like a hymn, and has a stirring rhythm. The words and ideas betray the climate of Gnostic piety. The contents seem to describe Hellenistic mysticism rather than Jewish knowledge of God, even if they have been given a Semitic colour. Does the poet of the parables speak like this? Is this the utterance of one who forgot himself because he was possessed by God? And yet, through this hymn of praise to God, so unique in its style, and through the self-expression of this song of praise, there can be heard the voice of Jesus, filled with the Spirit.

He is exulting in his eschatological victory on earth as he sings this hymn. God has done great things: he has let *him* appear, speak and act. Jesus speaks in a rush of unbounded ecstasy, as it were. It is the only place in the Gospels where praise of God bubbles over in such a way. A generation or two ago it was thought that Jesus must have been a psychopath, or a hysteric, or a megalomaniac because of such expressions. How absurd! What strange ideas! Jesus thanks God not only for the response which his words met but even for opposition to them as well. God has hidden his work from the scribes, the intelligentsia, the creators of culture, the mighty and the influential. Therefore, he has revealed it to 'infants', that is, those who have nothing to say, who have no organs at their disposal to express their opinion—neither press nor radio, as we would say—and who have fewer rights and are treated accordingly. That is why Jesus gives thanks! But he is not thereby giving thanks for failure? No, not at all: for he may be giving thanks for a success, which, in the eyes of men, however, is overshadowed by failure. Jesus affirms what is, humanly speaking, an ambiguity. For in it he sees no accident, no mischance, but God's will, God's plan. God's will is free. The secret of his plan is election. God takes the risk of losing. Both what happens and the manner of it are the result of God's gracious decision. For this reason he knows that as Son he is united with the Father. Only the Father knows who the Son is. Only the Son, and anyone to whom the Son reveals the knowledge, knows who the Father is. *We* would judge that God is hidden and Jesus stands in the light. But he says the opposite: he, Jesus, stands in the dark, known only by God; and as the one who stands in the dark, he shows us God. Only through Jesus do we know who God is, what God wills and what God does.

To repeat: the historical Jesus did not speak like this. But through the Spirit the exalted Christ creates in the community of the early Church a full knowledge of himself. On the evidence of the Spirit believers recognize who the historical Jesus was during his lifetime. They know now about the secret of his earthly existence: about his personal relationship with God, about the nearness of the coming God in his words and actions. With characteristic assurance he declares that the eve of God has arrived. Turning to the disciples he speaks the last strophe to them 'privately' (Luke 10.23-24):

> Blessed are the eyes which see what you see!
> For I tell you that
> many prophets and kings desired to see what you see
> and did not see it,
> and to hear what you hear
> and did not hear it.

7. *The Message*

The message of Jesus has only one theme: the kingdom of God is near. This is the message with which Jesus begins his ministry (Mark 1.15). This is the news he announces in innumerable passages. The content of this message is described and developed by Jesus through that teaching medium which the Gospel tradition declares to be most original from a literary point of view and most probable historically, namely through his parables.

The idea which is familiar to us from our Bibles as 'the kingdom of God' or 'the kingdom of heaven' was taken over by Jesus from the Judaism of his day. Both terms mean the same. 'Heaven' in the phrase 'kingdom of heaven', which Matthew favours in contrast to Mark and Luke, is only the Jewish periphrasis for the name of God which was avoided for reverential reasons. 'Kingdom of God' has a twofold meaning: firstly, it means the actual power of God by which God manifests himself as King; secondly, it means the visible order which God's rule exhibits and creates. The emphasis is on the first of these meanings—the personal rule of God, so that the expression 'kingdom' is best rendered 'rule'. God's rule is so very much God's own business, that one is tempted to see in the word 'rule of God' simply another expression for God himself, the Lord who acts in a kingly manner. At all events, the kingdom of God is not to be understood primarily in static terms as an area or district, like an earthly kingdom; but, at the same time, God's rule cannot be disposed of simply by talking of God's dynamic activity. God's kingly power is identical with the visible expression of it. In fact, it creates this visible order. If God comes then he comes with his divine world. For God is this world and cannot be God without it.

When ancient Israel spoke of God's power it usually preferred to do so in terms of his 'election'. But the idea that Yahweh is King, even where the description is not found, is very old. In very early days it was connected with the Ark of the Covenant, the visible throne on which the Invisible sat. In this connection it is important to notice Israel's peculiar view that *before* Yahweh was Israel's King, he was the King of a heavenly court of innumerable divine beings (I Kings 22.19–23). He was able to be Israel's ruler because he was 'Lord of hosts' first. This is how Isaiah saw him with his own eyes, 'the King himself' (Isa. 6.5).

This is how, long before, although the title of king was not used, he was called 'the Judge of all the earth' (Gen. 18.25). Later, Deutero-Isaiah made the idea of the God-King more explicit (Isa. 41.21; 43.15; 44.6). The fact that God was King over divine beings gave him an exclusive superiority over the divine kings of every heathen pantheon from the very beginning. Israel's God was always 'a great King above all gods' (Ps. 95.3). His praises ring out in the Psalms: 'The Lord sits enthroned as King for ever' (Ps. 29.10). Israel's worship celebrates the annual Festival of his Enthronement (Pss. 47; 93; 96–99). Israel's God is the Lord of the whole world. He comes to judge the nations and establish his authority over the world (Pss. 96; 98). In faith the worshipping community anticipates the future foretold it in the Promise. Only the late period speaks of the *kingship* of God (Pss. 103.19; 145.13; Dan. 3.33; 4.31) instead of God, the King.

In apocalyptic circles the 'kingly rule of God' became a basic concept. Its coming was awaited. Its arrival was prayed for. Different expectations—earthly and heavenly, political and religious—circulated; sometimes they ran parallel, sometimes they conflicted, sometimes they joined forces. They were mostly narrow, selfish hopes for Jerusalem. Very rarely they were broad, unselfish hopes for all the world. In Jesus' own day it was said (Assumption of Moses 10):

> And then his kingdom shall appear
> throughout all his creation.
> Then the devil will be no more
> and sorrow shall depart with him.

Unquestionably Jesus shared many of the views of Judaism about God's rule. Resurrection (Mark 12.18–27) and judgement (Luke 11.31–34) belonged with God's kingly power as a matter of course. It was taken for granted, too, that his kingdom was like a sumptuous banquet, where one would recline at table with the patriarchs, Abraham, Isaac, and Jacob (Matt. 8.11), eating and drinking (Luke 22.30). In the 'kingdom of heaven' there are differences of rank: small and great (Matt. 11.11), ordinary seats and seats of honour (Mark 10.35–40). The disciples will 'sit on twelve thrones and rule the twelve tribes of Israel' (Matt. 19.28). And yet, how sparing and how reserved are the pictures of this internally graded divine world. Compare with it a typical passage from the Syriac Apocalypse of Baruch (*c.* AD 100–130):

> The earth also shall yield its fruit ten-thousandfold
> and on each vine there shall be a thousand branches,
> and each branch shall produce a thousand clusters,
> and each cluster produce a thousand grapes,
> and each grape produce a cask of wine.
> And those who have hungered shall rejoice:
> Moreover, also, they shall behold marvels every day.
> For winds shall go forth from before me
> to bring every morning the fragrance of aromatic fruits
> and at the close of the day clouds distilling the dew of health.
> And it shall come to pass at that selfsame time
> that the treasury of manna shall again descend from high,
> and they will eat of it in those years
> because these are they who have come to the consummation of
> time.

Jesus says nothing about such a paradisical fairyland.

Even more important, however, is a second fact. Jesus knows that the day of God is dawning, but he forbids calculation of the hour. The apocalyptic calendar of the last days disappears. God's rule comes upon men without it being possible to calculate or observe it. This is the meaning of Luke 17.20, 'The Kingdom of God is not coming with signs to be observed', and of the saying, 'But of that day or that hour no one knows, not even the angels in heaven, nor the Son, but only the Father' (Mark 13.32). No one, not even the doorkeeper, knows when the master of the house will return home, perhaps late in the evening, perhaps at midnight, perhaps at cockcrow or in the morning: he comes suddenly (Mark 13.33–37). He comes like the thief—unannounced (Matt. 24.42–44). Because no one knows it is wise to be on the watch. The password is not 'Look around' but 'Look out'!

This is enough to show that Jesus is no apocalyptist. He is the very opposite, in fact; he makes a break with apocalyptic. It is not accidental that he takes his stand upon the prophets, when he reads the lesson in the synagogue at Nazareth (Luke 4.17). The spirit of the promise revives. The folly of pious calculation is done away with.

Nevertheless, Jesus is master of the apocalyptic vocabulary.

He is familiar with apocalyptic concepts and ideas. Of course, there was never a simple thing called 'Jewish apocalyptic', not, at any rate, as a conceptual system. What is usually so called is a many-sided and contradictory structure. Not only does book conflict with book and group with group but intellectual contradictions run through one and the same book, through one and the same group. And yet, there is something like a standard of reference which underlies all the different apocalyptic viewpoints; in other words, an overall structure within which even the contradictory views have their place. This standard of reference is presupposed by Jesus' message of God's rule.

All apocalyptic objects and events, for instance, could at one and the same time be thought of and expressed in two dimensions, which, according to our normal way of thinking, absolutely exclude each other. It is a question of the integration of time and space. The apocalyptic idea of God's rule also shares in this two-dimensional view. God's rule is as much an object in space as in time.

As an object in space God's rule is the beyond, which stands over against our world on this side. God's rule does not come into being; it *is*. It is in constant, permanent opposition to this world. It is the eternal heavenly world, where everything that will take place on earth is already in existence. The eternal, decisive facts are always related to everything here and now. Their present existence 'up there' is not beyond time but superior to time. If one wished to describe the relationship between this world of pre-existent beings and ourselves by means of a graph, one would have to let the perpendicular fall vertically.

As an object in time, however, the rule of God is the future, which meets our world as the present. God's rule only exists while it occurs. It occurs as the future which breaks into our present. It is the time when the forces of energy which have been damned up in heaven are released and burst forth. The decisive events are of necessity only related to the here and now while they are actually occurring. They are not above space but separate from space when they are in advance of 'tomorrow'. If one wished to describe the relationship between this world of future realities and ourselves by means of a graph, one would have to draw the horizontal straight across.

There is no doubt that when Jesus proclaimed the advent of

God's rule he understood this primarily as an event in time. The rule of God is the future of the world. It is the coming God. It is thoroughly 'dynamic'—a divine event. But it has a 'static' character at the same time—it conceals men and the world in its divine space. It can only use its powers on earth because from the beginning they are part of the existence of the heavenly world. God can 'let his will be done as it is in heaven' (Matt. 6.10). Only if his will is done on earth (i.e. if the future is revealed in the present) can the world and mankind have a genuine present. Then the horizontal of a period of time (*chronos*) meets the perpendicular of the divinely ordained decision at a point of time (*kairos*). The *kairos* is the 'acceptable time', the right moment when God realizes his rule here and now (Mark 1.15).

The following picture is an attempt—inadequate, of course, in the nature of the subject—to portray in a diagram what has been said so far.

Space: **BEYOND**   :Existence

```
              K  |
              A  |   Point
              I  |   of
Time:         R  |   time    :Event
              O  |
              S  ↓
←  – – – – – – – – – – • ←————————————————
              Period of time CHRONOS
```

PAST   **PRESENT**   **FUTURE**
                    (interregnum)
                    THIS SIDE

Did Jesus, then, usher in this world of God? Or did he only declare that it was coming later? The answer which the Gospels give must be considered under three headings.

First, at the moment when Jesus speaks and calls, God's rule is imminent. It has, on a strict definition of time, not yet arrived. It is still future. Otherwise there would be no need to pray for it (Matt. 6.10); no need to call 'Look out!' and 'Watch!' A large number of passages in our Synoptic Gospels, which we do not need to cite in detail, makes this clear. God's rule is to be under-

stood 'eschatologically'. Albert Schweitzer and others thought it
should be understood in terms of a 'thorough-going eschatology'.
All words which speak of the nearness of God's rule mean its
future—even if that future be ever so near. 'From the fig tree learn
its lesson: as soon as its branch becomes tender and puts forth its
leaves, you know that summer is near. So also, when you see
these things taking place, you know that he is near, at the very
gates' (Mark 13.28–29). 'The summer is close by, at the very
gates.' God comes like this—like the Palestinian summer which
follows the winter rains almost without a break, almost without
spring.

All the sayings which speak of the 'day' confirm the future
character of God's rule. The terrible day of judgement draws
near—a day even more terrible for those towns which reject
Jesus' offer than it was for Sodom and Gomorrah (Matt. 10.15).
Its coming is more terrible for the Galilaean cities Chorazin and
Bethsaida than for the Phoenician cities of Tyre and Sidon
(Matt. 11.21–22). It is, in fact, the day of the coming Son of Man
(Mark 13.32; Luke 17.24). The term, 'to enter' the kingdom of
God refers to the future (Mark 10.15, 23; Matt. 5.20). It is,
indeed, equivalent in significance to the future life (Mark 9.43–48).
Words connected with 'inherit' are also promises of something
to come (Mark 10.17). The blessed of the Father are to inherit
the kingdom, which has been prepared for them 'from the foundation of the world' (Matt.25.34). 'Fear not, little flock, for it is
your Father's good pleasure to give you the kingdom' (Luke 12.32).
The little flock which gathers round Jesus, the shepherd, in the
present, is promised the gift of the future. The gift is certain
because Jesus' promise is rooted in God's eternal decree. God's
rule is imminent and near, in both a chronological and a spatial
sense.

But, secondly, contrasting with all these and similar passages
is a series of other passages, which speak of God's rule as present.
In respect of his work Jesus says: 'If it is by the spirit of God
that I cast out demons, then the kingdom of God has come upon
you' (Matt. 12.28). Luke records the same saying, but makes
Jesus say 'finger of God' instead of 'spirit of God' (Luke 11.20).
This is not simply one of those archaisms which Luke is fond of;
it is also an interpretation. God's finger (Ex. 8.19) denotes God's
miraculous intervention in the rebellious world, just as his 'arm'

(Isa. 51.9) expresses the power with which God makes his saving presence active on earth.

When the seventy return from their mission and tell him of their charismatic triumphs over the demons, Jesus says to them, 'I saw Satan fall like lightning from heaven' (Luke 10.18). The saying is without parallel. Is Jesus referring to a vision? When did it take place? At the time of the achievements of the seventy? Or when Jesus himself healed the first possessed man? Or even earlier, when he overcame the Tempter? The saying has overtones of a special experience of the Spirit. At any rate, it understands the destruction of Satan's power in heaven and his expulsion from God's world as a present event and completed fact. Does this mean, now that he has been cast out of heaven onto this earth, that he is doing his work 'here below'? The Revelation (12.9) says that the birth of the Messiah results in the evil from heaven being yoked to the earth. Its expulsion from eternity is to be its resurrection in time. He is to live on his fallenness. Jesus' word says nothing of this directly. But it assumes that the successful dethronement of Satan is the reason for the fact that men can exorcize him in the name of Jesus. God's rule is already at work. Another proof of the fact that God's rule is already present, although 'God's rule' is not explicitly mentioned, is the answer which Jesus gives to the imprisoned Baptist (Matt. 11.4-5) when he sends messengers to ask Jesus whether he is 'the Coming One' (Ps. 118.26?):

> Go and tell John what you hear and see:
> the blind receive their sight and the lame walk,
> lepers are cleansed and the deaf hear,
> and the dead are raised up and the poor have good news
>   preached to them.

The allusions to the prophetic promises of salvation (Isa. 29.18-19; 35.5-6; 61.1) indicate the important connection. The day of God, to which the prophetic voices a thousand years before had pointed, has dawned. It is present in the activity of Jesus. 'Blessed is he who takes no offence at me' (Matt. 11.6).

The present nature of the rule of God is attested by two more sayings, although their interpretation is attended with special difficulties. The first is Luke 17.20-21. We have already mentioned how in answer to the question (of the Pharisees!) as to when the rule of God would come Jesus replied that it was impossible in principle to calculate or observe it. 'Nor will they say, "Lo, here it is!" or "There!" for behold the kingdom of God is here!' The word which we have provisionally rendered by 'here' is often translated as 'within you'. Modern scholarship, taking up Old Latin and Syrian translations, has largely opted for 'in the midst of you', on the grounds that Jesus could not have understood the rule of God in terms of 'inwardness' and that Luke would have expressed himself more clearly if he had meant 'inward'. Whichever interpretation is followed the rule of God is a present fact in both cases.

The interpretation of Matt. 11.2–13 is even more difficult. 'From the days of John the Baptist until now the kingdom of heaven has suffered violence and men of violence take it by force. For all the prophets and the law prophesied until John.' It is quite uncertain who the men of violence are. The world-rulers in the spirit world? Jewish opponents on earth? Or the Pharisees, who want to 'compel' the kingdom—in a good sense—by religious ardour and moral effort? Whatever the answer may be, the Prophets and the Law have had their day with John the Baptist; the day of God's rule has replaced them.

Finally, in spite of its present nature, the kingdom of God does not cease to be future! It is not yet here—and again it is here already—and yet again it is still not here. The fate of men, including the man who puts his trust in Jesus, stretches between the 'now' and 'not yet' of their existence. Similes and parables repeatedly summon men to watchfulness. 'Let your loins be girded and your lamps burning, and be like men who are waiting for their master to come home from the marriage so that they may open to him at once when he comes and knocks' (Luke 12.35–36). The marriage feast is already in progress, for the bridegroom is there (Mark 2.19). On the other hand, it is still in the future, for the young maidens are supposed to be waiting for it (Matt. 25.7–13).

Man's path is the path of judgement. Come to terms with your accuser on the way to court before it is too late (Luke 12.58–59). Be constant in prayer for eschatological righteousness. If the widow provoked the unrighteous judge to help her because of her cries, God will certainly help to acquit his own 'very soon' (Luke 18.1–8). The fact that Jesus is there certainly denotes the presence of God's rule, but in such a way that he is the last messenger in view of its definite imminence. 'The men of Nineveh will arise at the judgement with this generation and condemn it; for they repented at the preaching of Jonah, and behold, something greater than Jonah is here' (Matt. 12.41). It will be a case of gaining or losing one's own life (Mark 8.35). It will be a case of eternal life in God's kingdom or the inextinguishable fire of hell (Mark 9.43–48; Matt. 25.41, 46; Luke 16.23–24). It *will* be. The parables of the tares among the wheat (Matt. 13.36–43) and the drag-net (Matt. 13.47–50) expressly forbid anticipation of the future separation. The final judgement is reserved for the future, for a date which cannot be calculated.

How can the similarities and contradictions of the expressions be explained? Two answers suggest themselves. Both illustrate how Jesus exploded Jewish and apocalyptic concepts by his ministry and his message.

First, the sequence of the times was no problem for Jewish expectation. The evil time of the world was quickly followed by the time of God. Towards the end of the first century AD the succession of Roman and Jewish rule was prophesied under the picture of the two brothers who were enemies, Jacob and Esau: Jacob's hand held Esau's heel (Gen. 25.26). The times can be separated clearly: this age closes with the Roman Empire, the future age begins with Israel's Empire. The two ages are mutually exclusive; the one follows the other. Not so with Jesus: in him God's rule was present in the midst of this time. The old age still existed, but in his person the new had broken in. The ages (Matt. 12.32; Mark 10.30: probably composed by the early Church) are superimposed on each other like two pictures. To put it graphically the two periods are like two film-strips, the one being run off fading and the one being run on emerging more clearly. Of course, the situation in the New Testament is that during the earthly life of Jesus both ages run equally clearly and thus conceal each other. The normal eye cannot distinguish which sequence the future belongs to. The new pictures are there but not yet there.

Secondly, Jewish expectation could only speak of the presence of the heavenly time if it were visibly present in power. It proclaimed that God's rule would come 'in power' (Mark 9.1). This means its future form. This future form, however, does not exclude its present form; in fact, it includes it. The expression for this is not found in the Gospels. Paul supplies it; it is the phrase

K

'in weakness' (I Cor. 15.43). This idea of the difference, indeed antithesis, of the two forms of the rule of God is expressed in the parables. The present form is like the grain of mustard seed which is easily overlooked or blown away with the breath, the future form like the tall mustard shrub, the largest of all garden plants (Mark 4.30–32; cf. Dan. 4.11–12). The initial form is like the little bit of leaven mixed with a bushel of flour, the final figure like the great pile of leavened dough (Matt. 13.33). It is not the 'growth' of the kingdom that is described from time to time, but the contrast between its pitiful beginning and its prodigious end. Here the poor wandering preacher—the foxes have holes and the birds have nests, but he has nowhere to rest (Matt. 8.20), and his disciples are have-nots: there the judge of the world in the glory of heaven. Here the failure of the sower (three-quarters of what is sown is lost): there the abundant yield of the harvest (Mark 4.3–8). If Jesus were not there, there would be no contradictions. But in the contradiction of the lowliness and the majesty of God's rule lies the miraculous activity of the God who establishes his powerful rule out of nothing.

In the person of Jesus the rule of God is both present and future simultaneously. To change its weakness into power is the work of God alone.

Men cannot 'build' the kingdom or compel it to come. The Jews thought they could. The Rabbis taught that by works of love Israel could earn salvation. A single act of obedience draws down God's mercy: if Israel kept but one Sabbath properly, the Son of David would come immediately! The kingdom which Jesus preaches comes only through himself! It is like what happens in the field: the seed is sown and the earth brings forth fruit of itself—'automatically' says the text—first the blade, then the ear, then the full grain in the ear. While the earth is busy the farmer can lie down and go to sleep; but when the harvest is ready, he sends the sickle into the field (Mark 4.26–29). Present and future are united by God's activity. Jesus' own activity is only implementing God's activity. To be exact, Jesus does not bring the kingdom —the kingdom brings him. Jesus is so much God's tool that he does not know when his day will dawn (Mark 13.32). Obviously he reckoned with the possibility that he might experience the advent of the revelation of glory in his own generation: 'truly, I say to you, there are some who stand here who shall not taste death till they see the kingdom of God come in power' (Mark 9.1; cf. Mark 13.30; Matt. 10.23). The saying can hardly be attributed to anyone except Jesus. It is unthinkable that the early Church should have placed on his lips a saying which proved later to be in error. For it should be openly acknowledged that in this respect Jesus 'made a mistake'. There is more cause for surprise that this mistake did not damage the faith of the early Church in him and that the non-appearance of the day of glory, or more precisely its delay, in no way shook belief, according to all the statements of the New Testament. The apocalyptic calendar of the last days was abolished in principle by Jesus. The question of an end— which, incidentally, Jesus did not fix—was superseded once and for all. Interest in a chronology which could be calculated belonged to the old world period. Its natural death was due to the fact that for Christians God's rule was present in Jesus.

8. *The Conflict*

The future nature of the rule of God is illustrated by the fact that Jesus proclaimed it and commissioned others to proclaim it, and constantly pray for its coming (Matt. 6.10; Luke 18.1–8). Its present nature is shown by the fact that Jesus himself is here and his message unleashes a conflict. Anyone who proclaims the advent of the rule of God thereby challenges the defenders of the theocracy to battle. For the rule of God and the theocratic state are mutually exclusive and opposed to each other. The more the leaders of the theocratic state see it as the representative of the rule of God and think of it as the earthly expression of God's rule, the more they exclude each other. We shall discuss this opposition later.

Anyone who proclaims the advent of the rule of God, however, thereby challenges the whole world, in all its parts. For he asserts that the world is entirely corrupt and that it is evil in the worst sense of the word; indeed, he does this much more radically than the leaders of the theocracy could ever do. To be sure, Jesus does not come simply to establish the world's wickedness. This had been done continuously and very forcibly since the days of the prophets. He comes, rather, to defeat the world's wickedness. And in doing so he exposes it—as already defeated by him. All this occurs in the conflict with the world. The signs of battle belonging to the advent of the rule of God in the activity of Jesus are his miracles.

Jesus performed miracles. There are various views about the scope and nature of his miracles; but scholars are unanimous about the historically indubitable fact as such. We cannot, of course, approach the accounts in the Gospels with our modern views and ideas of 'miracle', if we wish to understand the circumstances which are under consideration here. For the 19th century 'miracle' denoted an event which temporarily interfered with the laws of Nature. This characteristic had been associated with the idea of miracle from the days of scholasticism in the Middle Ages. That the idea of a breach in the laws of Nature does not play any part in either the Old or New Testament is self-explanatory. Laws of Nature, unalterable laws at that, though able to be broken temporarily, are known only to theoretical reflection. In the Old and New Testaments men saw the activity of the living God, the Creator and Sustainer of the universe, not the lapse of 'laws'. God was not always active in the same way, of course. But his extraordinary acts, which made men prick up their ears when he wanted to reveal something special, are described in the Old Testament by an expression derived from the word for 'creating'; it actually means 'creation', i.e. creatively produced (Num. 16.30; Ex. 34.10; Jer. 31.22; Isa. 48.7). Other descriptions understand miracles as manifestations of divine power, which evoke surprise or fear, as mighty acts or simply as acts of God. Frequently, too, they are called 'signs', which foreshadow or point to an invisible power. Our modern concept of miracle seems intellectually thin and pictorially pale by comparison.

In the New Testament the Greek word for 'miracle' in the sense of omen, unusual phenomenon, or miracle is quite rare, and then either in quotations from the Old Testament or to describe extraordinary events of a demonic nature. Satan and his angels, false Messiahs and false prophets, spiritual powers and Antichrist perform 'miracles' (Matt. 24.24; Mark 13.22; II Thess. 2.9; cf. Rev. 13.13–14; 16.14; 19.20). Miracles as such are ambiguous. Their occurrence is not necessarily an expression of divinity. On the contrary!

Jesus' miracles are understood as 'signs' for the most part. They are inseparable from his person and his work. They are not only signs in the sense that they are omens of the future, but they are symptoms of a reality at present concealed. The 'signs' are indications of the advent of the kingdom of God. In them the 'reality' itself appears, not just evidence in advance. Jesus' 'signs' are anticipations of the imminent day of God: the energies of God are stored in them. Therefore, they are subject to the same rules as the kingdom of God. Just as the kingdom cannot be calculated or observed, so neither can the miracles offer proof of the verifiable presence of God's power. Jesus had rejected miracles as a means of proof when he met the Tempter. He repeatedly does the same when confronted by his contemporaries.

In itself there was nothing unusual in asking men with a divine claim to give some divine confirmation. Jesus, however, rejected such demands more than once. His mighty acts are God's acts and as such only to be recognized by the man who surrenders his standpoint as a spectator and is willing to be confronted by his words (Mark 8.10–13). The simple demand for a sign epitomizes for Jesus the wickedness and faithlessness of his proud generation. God will only give them 'the sign of Jonah'; i.e. he will only send the preacher of repentance. This messenger of repentance stands before them as the secret judge of the world, who will— die (Matt. 12.38–40). High-priests and scribes even demand a sign of power from him when he is on the cross (Mark 15.32). The Pharisees and Sadducees who demand divine signs (Matt. 16.1) do not realize that the production of a special sign 'from heaven' is superfluous. They can tell tomorrow's weather—fine or storm—by the red sky at night and the nature of the dawn. But the meteorological experts who are so good at forecasting the weather are blunderers when it comes to diagnosing the history of God: they cannot judge 'the signs of the times' (Matt. 16.3; Luke 12.54–56). *The* sign is incarnate before them; but they do not see it. They do not perceive that Jesus represents the sign of Jonah on a cosmic scale. He himself is the sign, in the centre of the fullness of time, in the centre of the *kairos* of God (Luke 12.56).

The signs of Jesus have connections on two sides: on the one side with his message of salvation, on the other with the assurance of faith. They cannot be separated from either. If one compares the miracle-stories of the Gospels with similar narratives from the ancient world or Judaism or later Christianity, one sees not only certain similarities but much greater differences. The passion for fantasy and grotesqueness marks the legend. What miraculous powers the Rabbis developed! But most of what they do serves their own glory. How many trivial occasions had to be used to prove their superiority. The correctness of an opinion voiced by a Rabbi is corroborated by a decision of God: a carob-tree uproots itself at a word of command. The looks, the movements, and the words of the teacher all have power to inflict punishment. 'The curse of a learned man, even if it is spoken without cause, is always fulfilled.' Thus, one miracle after another happens to men, objects and animals. It was said of the Rabbi Hanina ben Dosa, a holy man who lived about AD 70 and who had success as a killer of snakes: 'Woe to the man who meets a water-snake! But woe to the water-snake which meets Rabbi Hanina!' Anyone who wants to know what a miracle is, in contrast to one of Jesus' signs should read these little stories, which are sometimes entertaining, sometimes absurd.

This type of legend also infiltrates into later Christian stories of apostles and saints. In the so-called Acts of Peter, which were written in the third century, the victorious contest of Peter with the magician, Simon, is pictured as follows. When the magician, exercising great self-restraint, is announced by the doorkeeper, Peter uses the opportunity 'to perform a great miracle. He sends a large dog to Simon, and the dog deliver's Peter's message in a human voice.' While the Roman householder, with whom the magician is lodging, is converted by the 'miracle', the dog 'delivers a reprimand to Simon, comes to Peter, reports his dealings with Simon, prophesies to him that a severe battle with Simon awaits him and dies at his feet. Some of the people are converted by this miracle, others want to see another miracle. Peter grants their wish and in the name of Jesus Christ (*sic*!) brings to life a smoked tunny fish.' But enough is enough!

We leave this unhealthy atmosphere and feel that we meet a breath of fresh air as soon as we come near to Jesus. Jesus did no miracles of this sort. It is customary to divide his signs into three groups: the so-called nature miracles, healing miracles, and exorcisms of demons. The comprehensive expression 'miracle' has obviously only a limited significance. But all the events which are grouped together under the word 'miracle' have one thing in common: their polemical character. Jesus brings God's power to bear at every level of earthly existence; in opposing the cosmos, human suffering and the power of darkness. He 'threatens' the hurricane (Mark 4.39), fever (Luke 4.39) and demons (Mark 1.25) equally. The rule of God is attacking the powers which are opposed to it.

(*a*) Among the *creation miracles*, usually called 'nature miracles', the cursing of the fig-tree occupies a special position (Mark 11.12–14). It is the only occurrence in the Gospels of what one could call a punitive miracle. It is not done to help others (cf. Luke 4.29–30; Matt. 17.27) and it implements a curse of Jesus. It is similar to the parable of the unfruitful fig-tree (Luke 13.6–9). Has it perhaps been worked up out of a parable into a narrative of an event? At all events, it is meant symbolically and is by no means typical of the Gospel tradition.

Narratives such as the stilling of the storm (Mark 4.35–41) and the walking of Jesus on the lake (Mark 6.45–52), on the other hand, are typical. Historical events undoubtedly lie behind these narratives. Jesus was not only the doctor of men's bodies; he also revealed himself the helper of his disciples at other times of need. He came to their rescue when they were in distress on the lake; he was both support and comforter in situations where there seemed no way out. The important fact, however, is not that something extraordinary occurs. These miracles are not showpieces which allow the magician to demonstrate his skill. They are executed simply to bring help. They refer, of course, not only to what happened but to the words that accompanied the event: they disclose that this existence of Jesus seeks to open a dialogue. The glory of God, who is the Creator of the world of the elements and who ruled over the waters from the very beginning, is made known in the figure of Jesus and in his activity. The pentecostal character of the Creator-Spirit and the Easter character of the God who resurrects the dead are attested in these stories. Hence, they reach out far beyond pure history, the details of which we can no longer reconstruct. What actually happened is the point that secures the message. A message seeks to express itself meaningfully by means of historically consistent elements. What happened is not dissolved in empty symbolism. Jesus is neither a magician of late antiquity as seen by an eyewitness nor an emblem of power and love in the sense of mystic symbolism. He is the Lord, sent by God, who initiates the reign of God's power on earth by his battle.

Already by the time we come to Matthew (8.23–27) the story of the stilling of the storm recorded by Mark (4.36–41) has been interpreted with reference to discipleship and the difficulties which threaten disciples in the little boat of the Church by its connection with the story of the various people who wanted to be disciples (Matt. 8.18–23). Moreover by the way in which he has worked over the text of Mark, Matthew has made the story reflect the later position of the Church. In this way it first received the voice which has sounded through the centuries—a voice which it would never have possessed or would soon have lost as a straightforward narrative about a purely historical event. The unchanging needs and promises of the disciples of Jesus are the subject of the message. A remote miracle, which might otherwise have been preserved in the archives of past religious history, touches us directly. In a letter to one of his friends Luther asked: 'You are sitting in Christ's little boat. Do you expect the winds to be silent there?' Today, too, we are asked the same question.

The protector of life is also the Lord of death. The daughter of Jairus, the president of the synagogue (Mark 5.21–43), and the only son of a nameless widow at Nain (Luke 7.11–17) are raised from the dead by Jesus. Similar events are recorded in the Old Testament and in other religions. Elijah (I Kings 17.17–24) and Elisha (II Kings 4.18–37) are well-known instances of men who were able to raise the dead to life. The distinctiveness of the Gospel accounts (cf. John 11.1–45: Lazarus) can only be understood in connection with the message which embodies the time of salvation. Even raising a person from the dead is not by itself a miracle. As such there is nothing compelling about such an event; in fact it is rather repellent. They only receive their true meaning in the context of the eschatological event: ' . . . and the dead are raised up' (Matt. 11.5). The conquest of death, to which Israel had looked forward since the days of late prophecy (Isa. 26.19), is imminent. In Johannine language, 'I am the resurrection and the life; he who believes in me, though he die, yet shall he live' (John 11.25). The author of these words is at work.

(*b*) The *healing miracles* of Jesus are the most well-known to us. We have confidence in them. They affect us most deeply. If we were to omit them from the picture of Jesus the picture would be destroyed. And yet they are more than purely medical operations. They have certain parallels in healings which were practised in ancient—and modern—places of pilgrimage such as the shrine of Epidaurus in Greece or the sacred grotto at Lourdes in the foothills of the French Pyrenees. In the shrine of the 'divine doctor', Asclepius, in fact, cures were achieved not only by religious but also by medical treatment. Miraculous cures, which sometimes took months, were effectively supported by surgical operations and shock-therapy. Even if the accounts exaggerate what happened and make it somewhat fabulous, yet the inscriptions on votive tablets and thank-offerings leave no doubt that numerous successes were really obtained. The stereo-typed outline of the healing narratives which were edited by the priesthood is similar to that of the synoptic accounts. But in both cases the stylization simply underlined and strengthened the characteristics previously provided by life itself. The uniformity of the accounts is grounded in the uniformity of the events. The literary arrangement reflects the sequence of such events in life. It is no wonder that in Roman times throughout Asia Minor and North Africa, in several places of pilgrimage, honoured, Greek miracle-working gods were felt to be rivals of Jesus Christ. As 'Saviour *par excellence*' Asclepius long confronted 'the Saviour of the world' (John 4.42; I John 4.14) not only in popular belief but also in educated circles.

Nevertheless, the differences are fundamental. It is true that from time to time Jesus worked like one of the numerous Hellenistic wonder-workers. That he was accepted as such by his contem-poraries is also undeniable. This side of his activity should not, therefore, be rashly made light of or disputed on the basis of a spiritual concept of 'religion'. But the idea of a superior 'miracle doctor' does not do justice to the facts. His miracles took place spontaneously. They were not his prime aim. Sometimes they seem to have been elicited from him half against his will, as in the case of the woman with a haemorrhage (Mark 5.25–34; cf. 3.10; 6.56), or even to have been bullied out of him, as in the case of the Syro-Phoenician woman (Mark 7.24–30). At any rate, he certainly did not make a 'profession' of his healing miracles or use them to make a profit. But this external fact expresses something fundamental. His signs were exclusively in the service of his message. They are, therefore, invitations to faith, seals of God's salvation which he bestows. The Gospels sometimes create the impression that Jesus was implementing a programme point

by point by means of the healing miracles. But if there was such
a 'programme', it was the eschatological plan that had been
announced by Isa. 35.4–6 and was inseparable from his person
(Matt. 11.5).

An incomparable sense of freedom is traceable wherever Jesus
appears and sets to work. With unparalleled sovereignty in the
midst of a mediocre and ailing world he brings to men the great
health of God. The blind man of Bethsaida is brought to him (Mark
8.22–26) and, as he is leaving Jericho with his disciples, Bartimaeus,
a blind man who was usually begging by the wayside, overtakes
him with his cry for help, and will let nothing divert him from
his request (Mark 10.46–52). A deaf and dumb man in the region
of the Decapolis, a federal union of ten Greek cities of the Jordan,
when taken aside by Jesus, receives wonderful help from the
laying on of hands and the application of spittle. There is
much that is reminiscent of the methods of other healers; but
the important factor is the look towards heaven and the 'sign',
with which he himself receives the healing as a gift from God
(Mark 7.31–37). Thus, he heals the epileptic boy and in reply
to his disciples imparts the information that 'this sort of thing
can only be expelled by prayer' (Mark 9.14–24). Thus, with his
forceful touch he heals a man with dropsy one Sabbath in the house
of a leading Pharisee, while the experts in the Law lie in wait to
catch him (Luke 14.1–6). Something similar takes place in the
presence of Pharisees and partisans of Herod, again on the
Sabbath but this time in the synagogue, with a man suffering
from a withered hand (Mark 3.1–6).

Setting and environment, patients and spectators, and indeed
Jesus' own treatment of all these, vary. Time and time again
chance seems to take a hand. The only constant features are Jesus'
direct, compelling manner and the fact that in the 'sign' God
himself speaks his own language—the language of action. God
sets men free again in their struggle against the bonds in which
they are entangled by sin and suffering (Mark 2.1–12). All these
different healings are so many manifestations of a superior will
steadily pursuing its aim.

The gift of healing, according to religious belief throughout
the world, is the charismatic possession of the king. This is not
simply a matter of faith in magic, such as superstition at all times
is familiar with. The Emperor Vespasian (AD 69–79) is supposed

to have healed a blind man in Egypt, the classical land of royal power. The English and French kings used to heal scurvy, the 'king's disease', right up to modern times. Shakespeare, in *Macbeth* (IV.3), describes a conversation between the prince and the doctor as follows:

> *Malcolm*: Comes the king forth, I pray you?
> *Doctor*: Ay, sir; there are a crew of wretched souls
> That stay his cure; their malady convinces
> The great assay of art; but, at his touch,
> Such sanctity hath heaven given his hand,
> They presently amend.

This is certainly belief in miracles. And yet Jesus' healing miracles can only be understood if they are seen against the background of world-wide expectations. The hope of the Jews for the day of God and the longing of the Gentiles both find their fulfilment in Jesus. The battle against human suffering marks the dawning of God's kingly rule on earth.

(*c*) Among the accounts of healing miracles are the narratives of *demon-expulsions*, which seem particularly strange to us. But they are among the best attested miracles of the Gospel tradition. Even at that time, however, they were already felt to be so primitive that they were embellished with some of the features of a novel. Is this, perhaps, true of the weird story of the possessed man of Gerasa? Let us re-read the details of this unusual story of the man who dwelt among the tombs, wrenching apart every fetter with which men tried to bind his hands and feet (Mark 5.1–20). A demon or a group of demons—called 'legion'—is responsible for the disorder within him. Jesus drives the demons out into a herd of pigs that are grazing. The herd rushes headlong down the hillside into the lake. About two thousand animals are drowned. There is a sequel: the owners of the herd are too afraid to claim compensation but they ask Jesus to leave the district, which he then does by boat. But, however much fantasy has contributed to the shaping of the story, the situation is so uncontrived and unique that the historical basis is obvious. In another way this is also true of the other, more normal accounts of the healing of possessed persons which include an instance of healing at a distance (Mark 7.24–30; for healing at a distance cf. also John 4.46–53).

There is fairly unanimous agreement today that 'demonic

possession' is a form of nervous disorder. A period which used
to attribute all illnesses to the influences of evil spirits also
considered mentally and emotionally abnormal persons to be
afflicted particularly by demons. The spirits not only distressed
and tormented them from time to time, they also lived in them
and plagued them continually. This widespread conviction tended
to produce schizophrenia in those who were susceptible to such
illness.

The world-situation as interpreted by the apocalyptists included
armies of demons fighting against the good spirits of God in
order to control men. They formed an anti-God kingdom with
a monarch at their head; their Prince was called Beezebul
(= Beelzebul) which is taken to mean 'Lord of the flies' (Baal-ze-
bub, cf. Matt. 12.24). The name Belial, in Greek Beliar, was also
current. In the War Scroll from Qumran he commands the
army of the sons of darkness which is composed chiefly of Gentiles;
in apocalyptic he is a devil; in the New Testament (only II Cor.
6.14–15) he appears as Antichrist.

Jesus obviously shared the popular view as well as the apocalyptic
theory. He did not act like a modern rationalist, who interprets
the demons as fictions of a morbidly superstitious consciousness
and thus explains them away as non-existent. Even if—in spite
of Blumhardt—we can no longer go all the way with this mythological viewpoint, the demonic appearances can still be interpreted
in a way that makes sense. In many religions demons are associated
with the spirits of the ancestors and the dead. They are spirits
of the past—even older than the gods. In them invincible antiquity
with its narrowness and anxiety lies heavy on man. In Judaism
at the time of Jesus this past was an aggressive force. The great
traditions of a stirring and moving period had long grown hard in
the world of the temple-state. They were entombed in a museum-
like sham reality. This is the fate of all dogmatism, which
guards ancestral wisdom like a sacred relic. Living faith is con-
stricted by veneration of a creed fixed in the past. The theocratic
state is the end of living guidance by God, and of the confident
but daring step along God's path. The institution which is sacred
in itself helps the demonic to gain ground.

A nation nailed firmly to the bare past, a community surrendered
to bare tradition, is robbed of a genuine present. The demonic
means loss of the present. The demons are the spirits of yesterday,

which today evoke the illusion that they are the spirits of tomorrow. The future is then seen and treated as if it were something that had already happened and that could, therefore, be seen through. The future then becomes by calculation and planning a matter of arithmetic. When one holds the future in one's hands, when one has control of its disposal, this only proves that one is without a genuine destiny. The Jewish theocratic state and the temperature of its piety in every direction, not least in apocalyptic, is in this sense demonically moulded.

Was there ever a time not threatened by this danger? To study the past is to take this danger seriously. Historical research has to do with the exhausted possibilities which are impossibilities today: they had their day yesterday, today it is gone. True historical writing is like the task of conjuring the dead to life. Like the woman of Endor bringing back Samuel for Saul at dead of night and causing him to speak (I Sam. 28), it seeks to loosen the tongue of the past. Woe, if the past is silent! Even values become petrified like mummies, if they cease to be encompassed by the breath of the future. What does 'a Christian West' mean to mankind if the musty smell of death rises from it? For the serious-minded it is a nightmare, for the light-hearted a prince among demons.

The demon-expulsions of Jesus are simply limited actions in an all-embracing battle against the spirits which torment men. In the old apocalyptic prayer-book (Isa. 24–27), at a time when God's spirit no longer possessed present power, the 'Pious' had prayed:

O Lord, our God,
other lords besides thee have ruled over us,
but thy name alone we acknowledge.
They are dead—they will not live;
they are shades—they will not arise;
to that end thou hast visited them with destruction
and wiped out all remembrance of them (Isa. 26.13–14).

Jesus has dethroned the shades, which pretend to be realities, and deposed the dead, who give the illusion of being alive. None of his contemporaries denied that Jesus expelled demons. In fact, they are the kernel of his activity. But the meaning of demonic rule only becomes clear in the presence of God's rule, which

Jesus introduces. His opponents become unwilling witnesses of this activity of his. From Jerusalem, where they had heard of this strange wandering preacher who was a miraculous doctor and an exorcizer of devils, a commission of experts was sent down to Galilee. The result of their enquiry was to declare: 'He has Beezebul' and 'By the prince of demons he casts out demons'. Then Jesus calls the chief rulers whose authority exceeded that of the Rabbis in the province, and speaks to them in parables. 'How can Satan cast out Satan? If a kingdom is divided against itself, that kingdom cannot stand. And if a house is divided against itself that house will not be able to stand. And if Satan has risen up against himself, and is divided, he cannot stand, but is coming to an end. But no one can enter a strong man's house and plunder his goods, unless he first binds the strong man; then, indeed, he may plunder his house' (Mark 3.22–27). Matthew and Luke insert at this point the explanatory saying which we have discussed—'If I by the spirit/finger of God cast out demons, then the kingdom of God has already come upon you' (Matt. 12.28; Luke 11.20).

The meaning of this passage, which seemed so obscure at first, is now clear: the rule of God is overthrowing the rule of the demons. In the various victories from place to place and from time to time is sketched the decisive victory of God against the kingdom of darkness. God's future gains power over the enslaving might of the past. The coming of Jesus supplies the world, which is firmly nailed to itself, with a future and thus with a genuine present. The breath of freedom blows through the world in which, from a religious point of view also, despotism and the subordinate mentality hold sway. An atmosphere of freedom is traceable in the works and words of Jesus.

It is the freedom proclaimed in the prophetic words of Deutero-Isaiah (Isa. 49.24–26, omitting v. 26a):

> Can the prey be taken from the mighty,
> or the captives of a tyrant be rescued?
> Surely, thus says the Lord,
> 'Even the captives of the mighty shall be taken
> and the prey of the tyrant be rescued,
> for I will contend with those who contend with you,
> and I will save your children—

> Then all flesh shall know
> that I am the Lord, your Saviour,
> and your Redeemer, the Mighty One of Jacob'.

The probability that the words of Jesus, which take as their subject the very situation envisaged by the prophet, contain an indirect reference to himself, begins to make itself felt. In his victory over the 'prince' he is the Servant of God, who in the last of the four Servant-songs is pictured as the representative of God: he will bring the Lord's work to a victorious conclusion (Isa. 52.13–53.12). The demon-expulsions represent the victory of God's rule brought about by Jesus.

John Sebastian Bach's Reformation Cantata No. 80, 'A safe stronghold our God is still', was probably sung for the first time on the second centenary of the Augsburg Confession in the year 1730. Its text is based on the Gospel for the third Sunday in Lent (Luke 11.14–28; the parallel to Mark 3.23–30). Luke generally uses the same word for 'prey' that the Greek Septuagint text of Isa. 49 employs twice (Isa. 49.24–25; Luke 11.22). Thus the connection between the Old and New Testament is very strong at this point. Bach, however, interprets this Gospel by means of Luther's hymn on Psalm 46 and by means of the arias and recitatives which occur in between. The music and the text have to be heard together: the 'stronger' advances to overcome the 'strong'. He enters the world which is full of devils and overpowers the adversary. He robs him of his weapons. He binds him. He occupies his citadel. Who is the 'stronger'?

> Ask ye who is this same?
> Christ Jesus is his Name,
> The Lord Sabaoth's Son;
> He, and no other one
> Shall conquer in the battle.

We find ourselves in the centre of the gospel of God's kingly rule. It was probably this very Gospel which also provided the background for Luther's most important polemical work, *The Bondage of the Will*. Written in 1525 against Erasmus, it constitutes a unique hymn of praise of the will that is free—the will of God in Jesus Christ.

9. *Defeat and Victory*

In his conflict with evil Jesus experiences defeat as well as
victory. We have already mentioned the occasional failure of his
message (Mark 4.3–8). He saw and experienced the danger of
backsliding in the battle against the spirits (Matt. 12.43–45;
Luke 11.24–26). Behind the warning stands his own experience.
The works and words of Jesus are directed in their activity towards
the person confronted, the man for whom they are both intended.
Men may surrender to him. But what if they deny him? Or
another denies them to him?

We have noted above that Jesus' signs are inseparable from
his person and his message on the one hand and from the faith
of men on the other. This means, then, that the power of his works
is limited by unbelief. In one of the narratives which has been
separated from its context it is stated that Jesus was rejected in
Nazareth, his home town. 'And they took offence at him. And Jesus
said to them, "A prophet is not without honour, except in his own
country and among his own kin, and in his own house". And he
could do no mighty work there except that he laid his hands upon
a few sick people and healed them. And he marvelled because of
their unbelief' (Mark 6.3–6). When he sees the inability of the
disciples to heal the epileptic lad, he is full of indignation and says,
'O faithless generation! How long am I to be with you? How
long am I to bear with you!' (Mark 9.19).

He has to rebuke his disciples time and time again for their
'little faith'. All the occurrences of the word are in Matthew
apart from Luke 12.28. The disciples are afraid in the storm on
the lake (Matt. 8.26). Peter cries out in terror when he sees the
size of the waves (Matt. 14.30–31). The man of little faith is
worried, 'What shall we eat? What shall we drink? What shall
we wear?' (Matt. 6.30–31; cf. 16.8). The man of little faith
cannot help others. 'Truly I say to you, if you have faith as a
grain of mustard seed, you will say to this mountain "Move
hence to yonder place" and it will move; and nothing will be
impossible to you' (Matt. 17.20).

But Jesus can only help those who have faith. The work of Jesus
does not precede faith, but *vice versa*. But what is faith? Luther
understands faith as the 'ratification' of the effective word of God.
It is remarkable, however, that the oldest strata of the Jesus-

tradition in the Gospels does not understand faith as 'faith in
Jesus'. The historical Jesus of Nazareth never demanded that
men should believe in him as the bringer of salvation. One can
only really believe in Jesus (Matt. 18.6; 27.42), or the Gospel
(Mark 1.15), or the resurrection of Jesus (Luke 24.25; Mark
16.13–14) after the experience of Easter. It is only then that
baptism and faith—saving faith, that is—which were not yet
established during Jesus' lifetime, belong together (Mark 16.16).
It is only from then onwards that Christians can style themselves
believers (Luke 8.12–13; Mark 16.17). Only the Johannine Christ
can say, 'Believe in God; believe also in me' (John 14.1).

The faith which the events centring round Jesus presuppose
is very much simpler. It is unreflective, untheological and
undogmatic. One could almost say that on the whole it is not
yet religious faith at all. It is openness to the situation which has
appeared with Jesus. It has no definite object as yet. It is simply
faith—unconditional faith, so to speak. The world is full of light
through Jesus. Life is full of joy through Jesus. Hearts unbend
and open out of their cramped state and hardly know how it has
come about or what is happening. They simply open because
he is there. His existence is the reason for their faith. They find
plenty of help simply in his presence. That is why they believe.
They believe because they feel instinctively that in Jesus 'the man
of faith *par excellence*' has come into their midst. Thus in the
case of the paralytic it is not the sick man who believes in the
first instance, but only those who have brought him. When Jesus
sees *their* faith, he begins to speak (Mark 2.5). Faith is living
faith in the face of adversity and uncertainty; faith is fearlessness.
'Undismayed and without fear . . . ' (Mark 4.40). The poor
woman who had been maltreated by many doctors for twelve
whole years and who had spent all her substance on them, with
the result that her suffering was worse rather than better, pressed
shyly through the crowd from the back. She thought, 'If only
I can touch his garments I shall be healed'. Could there be any
worse superstition? Does such primitive magic belong to the
Gospel? But it is precisely then that the miracle occurs: she is
freed from the scourge of her illness. And then something even
more surprising happens. Jesus, feeling intuitively—like the
woman—the power depart from him, says to the trembling
creature, who reveals her identity by her manner, 'Daughter,

L

your *faith* has made you well; go in peace, and be healed of your disease' (Mark 5.25–34).

Faith can be obstinate, like the SOS of the Gentile mother pleading for her daughter (Mark 7.24–30). The faith of the blind beggar of Jericho is not faith in the Messiah, in spite of the way he addresses Jesus as 'Son of David', but unlimited trust in the power and love of Jesus (Mark 10.46–52). The silent prototype of this faith is the poor widow whom Jesus observes in the treasury of the Temple amidst the crowd of givers. She brings two small copper coins which together make up a penny. The rich bring a great deal more, as far as the actual amount of money goes, and yet they bring less, as far as the giver is concerned. They give something; she gives all. She no longer knows how she will manage to live the next day. In giving all she throws herself unreservedly into the hand of Another. Faith means giving oneself unreservedly like this, throwing oneself into the hand of God (Mark 12.41–44). Faith has to do with the whole man. Faith is always an elementary activity. One can say no to an order and yet carry it out. When that happens it is a sign of faith (Matt. 21.28–32).

In faith man becomes a person with a 'self'. Faith reveals the human value of man. Matthew, particularly, illustrates this aspect, in the way he selects the miracle-stories he wishes to record and expound: if a man believes, he becomes independent in will, spontaneous in action and responsible in prayer. Faith is independence, spontaneity and responsibility combined. As the essence of man's personal existence it is 'fundamentally praying faith' (R. Bultmann). As such it shares in the miraculous power of Jesus (Matt. 17.20; 21.21; cf. Mark 11.23; Luke 17.6). In faith the disciple overcomes his littleness of faith and his doubt (Matt. 14.31). Littleness of faith and doubt are characteristics not of the outsider or the spectator or the enemy but of the disciple. The believer is constantly experiencing the brokenness of his existence. He knows he is referred from defeat to the victorious power of Jesus. Faith becomes 'resolute looking to Christ' (Luther).

Wherever men have faith in this quite general and yet very significant sense, there Jesus is active and victorious. Only if there is such faith can Jesus be really active. When this happens, Jesus, *the* man of faith, has believers around him who open

themselves to the life of God. It should be noticed how nothing
is demanded here! Everything is a gift. There is no demanding
of a decision. For in its onset faith is not a human achievement
to which a person must rouse himself. We should be well advised
to attend the elementary school of Jesus before visiting the high-
school for faith presided over by Paul and John. Here we learn
the ABC of faith. All attempts to describe faith as an existential
choice of the individual mistake the character of faith as long as
they fail to understand first the elementary fact that faith is not
something cramping. Faith is freedom from cramp, including
cramping faith! Faith is relaxation before God and the world.
Faith is the ability to relax which is the mark of the existence
that knows God and the world are a free gift. To believe is to
clothe oneself with the freedom of God. To believe is to rejoice
in the evening of God which Jesus brings.

It is said of Jesus that early one morning, a great while before
day, he sought loneliness in order to pray (Mark 1.35). On another
occasion 'he went out into the hills to pray; and he continued
all night in prayer to God' (Luke 6.12). Faith—freedom—prayer
belong together.

What he himself possessed he gave to his own: rest after
restlessness. Once, when the disciples gathered round Jesus and
'told him all they had done and what they had taught', he said
to them, ' "Come away by yourselves to a lonely place *and rest
awhile*." For many were coming and going, and they had no leisure
even to eat. And they went away in the boat to a lonely place by
themselves' (Mark 6.30–32). The world is made in such a way
that it should finally rest. It is not the 'bosses' who possess the
last word but those who rest. The 'bosses' are invited by Jesus
to rest with him. They are not invited to share a rest which
would only be a means to an end; in this case the more strenuous
pursuit of business after the rest. Rest is much more an end in
itself. For it is rest in the fellowship of him who won the victory
over the world's uproar. This was the way he introduced the eve
of his coming.

5

THE EVE OF MAN

THE EVE OF God, which Jesus introduced, became the eve of man. It was not a case of their joining up with each other, however. Rather, man's destiny was revealed *in* God's activity.

1. *The Eschatological Horizon*

Jesus' appearance released a movement which in many respects was similar to that which had proceeded from the figure of John the Baptist. It is possible to speak of a religious revival. But it surged out beyond the limits marked by the activity of the Baptist. Jesus was different from the Baptist in two ways. The Spirit, God's gift of the last days, had descended on Jesus. Where he sojourned the presence of God sojourned. And where he worked, miracle ruled. But tradition knows of no sign worked by John. In fact, this difference is emphasized to the point of contrast (John 10.41). The first reference made by the Fourth Gospel to the Baptist has no historical purpose except to reveal John's intention. But in the tone of the message, which is perhaps polemical in its attitude to the sect of John, there does appear to be correct historical knowledge preserved: John 'came for testimony, to bear witness to the light, that all might believe through him. He was not the light but came to bear witness to the light' (John 1.6–7). Matthew interprets Jesus' appearance within the framework of scriptural proof (Matt. 4.15–16) as the fulfilment of the prophetic word of Isaiah (9.1–2):

The land of Zebulon and the land of Naphtali,
toward the sea, across the Jordan,
Galilee of the Gentiles—
the people who sat in darkness

have seen a great light,
and for those who sat in the region and shadow of death
light has dawned.

No stretch of the imagination can do justice to the response
which the preaching of Jesus evoked. Even allowing for stylistic
exaggerations the content of what is recorded makes it possible
to perceive the extraordinary nature of the events. The occasional
chorus-style ending of individual scenes only underlines and
gathers together what had impressed itself on the mind. The
emotional language of the narrative corresponds to the call to
decide. Eye-witnesses and listeners are astonished (Mark 1.22;
6.2; 6.51), amazed (Mark 1.27) and surprised (Luke 4.22). Fear
and trembling come upon them (Mark 5.33). Overwhelmed by
great fear they ask, 'Who is this, that even the wind and the
waves obey him?' (Mark 4.41). Fear and praise are mingled in
the comment, 'We never saw anything like this' (Mark 2.12).
'We have seen paradoxical—strange—things today' (Luke 5.26).
'And all men marvelled' (Mark 5.20).
Everywhere those seeking help crowd round Jesus. Everyone
is searching for him (Mark 1.32–33; 1.37). They come to him
'from every quarter' (Mark 1.45). The space inside the house
and before the door becomes inadequate so that the roof has to
be taken off in order to bring the paralytic to him (Mark 2.2–4).
Jesus is almost always to be seen surrounded by a crowd of people
(Mark 2.13; 3.20). A boat has to be kept ready for him in order
to keep the crowd at a distance (Mark 3.10). Often he escapes
from the massing throng like a man in flight (Mark 4.36; 6.45;
8.10). But sometimes the crowd wins the race (Mark 6.33).
When they moored the boat and got out, 'the people immediately
recognised him and ran about the whole neighbourhood and
began to bring sick people on their pallets to any place where
they heard he was. And wherever he came, in villages, cities or
country, they laid the sick in the market places, and besought him
that they might touch even the fringe of his garment; and as
many as touched it were made well' (Mark 6.54–56). The news
of his deeds is echoed far and wide (Mark 1.28; 3.8).
His deeds, of course, are only the expression of his call. But
his call is related to that of the Baptist in that it is a call to repentance. From the very beginning Jesus, too, is a preacher of

repentance (Mark 1.15). He is different from the Baptist, however, in that he embodied what John had only held out the prospect of: namely, the presence of God. Now is the time to decide! The imminent nearness of salvation is the reason for the call to repentance. The future which is now dawning is not empty future time which men have first to fill. In the words of Jesus the future comes to the listener with a quite definite content: it comes with deliverance where God rules. For the person who will not hear it comes as destruction. Jesus requires only one thing—repentance by the whole of man for his previous ways. Change of 'disposition'? Certainly, the disposition may complete the repentance. But the disposition which our fathers spoke of when they wanted to describe repentance is not something in men, but man himself! What is demanded is the man himself, personally and completely.

Jesus requires no confession of sin. John openly demanded it or at least accepted it (Mark 1.5). The early Church likewise demanded it (Acts 19.18). For the early Catholic Church the confession of sin, 'confession', belonged to the permanent nature of the repentance. Nowhere in the Gospels do we read of anything like this in connection with Jesus. He dispensed with a confession of sin not because he left sin out of account or because he regarded it as insignificant. Quite the reverse! He took it so seriously and considered it so important that he relied on God alone for its defeat and not on the will of man or the demonstration of his will. What could a man know about sin? What could he say about his sin? Now *he* had come he promised forgiveness of sins even to the man who had not asked for it (Mark 2.1–12).

God reveals what is in man and then, where man is open to this revelation, he covers it again. That is why Jesus never expected declarations of guilt from individuals or groups. The phrase is 'do repentance'! Although the word 'do' is not found in the original Greek, it is a faithful rendering of the Greek word which denotes activity. Repentance involves action, not just words, least of all words about repentance. The demand for this first occurs in James 5.16, 'Confess your sins to one another'. The possibility that to declare one's sins before God and one's fellow men may be a genuine form of activity is not excluded. But even such an activity will be complete without reference being made to it later. It cannot be used as a proof of readiness to repent. For repentance is an activity, not a description of an activity. It is a necessary condition of repentance such as Jesus demands that it requires action without words. Its wordlessness is its mark of authenticity.

Jesus is so very much the bearer of the decisive utterance of God that he is not interested in the style or manner of the human reaction. That man repents is everything. How he does so depends on his personal temperament. Only Luke took an interest in stylizing men's acts of repentance. It is noticeable how he enjoys describing the event or experience of repentance. This was the way to salvation later when Jesus' eschatological call to repentance was silenced, and the Church, set in the midst of the world, received men into its bosom by repentance and acts of repentance, as Luke takes for granted in the story of Zacchaeus, the chief tax collector (Luke 19.1–10), and of various converts at various times in the Acts (2.38, etc.).

For Jesus himself everything depends on the fullness of the hour, on the 'acceptable time' and on its liberating quality, which is the gift of his words. The arrival of the Son of Man, the judge of the world, is at hand. The eschatological horizon governs everything. The present is already within shooting range of the future that is dawning. The field of decision becomes the field of separation. Communities, occupations and families are all separated (Matt. 24.40–41; Luke 17.34).

> Then two men will be in the field;
> one is taken and one is left.
> Two women will be grinding at the mill;
> one is taken and one is left.
> In that night there will be two men in one bed;
> one will be taken and the other left.

How ominous it sounds! As if the decision had already overtaken them both! What if God in heaven had already decided that the one should be accepted and the other rejected? There can be no doubt that concealed behind Jesus' call to decision lies the dark secret of that great paradox, election. Fundamentally, its weighty silence lies behind every word of the Gospels. What Mark makes Jesus say of the parables is true of Jesus' message as a whole: it produces divisions between men. 'To you has been given the secret of the kingdom of God, but for those outside everything is in parables, so that "they may indeed see but not perceive, and may indeed hear but not understand, lest they should turn again" and be forgiven' (Mark 4.11–12). The meaning of this passage is restricted if it is referred, as in Mark, to the parables. In this case the purpose of the parables would have been to speak a secret language, understood only by the elect, while acting as a means to prevent the rejected from repenting. But election and rejection take place in the light of the ministry of Jesus as a whole in word and deed. The severity of the passage could be modified by rendering the last clause, ' . . . otherwise they would turn again and be forgiven'. This is linguistically possible. But the urgency of Jesus' words then loses much of its force.

Jesus understands prophetic activity according to the word of Isa. 6.9–10: Isaiah is called to preach to the stubborn and hard of heart. The gravity of that situation is still alive in Jesus' day. It is a matter of decision once more; in fact, the final decision. The issue is not, however, simply concerned with the religious convictions of men, but with God's decision, the eternal decision. This is not meant in the sense of any theory of predestination, at any rate not in the sense that in heaven everything is already fixed down to the last detail and that it only needs to run its allotted course on earth. This would mean that men had been delivered into the hands of an unalterable fate, that the fatalism of the Hellenistic period was right, and that Jesus could have saved himself the trouble of saying what he did, because everything takes place in the way it must. What he preaches, however, is not the unalterability of fate but the freedom of God. Men are not surrendered defenceless into the power of this freedom of God, but are actively confronted. God is not a puppet-showman, to whose will men must dance like marionettes. The men who wield power in the world and who seek to move individuals and nations this way and that by pulling strings, are the puppet-showmen. Men and women, whom the modern world of those days—as today?—made the object of its opaque plans, are set free from this gruesome puppet-show. They are challenged by the words of Jesus to stand on their own feet. They are invited to reply. The eschatological horizon affirms that they are free for responsibility before God. God's decision is the decision to save. Man's salvation is utterly unmerited. And man's destruction? It is paradoxically all man's fault!

If we were setting out to be strictly proportional in our thinking —as we must if we follow human logic—we should have to say that either man's salvation is all God's work, in which case man's destruction is all God's fault, or, alternatively, man's destruction is all man's work, in which case man's salvation is entirely due to man's merits. This is logically unassailable if the possibilities of God and man are balanced against each other. But the appearance of Jesus shatters all human logic, however clear and however devout. Thought and all its regularities are shipwrecked on God's eternal will. This is exactly what the New Testament says when it speaks of repentance and faith. Faith is utterly and solely God's gift: God himself opens our hearts and lips when we say 'yes' to him. But unbelief is utterly and solely man's fault: I myself exclude God if I say 'no' to him.

Jesus has to speak so severely because it is the final hour for decision. The perpendicular of eternity and the horizontal of the future that is coming to meet us make our position inevitable; what is already decided eternally is, paradoxically, only decided here and now. And, conversely, what is decided here and now carries eternal irrevocability. The apocalyptic standard of reference, which applies to the kingdom of God, also characterizes the decision-situation which Jesus' presence evokes (see the diagram on p. 141). This decision-situation is distinguished by the fact that the new world period already overlaps the old. This overlapping of eternity and time is 'the *secret* of the kingdom of God' (Mark 4.11). The insignificant conceals the occurrence of the conclusive. It is certainly not some mystery-rite that is being celebrated but something routine that is being done—and it is in this that the extraordinary takes place. 'The secret of the kingdom of God, its mysterious presence, consists in the *word* of Jesus. A sower goes out to sow (Mark 4.1–9)—nothing else; and this signifies the new world of God. Who listens, who understands Jesus' word? One can hear it without understanding it; it is like a foreign language to some people' (J. Schniewind). Because Jesus seeks to save, he avails himself of the severest language of the prophetic preaching about election.

Since his baptism Jesus is the man chosen by God to be his Son, his Servant, the Bearer of his Spirit. We could also say the Elected One *par excellence*. Jesus shares the conviction of the apocalyptists that with the Elected One the elected ones are also revealed. Therefore, he understands his activity as election. His words and actions will rouse the elected ones whom God gives him (i.e. men and women).

How does his election take place? Under no circumstances in a political manner or with political intent. Jesus does not belong to the large company of Jewish messianic rebels. How far does his election reach? Is it limited to God's people? Does it seek to include the whole wide world, the 'modern' world of his contemporaries? We cannot give any conclusive answer to this yet. But this much, at any rate, is clear: it does not stop at the borders of the Holy Land. Scholars today no longer talk of Jesus' 'northern journeys' as previous scholars did, understanding by this the different routes of his travels which could be mapped. The historical content of these geographical descriptions is small, because the reference to places and routes are inserted simply for the purpose of connecting the individual narratives loosely together, or else, as in Luke and somewhat differently in the fourth Gospel, of rounding off the total structure of the Gospel to fit the message. Nevertheless, even in their brokenness, the geographical references permit us to perceive that Jesus did not stay within the borders of Galilee; in the very nature of things he could not have done.

Jesus was not brought up in 'Arcady', but in Nazareth. Geographically, politically and economically Galilee was anything but a self-contained territory. Some four miles north of Nazareth in the hills was the Hellenistic capital of Galilee, Sepphoris. After its destruction in 4 BC it had been rebuilt by Herod Antipas with new splendour. Josephus called it the 'glory of all Galilee'. It was here that the petty prince held his court. Walls, arcades, temples and theatres were rebuilt in the new style. From the hills above the village of Nazareth one could see the palace with its marble buildings standing on high ground (Matt. 5.14b?). Later, in AD 17, the prince founded an even larger city near Lake Gennesaret, which he called Tiberias after the second Roman Emperor. It, too, had its outstanding buildings and its famous hot baths.

The Gospels do not record Jesus staying in these two royal cities. Did he deliberately avoid them? We do not know. All that we can be sure of is that he did not choose either of them for his permanent quarters.

Nevertheless, daily life on this side of the border brought him into constant touch with the life of the period. On the other side of the border and in the territories up to the border this was inevitable. Places on the other side of the Galilaean border that are mentioned are as follows: Syria generally (Matt. 4.24), particularly the region of Tyre (Mark 7.24) and Sidon (Mark 7.31), both ancient Phoenician lands; the villages of Caesarea Philippi (Mark 8.27) near the source of the Jordan and the shrine of Pan (Paneas), the shepherd god, where the Egyptians had been defeated by the Syrians in 198 BC. Herod Philip, the most human of Herod the Great's sons, built his royal residence here in the foothills of Hermon. It was here that Peter confessed Jesus to be the Christ, in the midst of a country occupied predominantly by Gentiles. Special importance attaches to the Decapolis (Mark 5.20), to which the land of the Gerasenes (Mark 5.1) and the northern part of Eastern Jordan (Mark 10.1) belong. The Decapolis, as the name suggests, was a federal alliance of ten cities, whose independence from the neighbouring states was basically the work of Pompey (64 BC). Strategically the federal alliance was a sort of glacis against the invasions of the Arabs; geographically it was an intermediary zone dividing the two Jewish areas of Galilee and Peraea (the southern part of East Jordan). Anyone going from Galilee to Jerusalem and wishing to avoid the outlawed country of Samaria had to go this way. Jesus seems to have stayed fairly frequently in these parts which border Lake Gennesaret. He was then in predominantly Hellenistic territory, where Jews had been in the minority for a long time, where every city was self-governing, and where the climate was saturated with Hellenistic civilization.

But what place was free from such influence? Even Jerusalem in the days of Jesus was a 'modern' city. Greek literature and knowledge had their place there, just as elsewhere. Not only the Jewish scholars of Alexandria knew their Plato and the legends and myths of Greece. The ancient synagogue was not completely unacquainted with 'Greek wisdom'. Even the Rabbis read Homer: 'Reading Homer is like reading a letter.' Even later, when the bloody fate of the Jewish state intensified opposition to non-Jewish culture and sometimes led to the banning of the Greek language, Greek education never fell into such disrepute that relatives and even the daughters of Rabbis ceased to learn Greek.

Naturally Jesus did not come under the influence of such an education. To what extent he did not shun it, the Gospels do not record. But our sources assume that he lived in this world and did not stand aloof from it, like the Qumran community or like John the Baptist; the crowds, whose actions he could observe so well—their natural humanity (Matt. 5.47), their thoughtless babbling in prayer (Matt. 6.7), their worry and anxiety in the struggle for existence (Matt. 6.32)—flocked out from such a civilization. Jesus must have been a very remarkable hermit if he knew the Gentile world only by hearsay. It is of such a world that we must think when a summary such as the following occurs: 'And a great multitude from Galilee followed; also from Judaea and Jerusalem and Idumaea and from beyond the Jordan and from about Tyre and Sidon.' This is not a geographical inventory, but a sign of the far-reaching movement which Jesus inspired by his challenge to men to decide.

2. *The Representative of Man*

Jesus' call to decide is at the same time a call to be man. Matthew attaches it as the call of the Saviour to the two strophes which Luke also preserved as a pentecostal cry of jubilation (see p. 135 above). It reads as follows (Matt. 11.28–30):

> Come to me all who labour and are heavy-laden,
> and I will give you rest.
> Take my yoke upon you and learn of me;
> for I am gentle and lowly in heart,
> and you will find rest for your souls.
> For my yoke is easy and my burden is light.

The words are stylized, as one can tell straightaway. The form and content of Old Testament themes and Jewish Wisdom poetry are adapted; notably, the invitation of personified Wisdom (Prov. 8), and the appeal of the teacher of the Law to the uneducated, with which Ecclesiasticus closes (51.23–30). Its cadences are reminiscent of Hellenistic revelatory oracles.

Nevertheless, the call of the historical Jesus reverberates throughout the hymn in spite of its stylization. He is the most human of men, who softens the harsh Law and replaces it by the gentle Law of God's rule, which fits the neck better. He binds and liberates at the same time. The freedom which he reveals to men is rooted in God's binding will. The effect of God's bonds is to revive and refresh. For God gives rest. Rest is the eschatological gift of God. Rest, here, is not to be understood either in the sense of Hellenistic mysticism or of Jewish legalism. It does not mean either the blessed vision of the pious nor the conclusion to which the ideal of the educator leads—the achievement of great success by little effort. Rest is much more the domain of God's rule. Rest is the highest and final gift that God bestows. It is the way in which God completes his creation (Gen. 2.1–3); it is the life of Israel as soon as it possesses the promised land (Josh. 21.43–45); it is salvation itself and the loss of it is the loss of salvation (Deut. 12.9f.; 25.19). As long as the community remains a worshipping body it has an obligation to maintain God's rest (Ex. 31.12–18). The Sabbath is the day of sacrificial rest. The Rabbis say that it is a sixtieth part of the world to come. During the exile the people of God came to regard the day of rest as the sign of God's covenant. The rest experienced and offered on this day is Israel's indelible seal. In the New Testament also the 'companions of Christ' are pointed to the promise of this divine gift of salvation and warned not to miss it (Heb. 3.7–19; 4.1–10). The 'new day', the 'new today' (Heb. 4.7), is the day of rest. The preaching of the early Church invites men to repent and turn to Jesus Christ, 'that times of refreshing may come from the presence of the Lord' (Acts 3.19).

Jesus' coming is an invitation to refreshment for mankind. The rule of God is the rule of great refreshment or it is not the rule of *God*.

We fail to understand the Gospels, if we fail to hear this mighty refreshing power rushing through their testimony and if we fail to be refreshed personally. From Qumran and John the Baptist to Jesus is a short step—chronologically and geographically. But what a gulf there is on either side. In the monastery at Qumran they were separated from the daily round, and were preparing for the eschatological war of vengeance. Others may 'wander the broad, bright streets'; they are children of wickedness and darkness who will meet the fate they deserve. John ventures the next step and advances from the wilderness to the edge of the world: sinful men come to him while the pious defenders of the Temple are surprised at his words of judgement. But the final step is taken

by Jesus. He does not retire from the world to live in the wilderness. He does not call men out of the world to himself. Jesus
returns to the world from the Jordan. He seeks men out. When
he returns from the solitude of the desert he is to be found in the
places where people are. In their towns and markets, villages
and farms, he goes after them. He meets them where they live
and work, in their job or profession. Jesus finds them and speaks
to them in the places where they experience joy and sorrow,
where their hopes and disappointments are. It is there that Jesus
helps them. It is essential to understand Jesus' turning away
from the Jordan to Galilee in order to know what he understood
by 'humanity'. It is for him something quite simple—a man
going after men, going to where they actually live. He does so in
a human way while giving himself to them without reserve. He
gives them the best gift that a man can give to others—time.

To have time for one another is, in this world, the true proof
of humanity. It is the 'essence of all the good deeds one man can
show another. If I really give anyone my time, then I give him
the most unique and ultimate gift that I could ever share—
myself. If I withhold my time, I am certainly in his debt, however
much I say I may have given him in other ways' (K. Barth). In
having time for others man gives himself, not just a part of himself.

Every story in the Gospels shows us Jesus as a man who was
utterly human; he is our fellow man. In the same way that he
forgets himself for God's sake, he forgets himself for the sake
of his fellow men. The divine possession of Jesus is expressed
and illustrated in what we could call his human possession. His
devotedness to men is not a consequence of his devotedness to
God. Rather, it is identical with it. It is not such that he turns
first to God and then turns away from God to men. Rather each
takes place in the other. In revealing God to men, he reveals his
own personality to men. Knowledge of God and knowledge of
man coincide in the words of Jesus. His having time for men is
his service of God. His manifestation among men of his humanity
is, in truth, his divinity.

The century-long efforts to express the divinity of Jesus are
fruitless as long as an abstract concept of God is involved and
as long as an attempt is made to assimilate Jesus to such an ideal
of God. This leads to imagining that Jesus' 'divinity' has been
proved as soon as he has been equated with man's own conception

of God. Whose judgement, in that case, is the standard? Obviously, ours. We have finally established a conceptual idolatry. If we wish to understand Jesus' 'divinity', however, we ought to hold fast to Luther's simple rule not to begin with our speculations in heaven 'above', but 'below' in the lowliness of man on earth.

What is the essence of Jesus' unique distinctiveness, that lifts him above all other men, including geniuses and saints and those whom we call 'authorities' (K. Jaspers)? In what way is Jesus authoritative for us? The Gospels tell us that Jesus is authoritative for us just because he is on the scene and at our service in a way that no other man is. Certainly, there are countless well-known and unknown men and women who spend their lives in the service of their fellow men. But there is no one of whom we can say that the very idea of his humanity is inseparable from his actually living for others. This, however, is true of Jesus of Nazareth; we cannot imagine Jesus any other than as the one who is always, everywhere and in every way *for* men. We cannot think of him under any circumstances as the one who took his stand against men and the true interest of men. Jesus is not the partisan of any abstract form of humanism. Rather, he is the partisan of man himself in the flesh. Jesus is the representative of man *par excellence*; hence he is the representative of humanity.

The fact that he is the Spirit-bearer chosen by God means that the promise of Jer. 31.31–34, the promise of the New Covenant, is fulfilled in him. What does this new covenant consist in? It consists in God placing his Law in man's inner being and writing it in his heart, and in man knowing God so well that he has no need to be taught about God's will from without. The Spirit of the Lord is upon him (Luke 4.18). The question of those who listened to him and saw him, 'Where did this man get all this?' (Mark 6.2–3), finds its answer in the fact that he lives within the Word of God and not outside it (Matt. 4.4). God and man, God and the world are not two separate worlds for him. The Law burdens man with this tension. It keeps the opposition of God and man, God and the world, constantly before his eyes. The Man of the last days chosen by God and endowed with his Spirit brings together what is irreconcilable. He will have nothing to do with either a godless world or a worldless God. God's will includes man and the world. Indeed, man and the world are the content of the good and great thoughts of God.

The Law written in Jesus' heart is the secret of his being. The Chosen One only needs to look into himself and to listen to the world for God's will to meet him directly. God's Law and the position of men interpret each other in turn for the archetypal charismatic man. The reality of the time speaks the language of eternity to him. The reality of God and God's will is present for him in every man at every moment. It should be noted that all this is only true of Jesus. It is not true generally of men or the world. But since Jesus' appearance the glory of the eternal world lies over the reality of men and the world.

Now we can understand what it means that Jesus can be wholly on the side of God and man at the same time—and *vice versa*. He helps men to their true rights. As he does so the eve of man begins. As he realizes human rights on earth, he establishes God's righteousness throughout the world.

God's righteousness appears in Jesus of Nazareth as God's goodness. This is the deepest difference between Jesus and his time, especially in comparison with the warriors of the holy army of Qumran, but also in comparison with the Baptist. The former prepared themselves for the coming war of vengeance, the latter expected the fire of judgement. Both alternatives are rejected by Jesus. On the occasion of his first sermon in Nazareth (Luke 4.16–30) Jesus limited himself in what he read (Isa. 61.1–2) to the words of mercy; he broke off immediately before the words of judgement. He invokes the 'year of mercy of the Lord', but not 'the day of judgement of our God'. Also, in Matt. 11.5, where Isa. 35.5–6 is quoted somewhat freely, the words 'Behold, your God will come with vengeance, with the recompense of God' are omitted. In Isa. 49.24–26, which is the exegetical background for the victory over demons (see p. 158 above), v. 26a with its terrible threats,

I will make your oppressors eat their own flesh,
and they shall be drunk with their own blood as with wine,

is excluded. Jesus embodies God's good, gracious will.

Jesus knows he is sent to minister to men, to the whole man. For Jesus man is not only soul, he is also body. Therefore he does not forget man's welfare in his concern for man's salvation.

We have already spoken of his help in the dangers of life, in illness, and in nervous disorders, even including schizophrenia.

Men know that 'he can do something' even in times of miserable distress (Mark 9.22). He saw the great crowd and 'had compassion on them, because they were like sheep without a shepherd' (Mark 6.34), 'harassed and helpless' (Matt. 9.36). The tiredness of the leaderless, exploited crowd and the beggarly poverty, sickness and sadness of the individual all touch his heart in a similar way (Matt. 20.34; Luke 7.13). The distinctiveness of this man consists in the fact that he always has a heart for other men in the midst of a world without feeling, which treats men as objects, as means to an end and at the best fits them into the great machine of existence.

But the whole man includes man as soul. The question of man's welfare is always subservient to the question of his salvation. The whole man is addressed in Jesus' words '*Ephphatha*—be opened' (Mark 7.34). Not only the deaf ear but the deaf man is to be opened in every respect. And the whole man is to be satisfied, not just the empty stomach. The miraculous feeding of the five thousand (or four thousand) is related six times in the Gospels (Mark 6.34–44 with two parallels, Mark 8.1–10 with one parallel, John 6.1–13). In each case the narrative is concerned with deliverance which God has in store for the whole man, but it is especially true in the case of the fourth Gospel. God's thoughts, which Jesus translates into action, 'keep us safe and sound, in time and in eternity'.

Jesus is conscious of being sent to all men, good and bad alike. We are familiar with the fact that Jesus goes to sinners— almost too familiar, in a sense; we can hardly imagine Jesus without the questionable figures of 'the sinners', but we think little or nothing of what this really means. We are much less familiar with the question—perhaps we have not even considered it— whether Jesus stood only in a polemical relationship to the good.

Dietrich Bonhoeffer has tackled this question in his unfinished *Ethics*, in the section 'Christ and the good'. He starts from Matt. 5.10, where those are called blessed who are persecuted not for the sake of Jesus Christ or God but for the sake of a just cause, 'a true, good and human cause (cf. I Peter 3.14 and 2.20)'. In times of established order, when law and order prevail, the Gospel may be most clearly seen in relation to the tax collector and the prostitute. In times of lawlessness and wickedness it would 'rather be in relation to the few remaining just, truthful and

M

humane people, that the gospel would make itself known. It was
the experience of other times that the wicked found their way
to Christ while the good remained remote from him. The
experience of our own time is that it is the good who find their
way back to Christ and that the wicked obstinately remain aloof
from him.' Other times would preach that a man must first
become a sinner, before he could find Christ, but today it would
be better to say, 'First become righteous, in order to know Christ.'
Both statements are equally paradoxical and in themselves
impossible. Both sinners and righteous belong to him and have
fallen away from their origins either in their wickedness or in
their goodness.

The good man, however, should not be equated unquestioningly,
as in the Reformed Churches, with the Pharisee or hypocrite.
And the Gospel should not become merely a call to drunkards,
adulterers and vicious men of every kind to repent. Since the
end of the First World War the justifiable protest against bourgeois
self-satisfaction has led to a dangerous distortion of the Gospel.
'The justification of the good has been replaced by the justification
of the wicked; the idealization of good citizenship has given way
to the idealization of its opposite, of disorder, chaos, anarchy and
catastrophe; the forgiving love of Jesus for the sinful woman,
for the adulteress and for the tax collector has been misrepresented
in order to make it a Christian sanctioning of anti-social "marginal
existences", prostitutes and traitors. The gospel of the sinner
became, unintentionally, a commendation of sin. And good, in
the sense of good citizenship, was held up to ridicule.' At this
point the argument breaks off.

Bonhoeffer's question is by no means disposed of yet. Far from
being answered it has yet to be considered. We shall be wise not
to dictate any answer from our moral experience but understand
it by means of the Gospels themselves. Bonhoeffer himself explains
that sin, in the eyes of the New Testament or rather the Synoptic
Gospels, is more precipitous than our distinctions make clear.
Sin is not exhausted by phenomena of moral or religious evil.
It is a 'component part' of every man, including the good. Luther's
'our works are but in vain, even in the *best* life' is an accurate
statement of the position. We block the way to understanding
sin, however, if we regard it as an individual trait and attribute
of man, however unpleasant. Sin is not a purely individual

failure any more than faith is an individual achievement (cf. p. 161 above); the individual failure is much more the manifestation of a superhuman power. Sin is 'not an attribute but a chain' (G. Wingren). In contrast to what is said in the Old Testament it is a *force* which enslaves a man (John 8.34) and to which a man becomes addicted (Rom. 7.23). 'From within, out of the heart of man, come evil thoughts, fornication, theft, murder, adultery, coveting, wickedness, deceit, licentiousness, envy, slander, pride, foolishness. All these evil things come from within and they defile man' (Mark 7.21–23). The passage is very specific. A whole catalogue of vices is given. But it is clear that individual sins (in the plural) are an expression of sin (in the singular). 'The personal sin', in which I constantly find myself involved, assumes palpable form in 'sins committed'. The wickedness of men does not exclude the possibility of their giving good gifts to their children (Matt. 7.11). But efforts to prove who Jesus is by a sign, efforts which are religiously justifiable, are, nevertheless, expressions of mankind's wickedness and lack of faith in God (Matt. 16.4). Sin can only be committed against God, in fact. One cannot speak *about* one's sins, one can only confess them in prayer to God, for he stands over against men in a personal relationship. 'Against thee only have I sinned' (Ps. 51.6). Confession is the first place where it is possible to speak correctly of sins.

As a result of Jesus' appearance sin in the real sense is exposed for the first time. This makes it easier to recognize the twofold nature of sin: rebellion against God and retreat from God.

Jesus exposes sin as rebellion against God. God limits us by his will and the intractable nature of the world. What Bonhoeffer says about sexuality in his profound exposition of the Fall and Original Sin (on Gen. 3.7) is true of sin as a whole. Sin is 'passionate hatred of every limitation'. Sin is self-exaltation. The Greeks warned men against *hubris*, blasphemous protestation against the gods, and its punishment. The wisdom literature of the Old Testament, also, has something to say about this (cf. Prov. 29.23). 'Whoever exalts himself will be humbled' (Luke 14.11). To trust oneself, consider oneself in the right and despise others (Luke 18.9) is sin. God sees through this self-esteem of man. 'For what is exalted among men is an abomination in the sight of God' (Luke 16.15). God meets pride with the sharpness of his judgement. He blocks man's every escape into imaginary horizons.

Jesus also exposes sin as retreat from God. This is to a certain extent the opposite tendency to the one we have just been discussing. Man is not defiant, but despondent. He avoids the distant horizons. He allies himself with restriction and confinement. He goes in for 'spiritual emigration'. He gives way to fear. He flees before the morrow, or at least he closes his eyes to it. This form of sin is called 'care' by Jesus. The 'cares of the world' choke the word (Mark 4.19). They make tomorrow a forbidding power (Matt. 6.34). They prevent one looking to the future of God (Luke 21.34). God meets such care with the offer of his help. He attracts men away from the barrier of tomorrow on which their gaze is fixed.

Both forms of sin are basically forms of unbelief, which trusts itself too much and God too little. When God is distrusted man's being disintegrates. It is in such disintegration that our lives originate, both good and bad alike.

From the beginning Jesus' call was to all men. The fact that he calls them, and calls them to himself, makes their sin known. To be a sinner does not mean being a specially wicked person in a moral sense, but to find oneself in the wrong place. Jesus invites all men, whether they are good or not, to the right place. To be a sinner means not being where Jesus is. This knowledge makes it feasible to differentiate between various sorts of sin, although basically they all refer to the same failure. Jesus did not avoid the good. Luke pictures Jesus being invited to a meal on different occasions by a Pharisee or even one of the leaders of the brotherhood of the Pharisees (Luke 7.36; 11.37; 14.1). As regards the host it is not surprising, for it was an honoured custom to invite any travelling preacher to a meal. Even if Luke wants to underline by these stories the way Jesus was open to the world this does not mean they have no historical basis. More probably the later decision to oppose Pharisaic piety suppressed recollections of more relations with pious Pharisees. The statement that Jesus called sinners and not the righteous does not mean that he bypassed the righteous, any more than the concern of the doctor for the sick betokens enmity towards the healthy (Mark 2.17).

Jesus tells the paralytic, although he 'only' wants to be healed, that his sins are forgiven (Mark 2.1–12). Sin and suffering are related. What the Old Testament expected has arrived. Jesus does what only *God* may do. For 'the time of the Messiah is the time of forgiveness' (J. Schniewind). To forgive sins, however, means to cancel the past which is marked by hostility and distrust towards God, so that it can no longer accuse us before God. Where forgiveness takes place God opens the future to man. Man receives the right to have access to and fellowship with God. Guilt no longer stands between God and man. The great parables from Luke 15 illustrate what it means when the man who is lost is restored to God. The straying sheep is brought home. The lost coin is swept out of the dark corner. The young man who wanted to assume responsibility for planning his life returns home: the figure of his father will not leave him until it has drawn him home again. Yet forgiveness creates thanksgiving not only in places where forgiveness has been received but also where it is expected. 'God must have forgiven her all her sins, for she has shown such great gratitude; but he who is forgiven little loves little' (Luke 7.47). Jesus had pronounced the forgiveness of sins; now the sinner came to him.

The distinctiveness of Jesus' activity, however, lies in the fact that he does not simply forgive sins generally or in particular and then let matters take their course. If so, forgiveness could have remained a distant experience and his words would have proved static, unable to affect anyone. But Jesus seeks fellowship with sinners and sees forgiveness corroborated as he lives with them. It is necessary to make clear for once what this meant for him and for the religious world of his day. We are familiar with the tax collectors, who were not only financial racketeers but also evil political informers. He lodges with them. He chooses one of his disciples from their number. He sits at table with them (Mark 2.13–17; Luke 19.1–10). He is on friendly terms with them and enjoys their company, 'a glutton and a wine-bibber, a friend of tax collectors and sinners' (Luke 7.34). The *am-haarez* believe in him—'this crowd who do not know the Law—curses upon them' (John 7.49). He not only observes the circumstances of those who are poor, despised and demoralized (Luke 16.19–22), but he stands by all those who suffer from oppression or loss of rights, including children (Mark 9.34–37; 10.13–16) and women, who at that time were excluded from public and religious life. The statement that Mary of Magdala, Joanna, the wife of one of Herod Antipas' officials, a certain Susanna 'and many others who provided for them out of their means' accompanied them either permanently or for part of the time (Luke 8.1–3) indicates that women in the circle of the Jesus-movement were given a new honour and inviolability. By summoning them to the kingdom of God Jesus gave women their charter of equal human rights. This should never be forgotten when we are discussing the meaning of humanity.

3. *The Law of the Creator*

In the Protestant world it has been customary to understand Jesus exclusively as the conqueror of the Law. The renewal of the Pauline recognition that 'Christ is the end of the Law' (Rom. 10.4) appeared to reinforce this judgement. Historical observations referring to the way Jesus differed from the legalistic piety of his day had the effect of confirming this judgement.

A more thorough examination of the position would be compelled to regard the one-sided emphasis of this view as a Protestant prejudice and abandon it. Jesus' relation to the Law cannot be expressed in a single sentence. At the least it requires two sentences —both logically exclusive—to describe it. Jesus' relation to the Law is not accidentally hostile, but essentially paradoxical. This has its origin not in any unclarity of thought or will, but in the nearness of the rule of God, which is, in turn, a paradoxical force —it is both present and future. Because the rule of God is already present the Law is annulled by it; because the rule of God is still in the future the Law remains in operation. Jesus is paradoxical because the eschatological nature of God, which brings the day of refreshment and yet constantly keeps men in suspense, is paradoxical.

Jesus' relation to the Law is positive. For the Law contains God's will. God's will is the presupposition of all humanity. Thus he subjects himself to God's will by subjecting himself to the Law. Paul was not alone in affirming this. 'God sent forth his son, born of woman, born under the Law' (Gal. 4.4). Paul was only able to affirm this because Jesus had already lived it.

By being subject to the Law Jesus was united with all men. This affirmation of the Law does not mean for Jesus the affirmation of an ancient, honoured institution holy in itself, but the affirmation of God and hence the affirmation of man. Living under the Law Jesus proclaimed his solidarity with sinners. Understood in this way the Law became the expression of humanity for him. At the head of his commentary on the Law, in the Sermon on the Mount, Matthew puts the saying (Matt. 5.17–18):

> Think not that I have come to abolish the Law and the
>   prophets;
> I have come not to abolish them but to fulfil them.
> For, truly, I say to you,
> till heaven and earth pass away,
> not an iota, not a dot, will pass from the Law
> until all is accomplished.

The saying may have been shaped by the conservative Palestinian community. In addition it presupposes the conflict with the Hellenistic community. But its intrinsic value depends on the fact that Jesus was no opponent of the Law. The nearness of the imminent rule of God made it seem unimportant to him, anyhow, to break up the Law shortly before this and to alter the commandments and pious practices. The decisive thing for him was to confront men with the will of God. For the sake of God and man Jesus was 'conservative' in matters of the Law. His concern was to fulfil the Law. This did not mean filling up gaps in the Law, or giving the Law a new meaning, or clarifying obscurities, but 'making it effective'. Jesus aims to enhance the value of the Law, the will of God. The Law should be recognized as the will of God, who is the Creator of the world and Lord of mankind. Jesus establishes the authority of the Law over men.

The Law stands and falls with the Creation. Jesus shared this conviction with contemporary Judaism. The pointed saying that not a single letter, not even the smallest letter, the Hebrew *yod*, not even the ornamental little mark that 'crowns' the letter, would pass from the Law, does not refer to the literal fulfilment of the Law but to its universal and eternal worth. It is metaphorically exaggerated, like many other sayings of Jesus, such as the words about the camel and the eye of a needle (Mark 10.25), or straining at a gnat and swallowing a camel (Matt. 23.24). It found adherents among the Rabbis of the third and fourth century to a certain extent. There is no reason to ascribe the *bon mot*, the point of which tallies with what we know of Jesus, to the school of Matthew. In spite of its narrow appearance it breathes the full breadth of his humanity. Jesus stands on the eschatological horizon and proclaims for the last time the majesty of God's will. When Jesus says, 'Until all is accomplished', 'all' means the holy will of God.

It is not surprising that Jesus gives little or no eschatological reason for the Law. He does not lure men with the future Paradise nor does he threaten them with the coming Judgement. He does not make hell hot or heaven desirable in his exposition of the Law. When he makes specific demands, the indication that God wants this or that done or not done is sufficient. The original presence of God in earthly life sustains all existence. God maintains and rules the world. He sustains and cares for the life of men. The Law is also a sign of his involvement in the world and his friendliness towards men.

Fundamental to an understanding of Jesus' attitude to the Law is the fact that Jesus does not practise a theology of the Law; nor does he possess any doctrine of the Law. He 'teaches' the Law, it is true, just as he 'proclaims' the rule of God. It is perhaps wise to notice this difference which is particularly prominent in Matthew: the rule of God is 'proclaimed', the Law is 'taught'. He teaches it in particular circumstances, without, however, being a casuist like the scribes. He teaches it in such a way that specific people are confronted directly by the specific will of God; never in such a way that a generally applicable rule which could be made prescriptive is substituted for the unique situation in which a person finds himself before God. Jesus was not a theologian, least of all a systematic theologian; nor did he possess an 'ethics', from which one could gather how one ought to act.

Problems which were discussed in detail later by Paul and which subsequent theology has never broken away from did not exist for him. The fact that God's will can be recognized unequivocally creates no problem for Jesus. Man and the world are God's creation. The Creator speaks not only through the written Law but also through his creation. The world as a whole and its individual phenomena are facets of the penetrating and manifold utterance of God. Existence itself possesses this character of speech, because it is governed by God's will as part of his creation. Man is constantly surrounded by evidence of God's will in nature and history. Above him stretch the heavens of the Creator. Around him and beside him are his fellow men. Situations attract, threaten and demand.

> Consider the ravens: they neither sow nor reap:
> they have neither storehouse nor barn,
> and yet God feeds them.
> Of how much more value are you than the birds!
> Consider the lilies, how they grow; they neither toil nor
>   spin.
> Yet I tell you,
> even Solomon in all his glory
> was not arrayed like one of these.

The earthly (Luke 12.24, 27) is not only a parable of the heavenly, but the manifestation of it. For the Jew there is a remarkable parallel between events in heaven and on earth: the bird which is addressed as 'free' by God in heaven escapes the net of the birdcatcher; the bird which is surrendered by God in heaven gets caught. But for Jesus God speaks much more directly. His speech through dumb creation is not only an expression of a perfect, divine thought, but it is always at the same time a proclamation. In personal relationship with men God works out his great good thoughts. This God is to be believed.

The moth which destroys clothing and the woodworm which eats away the clothes-press both whisper the threatening word of God in men's ears, reminding them that their life is hastening imperceptibly to its end. The secret plotting of thieves makes us aware of the vulnerability of earthly existence (Matt 6.19–20). Death destroys all plans (Luke 12.16–21). God's will not only preserves life; it also endangers life. This God is to be feared!

Situations are demanding. God is demanding in such situations. God desires in such situations that the deed of love take place without difference of person, race, class or religion (Luke 10.29–37). This God is to be obeyed and his will done! God demands humanity (Mark 12.28–33).

Jesus observes the Law, and respects the institutions and men that represent God's Law. He subjects himself—for the sake of his fellow men—to the Law. He is baptized, because 'it is fitting to fulfil all righteousness' (Matt. 3.15). He left the cultic law, along with the sacrificial gift and the altar, untouched (Matt. 5.23–24); the Palestinian church could not have misunderstood him on this point. The leper who has been healed is sent to the religious 'medical police': 'Go, show yourself to the priest, and offer for your cleansing what Moses commanded, for a proof to the people' (Mark 1.44). The man who asks after God's will is pointed to the Ten Commandments of Sinai (Mark 10.19). Jesus and the disciples feel no obligation in respect of the temple-tax; it ought to be paid voluntarily. The fact that the rule of God frees men from the theocracy of the Temple does not do away with the holiness of the Temple. Even for Jesus and his disciples the Temple remained the focal point of their earthly existence (Matt. 17.24–27). The strange miracle-story of Matt. 17.24–27, in which a genuine miracle is recorded, underlines the meaning of the decision taken by Jesus. The piece of money in the mouth of the fish that has been caught, which reminds one involuntarily of Polycrates' ring, affirms that 'God himself, who sent his Son and subjected him to the Law, finally pays the price demanded by the Law, while working a miracle' (K. L. Schmidt).

The Temple is more than the gold with which Herod decorated its inside and its façade. The altar is more than the sacrifice, which is consecrated by the altar. But heaven is God's throne as the earth is his footstool; it is higher than Temple and altar together, higher even than Jerusalem, 'the city of the great king' (Matt. 23.16–22; 5.34–35). But the Temple is not unimportant! Even the tithe of the most insignificant plants of the kitchen garden— mint, anise and cummin—is not unimportant. These small precepts are not absolutely vital but of secondary importance. The decisive qualities are 'righteousness, mercy and faith'. 'You ought to have done these things without neglecting the others!' (Matt. 23.23). This proverbial utterance contains some profound wisdom. Jesus knows that the world is a very varied reality. But at all levels it is subject to God's will. There is not only an 'ultimate' in the world, there is also a 'penultimate'. The penultimate is derived from the ultimate and points forward to it. What is small serves what is great, the object serves the person. Jesus' visit to the synagogue on the Sabbath is one of his customary practices (Mark 3.1; 6.2). Accordingly the early Church in Judaea held fast to the celebration of the Sabbath (Matt. 24.20). The prophetic protest, 'I desire mercy and not sacrifice' (Hos. 6.6), is Jesus' test of all human actions (Matt. 9.13; 12.7).

Jesus does not even assail the office of those who declare the Law. He knows how to distinguish between office and person; this distinction did not originate with Luther. 'The scribes and the Pharisees sit on Moses' seat; so practise and observe whatever they tell you, but not what they do; for they preach but do not practise' (Matt. 23.2–3). Jesus establishes this without either bitterness or scorn. They do not live according to the will of God; they lecture *about* existence. At best they make such a fine show of existence in words that they make it utterly impossible. 'They bind heavy burdens hard to bear and lay them on men's shoulders; but they themselves will not move them with their finger' (Matt. 23.4). The distinction between person and office is one of the fundamental insights mediated by Jesus to the world. It represents the axiom of objectivity which must be authoritative not only in the Church but also in contemporary civilization, if the Church desires to be Christian and civilization to be human. The Reformers saw in Matt. 23.2 the possibility of distinguishing between life and doctrine without losing sight of the majesty and holiness of revealed truth above the doubtfulness and corruptness of life. The holiness of the Church, its message and its sacraments did not for them depend on the holiness and worthiness of the persons (Augsburg Confession, article 8). Only where this axiom is applied does the struggle for eternal values remain unsullied. The distinction of office and person guarantees the sincerity of the intellectual search for truth. It acts as a check on every form of fanaticism, including religious as well as political fanaticism. Slogans and jargon are both proscribed, religious jargon and ecclesiastical slogans not excepted. We are given a sharp reminder not to lose sight of the importance of the subject-matter in the presence of our opponent when he presents his case all too unobjectively. Where the axiom of objectivity is applied, eyes and ears are opened to observe the adjacency of truth even in the distortions of lies and to perceive humanity's cry of alarm in the shrill discord of human passions. For the axiom of objectivity rejects all possessiveness, all distrust, and all malice and substitutes 'righteousness, mercy and faith' (Matt. 23.23). The axiom of objectivity is equally the axiom of humanity.

It is only from this point of view that one can understand how Jesus stood not only in a positive but also in a critical relationship to the Law. The period of the Law has been superseded through the arrival of the period of God's rule (Matt. 1.12–13). Jesus protests first of all against legalism. In doing so he protests not only against incidental abuses of the Law but against the primary abuse of the Law, to which the Judaism of the theocratic state owed its existence. The kingdom of God and the theocratic state are mutually exclusive, for theocracy makes the Law a necessary prior condition of fellowship, but the kingdom of God knows no conditions other than itself and man's acceptance of it. 'But woe to you, scribes and Pharisees, hypocrites! because you shut the kingdom of heaven against men; for you neither enter yourselves nor allow those who would enter to go in' (Matt. 23.13.)

The one who is summoning men to the kingdom of God is on the attack against the guardians of the theocratic state. He attacks the spirit of legalism which conceals the purely formal correctness of its 'inwardness'. Statements from the Bible and catechism are learned off by heart; God's word brings liberation from life in the sight of others and of God. The prayer-book is used for prayer and the psalms are sung according to their various musical modes, but the Spirit is no longer in control of life apart from these observances. In spite of much work on regulations for faith and practice applying to both ordained and lay members of the church there has been a failure to go beyond the blue-prints to life itself. In short, men rack their brains and speak and write *about* life, but refuse to live. Synods and conferences are held to discuss the tasks which Christ and the Church face in relation to the world of today; but while this is happening the world is being left to its own wisdom and its own devices.

There is a great desire for information of all sorts drawn from the Bible, but it is a Bible taken over uncritically from a pious generation that is now gone, without any personal confrontation or conversation. What lies in our homes under the name of the Bible is by and large only an *image* which we have of the Bible. Woe to the man who uses the equipment of critical scholarship to make it speak afresh! Woe to the man who tells the 'Church' that not every recorded word of Jesus stems from Jesus, because the words of Jesus have been given shape and sometimes content by the Church! Woe to the man who destroys the illusion that Jesus delivered the Sermon on the Mount on a tape recorder and that the miracle-worker was accompanied by a film-unit making a news-reel! These biblicists who call 'Woe' also have their own 'Woe': the 'Woe' of Jesus in Matthew 23.

The battle of Jesus against legalism raged most fiercely against the prescriptions of the ritual law and observance of the Sabbath.

In both cases he is concerned to make the stipulations of the Law serve man's welfare.

The dispute over the so-called 'clean and unclean' (Mark 7.1–23) centres round the validity of the ritual law, which requires the purity of the cult to be applied to daily life also. This ideal of realizing cultic purity in daily life also had been familiar in the circles of the 'Pious' since Maccabaean times. Anyone who wanted to represent 'the kingdom of priests' (Ex. 19.6) had to gather the pure community together. The baptismal and repentance movements of the time, especially the Qumran community, were vitally concerned with such purity. These purification ordinances, which went back to the Levitical laws of the Old Testament, were religious rites, not hygiene laws. It is true that at mealtimes, since food was eaten without cutlery, cleanliness was a very sensible requirement in view of the routine work of house and home and in view of the climate which was the regular background of this daily routine. But the rite itself could be no less unhygienic. At all events, Jesus' disciples ate with unwashed hands. When questioned about this by the scribes and Pharisees Jesus not only defends his disciples but attacks their attackers. The commonest interpretation of Jesus' polemic is that he did away with the difference between 'clean' and 'unclean', 'holy' and 'unholy'. But there is nothing of this in the text (cf. Matt. 15.1–20). Rather, Jesus does not refer to external appearances but to inner realities. A man must keep himself 'clean' before this inner reality. And from the contrast of 'clean—unclean' he moves straightaway to the contrast of 'God's command—the tradition of men'. This is another instance, however, where we must place the accent correctly. The tradition of men is not to be despised because it stems from men but because it renders God's command ineffective. The obligation of the command to honour one's father and mother is being evaded by means of a vow. Parents are being left to starve for the sake of the Temple. People are being forgotten because of the cult and its ritual.

It has been rightly observed that Jesus not only attacks the Jewish tradition here, its theory and its practice, but the letter of the Law itself. This should not be made light of. Rather, it should be examined in the light of the contrast of Mark 7.9–13 and Num. 30.2–30 together with Deut. 23.21–23, and of Mark 7.15 and the innumerable stipulations of the Levitical purification laws in Leviticus (cf. also the contrast of Matt. 5.38–39 and Lev. 24.20). If Jesus cites Moses (Mark 7.10: Ex. 20.12 and 21.17) then it is a case of 'Moses against Moses'. It is impossible, however, to understand this as a dispute about the Law as such, rather than a sharply different interpretation of the Law. Only those parts of the Law that serve the glory of God *and* the salvation of man are valid. The man who evades the service of man by means of the Law or substitutes an altar-sacrifice for compassion is guilty of an 'unholy' action. The man who recognizes the correspondence between God and man and practises humanity does what is 'holy'. The contrast 'holy—unholy' remains. But it is raised to a different level. Humanity is the measure of the Law.

The narratives about breaking the Sabbath-law point in the same direction. The disciples who are walking through the corn-fields with Jesus on the Sabbath pluck the ears as they go (Mark 2.23–28). In doing so they desecrate the Sabbath. That, at any rate, was the judgement of all pious Jews at that time, not only the Pharisees and Rabbis but also the apocalyptists and members of the Qumran community. For the 'community of the New Covenant in the land of Damascus' the Sabbath belongs to the revelations brought by the teacher of righteousness. The Sabbath regulations which go back to him increase not only the number of the previous stipulations, but also their severity; in cases of deliberate desecration the punishment of death is to be inflicted. According to the teaching of the Rabbis the Sabbath is kept holy not simply by celebrating the cult but by resting and by studying the Law. As a day of joyful participation in God's heavenly world it is celebrated by festal eating and drinking and by wearing special clothes. Cooking is not permitted, though feasting is. Jesus defends an action which in his day counted as a violation of the Sabbath. His reference to David (I Sam. 21.7) is anything but a literal biblical proof. It is a reference to the unique king who was closely associated with Messianic expectation: the coming freedom which is now dawning is already foreshadowed in his actions. This is followed by the regal statement, 'The Sabbath was made for man, not man for the Sabbath' (Mark 2.27). A saying of the Rabbis (about AD 180) declares, 'Observe the Sabbath, because it is holy *for you*.' This 'for you', in the sense of 'for your good', is stating the exception, not the rule, however;

when life was in danger a man could be saved. But for Jesus this was the rule; the Sabbath is the servant of men—not, of course, for doing anything one may please but for doing good.

This is underlined by the following story of the healing of the man with the withered hand (Mark 3.1–6). Jesus heals him on the Sabbath. This leads to another conflict with the Pharisees who are watching him. The question in this case is not for Jesus 'holy or unholy', but 'good or evil'. 'Is it lawful on the Sabbath to do good or to do harm, to save life or to kill?' The question is put in the most extreme form possible. It presents an alternative which must be rejected. His opponents are silent. Casuists, expert in distinguishing between shades of meaning, find Jesus' question too trenchant. Behind his angry look is his knowledge of the good which every man is called to do—and his sadness at how dead the human heart can be. The Sabbath was intended to quicken the heart. The Sabbath gives the signal for humanity to be practised.

It is impossible to attach too much significance to the central words of these two narratives. Mark 2.27 and 3.4 are the Magna Carta of all humanity. Little did men suspect that a new picture of the possibilities of human existence was being established here. This is the answer to the question of the Hellenistic, modern world about man and his day. The day of God is the day of man. The eve of that day is already present wherever Jesus acts as the representative of man. Not the day of the 'Pious', but the day of man who is really man has dawned.

Jesus is very concerned with what Harnack, using the thought-forms and expressions of the last century, called 'the eternal value of the human soul'. Today, of course, we know that man is a psychosomatic (soul-body) unity. 'Soul' is not what a man possesses, but who he is. It is precisely so, in his natural wholeness, just as he is, that God promises him the Sabbath to be a great help in life. Jesus proclaims this Magna Carta: man does not exist for the sake of this or any other institution, but the institution exists for the sake of man. The sick person is not just a 'case' for the hospital, the doctor, the nurses, but all these, together with all their apparatus, exist to serve the sick person. The authorities are there to serve the public—otherwise we call it a bureaucracy, which is simply the secular form of theocracy. Knowledge has to serve human life—and not *vice versa*, otherwise knowledge becomes superstition. Man was not made for the state or society, but the state and society were made for man—otherwise society becomes a demon and the state becomes 'the coldest of all monsters' (Nietzsche). In fact, not even the criminal, within the framework of constitutional justice, exists to serve the legal code and the judge, but both of these exist to serve him. All abstractions are of the devil: knowledge, culture, the state, the church, the law. The concrete reality, which appears in Jesus, is of God, for Jesus is Man, in the sense of the Son of Man who is Lord of the Sabbath.

When this is understood, the alternative 'to do good or evil' is understood and already answered.

4. *The Duty of Man*

The essence of the Law is love. Jesus brings this love in the course of acting as the representative of man. What the Law demands he does. In his actions he reveals to men the love of God. Anyone who has received this love lives in it and shares it. The good news of Jesus proclaims the fulfilment of the Law and thereby the new existence of man. Man is given the power to love through the gift of God's humanity.

Jesus is not only the man of faith, i.e. the one who is open to God's reality, but he is also the one who is open to man's reality, i.e. the man of love. English only possesses the one term 'love' for the force which is meant, and this conceals several different nuances. Greek, however, is able to distinguish three different sorts of love. *Erōs* is desiring love, including love between the sexes, as well as the desire for possessions and objects of value— love which inclines to ecstasy, but also to religion. Secondly, there is *philia*, the love of the gods for man, sympathy between friends, reverence for everything human. Sophocles' Antigone, faithful to the law of death, epitomizes this love:

> I am here to love, not hate.

Finally there is *agapē*, love which does not use force, but manifests itself in free choice or 'preference'. The New Testament does not even mention *erōs*, passionate love, and the word *philia* only occurs in a derogatory sense (James 4.4). The New Testament expressed Jesus' concern by the Greek word *agape* which up till then had been a fairly colourless word. This love means

God's choice. As the Chosen One Jesus is the 'beloved Son'. God's choice, however, is God's work, which is free and allows mercy to take precedence over justice. God's love is God's creative activity.

The love which is required of men is to be measured by this creative activity. The word 'love' usually has a sentimental and somewhat effeminate sound in English. For the New Testament love is an austere and sober reality. It is not a feeling, although it does not occur without feeling. It is not an emotion although it is an experience mediated through emotion. It comes from the centre of the personality, 'the heart'. It is something done—by the whole man; a surrender which knows no obstacle and fears no sacrifice.

The love which Jesus means is obligatory love. It is, in fact, the content of the Law. It is expressed in the double commandment: 'You shall love the Lord your God with all your heart, and with all your soul, and with all your mind, and with all your strength; and, you shall love your neighbour as yourself' (Mark 12.28–34). Matthew however adds: 'Everything in the Law and the prophets hangs on these two commandments' (Matt. 22.40). Everything hangs on these just as the door hangs on its two hinges. Neither is greater than the other, neither is less important. Both are equally binding on men. In the will of God—as we have noted—God and man are bound together and can only be honoured or dishonoured together.

The double commandment is not new. Jesus is certainly not original. The double commandment occurs in the Old Testament, even if never brought together. The command to love God has its place in ancient Israel's confession of faith, which the pious Jew had to recite twice each day, once in the morning, once in the evening. It was given special emphasis (Deut. 6.5). The command to love one's neighbour occurs in Lev. 19.18 as love of one's fellow countrymen. Luke 10.27 assumes that Rabbinic Judaism of those days was familiar with the combination of the two commandments. In this case not even the union of the two commandments was the work of Jesus. The new feature which Jesus brings to light, however, undoubtedly consists in the fact that he affirms the superiority of the first commandment to the second, but above all in the fact that he achieves the unity of the two commandments in his own person. His personal existence

N

is 'comprehended' in this word and attached to it. Jesus' activity makes it possible to understand how the required love is something to be done by the whole man.

The requirement of love is understandable without further explanation. Everyone knows from personal experience what it means to be loved, and also to show love. This is the meaning of the 'golden rule' (Matt. 7.12): 'So whatever you wish that men would do to you, do so to them; for this is the Law and the prophets.' The ancient Jewish scriptures knew the maxim in its negative form. It was a familiar truth in the Wisdom literature, where it was one of the rules of the good life. 'Do not do to anyone else what you yourself would hate' (Tob. 4.15). But the positive form also occurs. The *Letter of Aristeas* (see p. 41 above) makes the Jewish scholars answer the question of the Egyptian king about the 'teaching of Wisdom' as follows: 'As thou desirest that evils should not befall thee, but that thou shouldst partake of all that is good, thou shouldst treat thy subjects and offenders in the same way and shouldst very gently admonish such as are virtuous; for God draws all men to him by gentleness.' In spite of the religious reason given the rational-moralistic ring is obvious—one ought to treat virtuous men gently. Are not all men, even offenders, basically virtuous? Jesus' command has the force of his own directness and can be understood from the total ethos of his teaching. No moralistic evaluation is applicable. Not even the Law applies. The principle of justice is superseded in the teaching of Jesus, as the parable of the owner of the vineyard demonstrates (Matt. 20.1–15). God has complete freedom to do what he likes with what belongs to him. But his freedom is everlasting, generous goodness.

The man who loves lives on forgiveness. His love depends on readiness to forgive. Primitive days echo the drunken song of Lamech's defiance (Gen. 4.23–24):

> Give ear;
> I have slain a man for wounding me,
> and a young man for striking me.
> If Cain is avenged sevenfold
> truly Lamech seventy-sevenfold.

Braggart songs of vengeance and the sword have been a constant theme of human existence and world history in one form or another. The law of Hellenistic history and 'modern' man is 'retaliation'. Weapons for offence and defence become weapons of revenge. Attacks of reprisal keep the powers ready for one another. They force their way into 'power politics'. But the daily life of the ordinary citizen is not free from the desire for revenge; all that is lacking are the actual means to inflict more than pinpricks. Jesus sets this thinking and planning aside. The place of the law of revenge is taken by the law of forgiveness, which supersedes every law. Peter persists with his question about the specific number of times one should forgive a person: 'up to seven times?' Jesus replies, 'I do not say to you seven times, but seventy times seven' (Matt. 18.22). In the age of measurement and counting, Her Majesty Queen Number is dethroned. This saying of Jesus is followed by the parable of the brutal satrap, who was offered a free pardon by the Great King, although his debt from the province ran into millions. Subsequently he brings an under-official, a small, starving beggar, to trial and is himself, this time permanently, mercilessly condemned by the supreme judge. Anyone who does not share the forgiveness he has received falls foul of the law of revenge. This is justice, it is true, but by that very fact it is not mercy.

To love means to live on humility. The tax-collector stands afar off and will not even lift up his eyes to God (Luke 18.9–14). Jesus advises a man not to strive for the seat of honour at table but to take the lowest seat. 'Whoever humbles himself will be exalted' (Luke 14.7–11). When a feast is held, the host is not to invite the guests according to whether this is conducive to his own interest. 'Do not invite your friends or your brothers or your kinsmen or rich neighbours, lest they also invite you in return, and you be repaid. But when you give a feast invite the poor, the maimed, the lame, the blind, and you will be blessed because they cannot repay you . . . ' (Luke 14.12–14).

To love means to act on hearing. In the story of Mary and Martha Luke has discussed the secret of Jesus speaking and man hearing (Luke 10.38–42). From early days the two sisters were seen as types of the 'contemplative' and 'active' life. But they are more than embodiments of two virtuous modes of behaviour, one of which is more excellent than the other. It is not a character-sketch of two people but an affirmation of the power of what Jesus says. The self-forgetful one produces self-forgetfulness.

The man who forgets himself because of the word becomes human through listening. To be human means first of all to be receptive. Once again Luther has reminded us that the listening man of faith is 'purely passive'. God's divinity consists in his activity and giving. Man's humanity is rooted in his stillness and receptivity. Listening and receptivity lead to real activity.

Love means not making God the means to an end, however justified the end. Jesus' cause is certainly 'justified'. Jesus' request for lodgings in a Samaritan village is refused by the long-standing racial and religious enemies of the Jews, because he is going as a pilgrim to celebrate the Passover in Jerusalem. The 'sons of thunder' (Mark 3.17), James and John, ask him whether they ought not to call down fire from heaven, like Elijah (II Kings 1.9–16). 'But he turned and rebuked them,' and they went on to another —a Jewish?—village. The abrupt conclusion of this story points to a later interruption; perhaps it contained a word of rebuke for the disciples which appeared derogatory to their later calling. Later texts contain the addition, 'You do not know what manner of spirit you are of; for the Son of man came not to destroy men's lives but to save them'. This is the language of a later period. But even here we can see that Jesus himself is the source and standard of love (Luke 9.51–56). Jesus is the end of the curse of the Law (Gal. 3.13). Therefore he is also the end of cursing. Here is something 'more' than Elijah.

Jesus' love is love of one's enemy. That is why he can constantly call upon his followers to love their enemies (Luke 6.27–28):

> Love your enemies,
> do good to those who hate you,
> bless those who curse you,
> pray for those who abuse you.

Matthew gives the reason for this advice by referring to the creative activity of the Father (Matt. 5.45):

> For he makes his sun rise on the evil and on the good,
> and sends rain on the just and on the unjust.

The God who is worshipped at Qumran does not do so. At least he is not allowed to.

Jesus' love lives by rejecting vengeance. This is repeatedly shown by the tradition of his praying. He does what he requires of others. Luke makes him pray on the cross for his executioners. 'Father, forgive them; for they know not what they do' (Luke 23.24). Anyone who wants to know what is new about Jesus must compare the Lord's Prayer with the corresponding formulae of Jewish prayers. Both pray for the forgiveness of sins, but the Jew prays that God will destroy the sinners. The fifth petition of the Lord's Prayer, on the other hand, is linked with the proviso, 'as we have forgiven our debtors' (Matt. 6.12). An additional comment explains that God will refuse to forgive, if Christians do not forgive their fellow men (Matt. 6.14–15).

Jesus' love is experienced as compassion. Jesus' own activity shows us what compassion is. Anyone who wants to know what it is *not* should read the parable in Luke 16.19–31. Anyone who wants to know what it is should read the parable in Luke 10.29–37— and 'do likewise'! Only by doing the will of the Father can one know whether Jesus' teaching is from God or not (John 7.17). The deed is the criterion of the truth.

Jesus' demand for love is a unique demand. What is demanded is not a virtue or latent ability, but man himself. Man is challenged to make the choice of human existence—between neighbour and enemy. Who one's neighbour is cannot be decided beforehand; it can only be settled in particular cases in the actual context of a definite moment. Fundamentally my neighbour is every fellow human being who is referred to me for help. The great fundamental question of all ethical inquiry which is more than theory is this: 'Where is the man who is referred to me for help at this moment—even if perhaps he does not want it?' Where will he meet me? I may wake with this question tomorrow. It will accompany my daily work. It will continue to keep me in suspense while I plan and work, lest I forget my daily resolve to be a man.

In the conclusion of the parable about the man who fell among robbers Jesus gave a distinctive twist to a question which had been framed one-sidedly. The parable was supposed to answer the question, 'Who is my neighbour?' Jesus answered the bold, almost provocative question with a parable, which was itself a challenge. It was not the sort of answer which is really a counter-question seeking information and is simply another way out of a difficult situation. It leaves the level of cheap discussion far behind. The question appears to be on a level of ultimate serious-

ness. It changes the direction of the original question and takes
the questioner by surprise. Jesus asks, 'Which of these three—
priest, Levite, Samaritan—do you think proved neighbour to the
man who fell among the robbers?' By means of the question
about the man who needed help the question of the man who gives
help is raised. The neighbour is the one who gives help—says the
answer. Hence the question is given an unusual urgency. I do
not simply need to ask who is my neighbour. For I bring the one
who is neighbour with me into every situation. The one who is
neighbour is not anyone standing nearby—it is *myself*. If I
understand myself as a neighbour to others because of Jesus'
word, I am beginning to live, in the truest sense of the word.

And who is the 'enemy'? Jesus is certainly not thinking of
what we have become accustomed to understand by 'enemy' in
recent centuries—the enemy of the nation, the enemy of the
motherland or fatherland. That is an artificial concept constructed
to suit certain political aims. The same applied to other 'enemies'
of other groups and societies. Modern man began to vegetate
in an empty world, so he populated it with the products of his
anxieties and dreams. Anyone who alleged that he desired to or
felt compelled to love the 'enemy' was branded as a 'pacifist' by
some or a 'traitor' by others. When the question about the enemy
was posed by this world of abstractions, it naturally could not be
answered satisfactorily by the Gospel. The Gospel thinks in
concrete, not abstract terms. Meaningless questions cannot be
given a meaningful answer.

By 'enemy' Jesus means a fellow man who makes my life a
burden, who begrudges my success, and who makes my life a
torment or, at any rate, is always threatening to. Enemy means
concrete danger. There is no such thing as *the* enemy, but only
my enemy. It may be that as a Christian I understand ideological
opponents better than companions in the faith sometimes. But
it may be the very opposite sometimes. The demand of Jesus,
however, never varies—I must seek the good of my enemy. Only
the person who knows how difficult such an attempt may be has
understood Jesus' word and has realized that Jesus' command
to love is not a special, radical form of a general ethical maxim,
a special case, so to speak, of a general moral duty. Jesus' command
to love is inseparable from his person. This constitutes its uniqueness and originality. And Jesus' person knows no failure.

5. *The Conquest of Man*

Jesus opened a new dimension in human life by his coming—the dimension of love. By his demand of love he challenged men into becoming men. How did he develop this challenge to comprehend all mankind? He didn't. The impulses towards mission which came from him were anything but techniques of organization. But did he not draw any conclusions for communal life from this newly opened dimension of love? No. The dimension of love is not a position to be built upon. Did he not, then, usher in the day of Man? If we mean by this a new form of society, then again the answer is no; one could not even speak of an 'eve of man', if this were what he brought.

Jesus does not bring any new ethic to mankind, least of all a new social ethic. Jesus does not bring forward a programme which he tries to realize. Judged from a modern standpoint Jesus' field of vision in the matter of social ethics was marked by a complete aimlessness. The leaders of the theocracy, the cool calculators of Hellenistic modernity, must have considered what he did, or rather what he did not do so far as they could see, complete anarchy. Jesus was a nihilist of social ethics in their eyes.

He paid no attention to questions of communal life, apparently. Was he a dreamer, a child, that he could overlook them in this way? Was he so blind to the problem that with a naivety which was almost criminal he did not even consider them? Did he live so far removed from reality that he hesitated to lay hold of this 'hot iron'? Simply to put all these questions is to receive the answer no. Let us consider a few examples at random.

We shall begin with the problem that constituted the greatest disgrace in the Hellenistic world, the problem of slavery. Jesus' parables show that he was acquainted with it. It went without saying that the household of a man in authority contained slaves (Mark 13.34). In large households slaves of both sexes presented a motley array (Luke 12.41–48). There is the loyal slave on whom the owner can rely; alongside him is the unreliable slave who uses the absence of his owner to tyrannize the other servants of both sexes and to provide himself with some nights and days of enjoyment. Finally, there is the slave who has become a drudge on the treadmill of a joyless existence and whose faculties have been dulled in the process. Perhaps the setting is coloured by the differences between the Hebrew slaves who had certain rights and the Canaanite slaves who were treated like cattle. Even in Palestine, however, the slave trade was a dark chapter. The Rabbis knew that 'a dog was more valued than a slave'. Men were not embarrassed about even the most intimate functions in the presence of such 'donkey-people'. The master can do as he wills with his slaves, as the parable shows. He can have them whipped or tortured or even killed (Luke 12.46–47).

The old, useless slave who is past working can be driven from the door or turned into a beggar. Day and night the slave has always to stand at the service of the farmer without regard for the work he may already have done. No word of thanks is due to him (Luke 17.7–9). Slaves are rewarded or punished, as the rich merchant thinks fit (Luke 19.11–27).

Jesus describes life as it is. He does not offer any social programme to deal with the question; he does not even indicate how the position of the slaves can be improved. The dark chapter which confronts us with the question of the nature of human existence remains dark.

The question of property was another subject which Jesus did not deal with, let alone answer. Possession is a power which enslaves men. Wealth (i.e. money) holds sway over men like a rival of God. As an idol 'mammon' brings men into conflict with the living God. As 'capital' it exercises its tyranny. One cannot serve both God and mammon. One must decide: either—or (Matt. 6.24). Riches bring danger, not for the community but for the owner (Mark 10.23–27). Jesus warns his hearers not to succumb to the mania for possessions. He says nothing about the wheel of circumstance, he does not even touch the spokes. The trouble lies not with circumstances but with men who are possessed by greed (Matt. 6.9–11). Thus, there is no land-reform in Galilee; the system of *latifundia* remains. God will fetch the great landowner who has forgotten God when he dies—perhaps even this very night (Luke 12.16–21). The moral of the story? 'Take heed, and beware of all covetousness; for a man's life does not consist in the abundance of his possessions' (Luke 12.15).

In town and country everything remains as of old. The rich man clothes himself in purple and linen and 'lives all his days in splendour and joy'. And poor Lazarus lies at the door of his house, covered in sores and his stomach empty. He is glad for stray dogs to lick his wounds and drive away the swarms of flies. Such is life. In eternity the positions are reversed—but not before (Luke 16.19–31). The foolish request that he should arbitrate in the matter of an inheritance is brushed aside by Jesus. He has not studied case-law or been ordained for such matters (Luke 12.13–14). In the parable of the cunning steward who was a rogue of the first water, Jesus expresses himself about money in passing. 'Did Jesus pronounce a blessing on money? No. Did Jesus pronounce a curse on money? No. He made a joke about it. As a result of the joke, what he was laughing at was done away with, devalued and brought to an end. He told a story about a knave, a wangler. This is how it is done, this is the way men act, this is the way they are. This is the world . . .' (L. Fendt).

And questions of political ethics? Here, too, Jesus perceives the real position of power and the factors which produce it. He is not unaware of the luxury and the enervating climate of the courts of Hellenistic princes (Matt. 11.8), or the cunning and brutality of His Serene Highness (Luke 13.31–32). The nations are not free; tyrants enslave them. Might prevails over right. This is the way of the world. Among *you* it shall be exactly the reverse; anyone who has the ambition of being first must be slave of all—like myself (Mark 10.42–45). The kings of the nations are styled 'benefactors' (Luke 22.25). In fact, a great many Hellenistic princes added this title with its aura of divine glory to their own name. 'But you shall not do so.' The procurator, Pontius Pilate, was responsible for the callous massacre of certain Galilaeans, probably in the Temple-forecourt, by his legionaries. Perhaps they were Zealots who wanted to introduce direct action with a sacrifice. Who knows! At any rate their blood flowed with that of the sacrificial animals (Luke 13.1–3). World history took no notice of this blood bath. The pious read into the horror of the massacre the sinfulness of those who had been murdered. Was not the collapse of the tower also such a judgement of God? The collapse took place in the vicinity of the spring of Siloam, where an aqueduct was probably being constructed; eighteen peopled were killed (Luke 13.4–5). Jesus does not deny that there is a connection between guilt and fate—like that between sin and sickness (Mark 2.1–12). God really has used the building tragedy and the bloody action of Pilate as a punishment. God speaks, in fact, through catastrophes in nature and history. But *what* does he say—both in major and minor political issues? He does not say anything about the events or the people involved. He speaks through the events to men. He speaks to you and to me. Pilate is his mouthpiece. 'Do you think that these Galilaeans were worse sinners than all the other Galilaeans, because they suffered thus? I tell you, No; but, unless you repent, you will all likewise perish.'

It is not enough to change circumstances; it is man who needs changing. Circumstances cry out. But they do not call to heaven, as the saying goes. They call from heaven to earth. They cry out for the reformation of man himself.

The call to repent also rings out from the story of the tribute-money (Mark 12.13-17). The Pharisees and courtiers of Herod seek to trap Jesus in their dialectic. They begin eulogistically; they address him as 'Rabbi' and appeal to his truthfulness and impartiality. They use the question of the poll-tax to ask about the rightness of political revolution. Jesus sees through their cunning. They are playing with fire. The party of the Zealots had left the radical wing of the Pharisees on the occasion of the taxation in AD 6. Eschatological expectation of the Messiah had driven them to revolt against Quirinius, the Imperial governor in Syria. Religion and politics were fused in the attempt to realize the First Commandment on earth. Unlimited theocracy was to be realized by force of arms in the political sphere. The Galilaean Judas had wanted to establish the right of the Jewish 'king' against the Emperor in Rome. If Jesus were to affirm that taxes should be paid, he would have not only public opinion which was swayed by nationalism against him but he would also be offending religious principles and would be branded as 'unpatriotic', and a preacher of apostasy at the same time. If, on the other hand, he came down in favour of not paying taxes he would be siding with the party of the Zealots and exposing himself to the Roman sword. However he decided, he was caught in the net of their dialectic.

Jesus surprises his opponents with the request, 'Bring me a denarius and let me look at it'. He had no money with him, presumably. He is poor (cf. Matt. 17.27). For the preacher of the kingdom of God the problem doesn't exist. The questioners, however, have their purses full; if it was to their advantage or profit or for the sake of business they willingly used Gentile money. Jesus mocks them and exposes them. They bring him the small, silver denarius which was worth about sixpence. On the front is the head of Tiberius with a finely engraved profile, wearing a crown of laurel, with the customary inscription, 'the illustrious . . . son of the divine Augustus'. The back showed a figure with a sceptre and olive branch on a divine throne with the inscription 'Pontifex Maximus' (i.e. High Priest). The emblems may have evoked religious thoughts in the 'Pious'. But only if the money were paid in taxes, not when it was used for business? 'Whose image and inscription is this?' 'Caesar's.' 'Render to Caesar the things that are Caesar's and to God the things that are God's.'

This really amazing word not only demonstrates the sovereign skill of Jesus in coping with his opponents; it was also a decision in principle about the relation of Church and State. There is no talk of parity or friendly co-existence. Money, which is minted, issued and recalled again, belongs to the State. Apart from this the State possesses nothing! What, then, belongs to God? Not something but—everything. For man himself belongs to God. As the image of the despot is imprinted in the silver, so is the image of God in man. This incredible image proclaims that man is eternally the property of God. There is a devastating contrast between the ruler who is allotted the domain of petty cash and Almighty God. The incidental joke about ownership was well worth making. The State is disposed of with an ironical *bon mot*. In the light of the imminent rule of God the State is such a trivial matter: it is not worth laughing at it or rebelling against. It should be given what it owns. The rejection of the State corresponds to the call to men to be converted. If we are really converted from our false questioning and activity and turn to God, we shall give him what belongs to him, namely ourselves.

Why did Jesus show such little interest in the environment? Why did he not bring any programme for removing the problems of society? Various answers can be given. They all point to the same conclusion.

First of all, the last days are here. God's rule is coming. It is no longer worth while changing the world by a programme to improve environmental circumstances. God will not change the world, but do away with it. What would be the point of a new programme for a world that was finished? Would it not be like patching a threadbare garment with a piece of cloth not yet milled?

Would it not be like new wine which breaks old bottles? (Mark
2.21–22). The sequence of their programme, their faith in the
truth of their system, their '——isms', show how senile the world
is and how ripe it is for the kingdom of God.

Secondly, the world already has its programme, the law of
the Creator. Jesus is not preaching pessimism when he invokes
the kingdom of God. The watchword of cynicism, 'All that is
created is only fit to pass away', is not the wisdom of Jesus but
the cold cleverness of Mephistopheles. For Jesus, the world is
God's. The Creator and his creation are visible again on the
eschatological horizon. What is hidden from the sarcasm of reason
is perceived by the intellect illuminated by God. The will of the
Creator is revealed to the latter. To perform it is no problem for
Jesus.

Finally, the last days and the Law both have man as their aim.
Set into operation by Jesus they introduce the eve of man. This
means the end of men's planning. The 'redemption' of man also
means that man must be liberated from the delusions of his plans
and programme. His plans deceive him by raising false hopes of
the happiness of freedom. Without the narcotic of his plans man
could not endure the pain of time. Marx was quite right when
he called religion the 'opium of the people'. For 'religion', introduced as an object of faith to cure earthly misery, has the character
of a plan. Jesus with his message of the kingdom of God heralds
the end of such 'religion'. But it is not the only 'plan'. It is no
accident that the general projects of an economic, social and
political nature which seek to change the environmental circumstances of the world are offered to men on a practical level as if
they were religions. They all arise in the name of man—and
proceed to sacrifice him on their altar. They may not intend this,
but they do it, nevertheless.

Jesus breaks the curse of the brave new world of planning,
while taking man seriously, more seriously than he was accustomed
to take himself. Jesus overthrows faith in planning, that is,
planning as a means to salvation. As a result he makes the way
clear again for original existence as it should be. He wrests
planned man out of the straitjacket of his audacity and despair.
He opens the future of God to him. The destiny of man is not to
be found in economics or politics, but in the coming God.

Anyone who says God and means God hears from the mouth

of Jesus something of the laughter and derision of him who is
enthroned in heaven (Ps. 2.4). The Lord laughs at the godless,
'for he sees his day coming' (Ps. 37.13). This was known in the
Old Testament. But on the lips of Jesus the laughter of God
loses its bitterness. It receives a brightness which animates not
only the combatant but the victor. The person whom Jesus has
impressed is no longer impressed by the noisy actors and actions
which promise to usher in a new era. Neither is he frightened
by them, for it is only their appearance that is so imposing and
threatening; from the eschatological viewpoint Jesus has dealt
them their death-blow.

Jesus is not concerned with changing the surroundings, but
with the conversion of man. 'Man is something that must be
conquered' says Nietzsche's Zarathustra. But for Nietzsche this
presupposes the death of God and the epiphany of the Superman.
Jesus would agree with the aim, but dispute the presupposition.
Jesus is, in fact, concerned with the conquest of man. But this
happens when man submits to the living God, and looks to Jesus
himself, who is the representative of man from the beginning.
Jesus will conquer man in such a way that he conquers the Superman in him. For the Superman is the tyrant *par excellence*. Man
can only live if the Superman is dead. The Gospel is the good
news of victory: the Superman is dead. In practical terms, however, this means that I myself must die. My own self-will must
be put to death by Jesus. We shall return to this again later.

It does not help Christianity to give way to concrete programmes
at this point. In his *Ethics* (Eng. trans., pp. 318–26) Bonhoeffer
thought very seriously about 'the possibility of the Church
addressing the world'. His most important conclusions could be
abbreviated as follows:

(a) Jesus was not concerned with the solution of the world's
problems. His words bring salvation, not solution.

(b) Whoever said that all the problems of the world ought to
be solved or could be solved? Perhaps for God the in-
solubility of these problems is more important than their
solution, because it reminds men of their sin and God's
salvation. Perhaps the problems of men are so entangled
and so badly formulated that they cannot, in fact, be solved.

(c) The organized struggle of the Church against certain evils

of the world in 'campaign' or 'crusades', a continuation of
the mediaeval idea of a crusade, which has died out almost
completely in Lutheranism, is one of the characteristic marks
of the Christian life in Anglo-Saxon countries. Examples of
this are slavery, prohibition, and the League of Nations.
These examples also show the critical weakness of these
crusades. The ending of slavery coincided with the rise of
the English industrial proletariat (one might say that the
world was not able to bring itself to abandon the privilege
of slavery). Prohibition, chiefly enforced by Methodists,
led to even worse trouble than already existed, so that the
Methodists themselves supported the ending of prohibition
(a decisive experience for the American churches). The
League of Nations was intended to overcome national
antagonisms, but its result was to intensify them to the
highest pitch. Such experiences must give food for serious
thought about the question how far the Church is called
upon to solve the world's problems. 'God in their hand'
(Job 12.6).

(*d*) It is necessary to free oneself from the way of thinking
which sets out from human problems and asks for solutions
on this basis. Such thinking is unbiblical. The way of
Jesus Christ, and therefore the way of all Christian thinking,
moves from God to the world, not from the world to God.
This does not mean, however, that the Church has no
responsibility to the world in this respect.

Bonhoeffer regards the starting point for validating the Church's
activity in the world as the message of God's coming in the flesh,
which establishes responsibility and declares God's love for the
world in Law and Gospel. The Ten Commandments mark out
the sphere of the Church and the sphere of the world. Before
God there is no autonomy of worldly ordinances. Horizons which
are not yet visible in the Gospels themselves are outlined briefly
by Bonhoeffer. It is not the call of Jesus which gives us advice
about this, but early Christianity which is the response to Jesus'
call in the great anthem of the New Testament.

6. *The New Righteousness*

It would be a completely wrong impression, however, if Jesus were thought of as an apostle of aimlessness. He was certainly not that. His whole ministry was shaped by God's word and its constant theme was the salvation of man. His intentions are characterized by a definite structure. His actions are marked by vigour and method. Jesus is no chaotic spirit. His thoughts are clear, not woolly. His advice is relevant, not vague. This orderliness was conveyed to Christianity and the world long ago in the large block of material which we call 'the Sermon on the Mount'.

This contains Jesus' advice to the community in the world. It was obviously not spoken by Jesus as it stands either as a whole or in its separate parts. What is true of all the sayings and narratives in the Gospels is especially true of the Sermon on the Mount. Jesus' words are never words suspended in empty space—soliloquies. They are always part of a conversation with someone else, in this case his circle of disciples, the early Church. What he says is always heard, understood and believed, and in the affirmative of faith it is an answered word. Only so, as a word which has found a hearer, is it preserved and handed on; it would not have been written down if it had not been for the witness of the early Church.

From the very beginning the response of faith found its way into the recorded words of Jesus. This response became so inter-woven with Jesus' call that it is no longer possible for us to make a clean break between his own words and those of the early Church. But even when we are able to do this, it is still the believing community which transmits the words of Jesus. Anyone who is looking for Jesus' words as a sort of original and authoritative exposition is looking in vain; the exposition is the commentary of the Church. Jesus does not come forward to speak apart from the community. It is true that the community misunderstood a great deal or formulated his words afresh for their special position under different conditions of life. Later intrusions followed earlier differences of presentation. Comparison of the sayings of Jesus in the three Synoptic Gospels proves that hardly a single saying is preserved by them in exactly the same way.

Every reader of the New Testament, by comparing the parallel passages, can examine the divergences and ask himself what

motives occasioned the alterations, omissions, additions or assimi-
lations. It is time we learned that it is simply an acoustical delusion
to accept the possibility of sayings of Jesus which can be detached
from the community or treated as soliloquies without context. If
we were to disregard this basic feature of the recorded sayings of
Jesus our reading of Scriptures would be nothing less than dis-
obedient. This conclusion is not the product of scepticism. The
seductive snake is to be found in the thoughtlessness by which
we misjudge the essential nature of Jesus' words when we forget
that they are shaped and filled by the community.

The Sermon on the Mount recorded in Matthew (Matt. 5–7)
is a free composition of the evangelist or the circle concealed
behind his name. Jesus never delivered it as it stands. Try to
imagine what excessive demands such a 'sermon' would have
made on those who listened! Luke has incorporated substantial
portions of Matt. 5 and 7 in his 'Sermon on the Plain' (Luke
6.20–49). In addition, there are parts of the Sermon on the Mount
scattered throughout Luke 11–14 and 16. Correspondences with
Mark are rare. Matthew worked from the same source as Luke,
therefore, but grouped the sayings differently.

He loves large blocks of discourses, such as those on missionary
evangelism (Matt. 10), parables (Matt. 13), discipleship (Matt.18),
judgement (Matt. 25), and the Sermon on the Mount (Matt. 5–7).
The conclusion of each of these discourses is stereotyped and
makes use of the following formula, 'and when Jesus finished
these sayings . . .' (Matt. 7.28; 11.1; 13.53; 19.1; 26.1).

The Sermon on the Mount is closely linked with the two
following chapters, Matthew 8 and 9, which contain stories about
Jesus rather than sayings of Jesus. Matt. 4.23 at the beginning
and Matt. 9.35 at the end both say the same thing, 'and Jesus
went about . . . teaching in their synagogues and preaching the
gospel of the kingdom and healing every disease and infirmity
among the people'. These two sentences form the framework of
the intervening five chapters. They set out to teach men to understand Jesus as the Messiah of Israel. The Messianic deed (Matt.
8–9) is preceded by the Messianic word (Matt. 5–7). Such is the
interpretation of Julius Schniewind.

This brief survey leads one to expect that in the Sermon on
the Mount we shall be dealing with a stylized composition. Its
broad outline may be represented as follows:

Matt. 5. Beatitudes—sayings to the disciples—theme of righteousness—contrast between Moses and the Messiah.

Matt. 6. Works of righteousness, such as almsgiving, praying
and fasting—laying up treasure—anxiety.

Matt. 7. Advice and exhortation based on scattered separate
sayings.

What is the meaning of the Sermon on the Mount? This
question has raised its head in every century, or rather every
vigilant century has found itself faced with this question. It
would bode ill for an age that no longer understood this question.
Let us consider some important answers. They can be arranged
in four groups.

First, the neutral answer. The Sermon on the Mount has a
purely historical character. It is to be explained in terms of Jesus'
opposition to the theology of the Pharisees. Rabbinic formulas
and requirements are surpassed by Jesus' exaggerated demands.
The piety established by cultic law is decisively rejected. How
far the Sermon on the Mount is still binding today is another
question. Albert Schweitzer's starting point is similar, but different
in its exposition. He interprets it as an 'interim-ethic' for Jesus'
companions, who by their extraordinary achievements are to
bring in the last days which are directly imminent. His followers
'stand under the exceptional law of the final decisive battle'
(Johannes Weiss).

Secondly, the radical answer. The Sermon on the Mount
demands literal fulfilment. It is the 'new Law', which Jesus
establishes as the basis not only of life in the Church but of life
in the world. The pietists and biblicists of all times, right up to
Tolstoy, regard it as the programme for a revolution of the world
in all areas of life. The new order of mankind is to be won by
rejecting the state and its justice and by attacking the existing
order. Variations of this view see Jesus as the champion of the
economically deprived and exploited (Karl Marx; Karl Kautsky;
Leonhard Ragaz).

Thirdly, the answer of compromise. The Sermon on the Mount
is to be fulfilled but not by everybody, only by the spiritually
mature. It does not contain commands for the faithful, but advice,
i.e. counsel for the pious *élite*. In the early period this consisted
of the disciples and apostles, later the monks. They gain special

merit for themselves by fulfilling the special demands. This Catholic teaching found unintentional confirmation in the Protestant position. Friedrich Naumann considered the Sermon on the Mount applied only to Galilee, or at least only to monks in Europe. Johannes Müller considered it was an ethic of intention, which possibly required the opposite to be done in actual practice. This view also blunted the edge of the Sermon on the Mount.

Fourthly, the paradoxical answer. The Sermon on the Mount sets out to awaken a consciousness of sin. Its demands are deliberately impossible. The intention and the effort to fulfil them are a delusion and a rebellion against God. This is the orthodox Lutheran view, and also that of certain modern scholars (Gerhard Kittel; Karl Stange).

The third of these answers can be separated from the rest straight away. Jesus does not recognize the compromise of a twofold morality. Anyone who listens to him, disciple or not, is addressed by him. Jesus is not after man's opinions; he is looking for men of action.

The second answer is also incompatible with Jesus' message. It is true that the radical seriousness of his intention is recognized. But Jesus releases man from the curse of planning and does not place him under the curse of a new 'Christian reform programme'.

The first answer is historically correct. It is false, however, in limiting Jesus' demand to his own generation and thus neutralizing it. Its truth slumbers in its eschatological tendency. If it is understood not in the sense of work (Albert Schweitzer) but of sacrifice (Johannes Weiss) it can give a genuine stimulus to the modern world.

The fourth answer seems restrictive in its influence at a first glance. It seems to be dazzled by too much light from Paul. Does the Jesus of the Sermon on the Mount regard God's law as impossible to fulfil, or does he regard efforts to fulfil it as sin? Is it not truer to say Jesus expects conversion when man is addressed? He calls upon man to let himself receive the miracle of forgiveness. If one understands the Sermon on the Mount as the call of Jesus himself together with the response of the early Church, and not as a programme, then it is inseparable from his person. His person, however, should not be isolated from his other words. We must listen to the Sermon on the Mount in the context of his total message, which is a message of action. Jesus only demands from men what he himself fulfils. In going to his death, however, he fulfils God's will. He takes man with him as he goes. The Sermon on the Mount is the call to go with him on this journey.

Recently studies of the New Testament have been able to use manuscript discoveries to emphasize this meaning of the Sermon on the Mount which was rediscovered by Luther. Without foisting Paul's teaching about justification on to the Sermon on the Mount, as Luther did, it can now be said that the Sermon on the Mount is 'evidence of the coming Kingdom', 'not a new law comprehending every sphere of life' (M. Dibelius). One does not become a Christian by fulfilling a number of regulations but by believing in the nearness of God's rule. The nearness of God is terrible, yet full of promise in Jesus. In him the powers of the new world are released and they show the man of faith to what sort of existence he is called. The Sermon on the Mount aims to encourage us to ask of it, as of all the words of Jesus recorded in the Gospels, what sort of man Jesus was. For his image is reflected in his words. And ours, too, perhaps.

All interpretations of the Sermon on the Mount regard it as a whole, but basically they limit their attention to Matt. 5 (sometimes only to verses 21–48). Matthew's careful composition is really a sort of catechism which brings together sayings of the Jesus-tradition which have a special shape and emphasis. We met some of these sayings earlier. In describing the Sermon on the Mount, we are describing a whole string of passages in addition to Matt. 5–7.

What is the theme of the Sermon? Matthew has composed it as a speech of the 'Messiah'; he has contrasted it with the speech of Moses and yet related it to it. Perhaps the same is true of the contrast and relation of the 'mountain' (Matt. 5.1) to Sinai. Yet the Sermon contains no Messianic claims. Jesus does not proclaim himself but God's will. The theme of the Sermon is the new and better righteousness. Jesus is not issuing a new law. Rather he is declaring and teaching a new righteousness, i.e. the way of life which the Law demands and which corresponds to the Law.

The righteousness which Jesus proclaims and teaches is neither moralistic nor legalistic. It is neither a virtue nor a code of upright behaviour. The famous definition of Ulpian (d. AD 228), 'righteousness is the perpetual and unchanging will to render to each man what belongs to him', is on a different level. The righteousness meant by Jesus is essentially *God's* righteousness, even where it refers to the behaviour of men. If a man thinks of it he is thinking of the kingdom of God—and *vice versa* (Matt. 6.33). This does not mean, however, that human ideas of distributive or punitive justice are being attributed to God. Even in the Old Testament righteousness is the province of God. God's righteousness is regarded as spatial to a remarkable degree, like a field of force into which men are drawn and thereby empowered to perform special deeds. Men 'are exalted *in* thy righteousness' (Ps. 89.16). 'Let the mountains bear prosperity for the people, and the hills, *in* righteousness' (Ps. 72.3). Men pray to God that their enemies 'might not come *into* thy righteousness' (Ps. 69.28). A sphere of power, in which social conduct is possible, is always meant. Righteousness is to a certain extent a social blessing. Jesus brings this blessing. It is a blessing worth fighting for.

But how can righteousness be said to be brought and yet fought for at the same time? The paradox, that righteousness—including the social conduct of man mentioned above—is exclusively God's gift and yet exclusively man's task, is only intelligible to the person who knows about the paradox of the kingdom of God and God's Law (see p. 182 above). Because the kingdom of God is present and the Law has already been brought to an end, the righteousness of man is entirely God's free gift. Because the kingdom of God is still in the future and the Law is still valid, the righteousness of man is man's task. This is the explanation of the distinctiveness of Jesus' message. It speaks of an 'is' that encircles man and also of an 'ought' that he has to fulfil. This fundamentally paradoxical message of Jesus is the root of the paradoxical interlacing of moral indicative and moral imperative, to which his life is subject. The Sermon on the Mount is itself evidence of this unity.

The 'is' of Christian righteousness is the person speaking— Jesus. Every 'ought' is grounded in his person. Every demand presupposes his gift. The Beatitudes express this 'is' in their indicative, describing the present situation of expectation (Matt. 5.3–6) and behaviour (Matt. 5.7–10). Even if the second group— mercy, purity of heart, peacemaking, and persecution—is meant to describe 'conditions' for entry into the kingdom of God, yet these conditions are completely encompassed by the divine indicative. 'You ought . . . you shall . . . ' It is a constant pointer to the future of God and an act of God (sometimes expressed by the use of the passive mood) which will happen to them. They are called 'happy' even today because of this future of God. The similes of salt, the city on a hill, and light are in the indicative; three times it is said 'you are . . . ' (5.13–14). But the three indicatives carry an imperative, 'Let your light shine before men!' (5.16). The similes of the eye (6.22–23) and serving two masters (6.24) are in the indicative. The criterion of righteousness is expressed by means of a picture from the sphere of the 'is', or more precisely from the sphere of growth: thorns and thistles, good and bad trees, do not have to be compelled to grow. The good tree brings forth sound fruit, the bad tree brings forth evil fruit. The thorn does not produce grapes or the thistle produce figs. Both in positive and negative situations the order of the 'is', which cannot be enforced, prevails. One almost has the impression that a predestinatory necessity is at work in everything, a necessity which is in turn derived from the activity of the powers of light and darkness. But the expression of this circumstance is simply meant to heighten the urgency of human responsibility. The final indicative occurs in the concluding parable about the wise and the foolish builder, promising and threatening by reference to the existing facts (7.24–27).

The 'is' of Christian righteousness which is present in the speaker, in Jesus himself, brings about the development of the 'ought'. The indicative releases the imperative. It is well known that the Sermon on the Mount contains predominantly imperative clauses. The numerous interpretations that we examined were based on this. The six antitheses of ch. 5, about murder, adultery, divorce, oaths, vengeance and love of one's enemy, are in the imperative (5.21–48). Only twice does the light of the divine indicative shine into the darkness engendered by the bank of clouds which are demands of unheard-of severity. Heaven . . . is the throne of God, earth is his footstool; Jerusalem . . . is the city of the Great King (5.35); your father in heaven sends sunshine and rain on the just and on the unjust (5.45).

These sayings about opposites are followed by rules about works of righteousness corresponding to the Jewish tripartite division: almsgiving, praying and fasting (6.1–18). The directions seek to regulate existing usage. They demand something from men. But they also point to existing facts, both on earth and in heaven, such as the conduct of the 'hypocrites', who represent false show (6.2, 4, 16), and the activity of the Father, who sees into what is hidden and who will requite, i.e. reward (6.4, 6, 18). The warnings about laying up treasure (6.19–20) and worrying (6.25–34) are exacting. The references to the birds, the anemones and the grass, however, bring words of comfort; they declare God's concern (6.26, 28–30), like the references to the Father, who 'knows that you need them all, . . . and all these things shall be yours as well' (6.32–33).

Chapter 6 seems milder in tone than ch. 5. In fact, however, its demands are equally strenuous. It is concerned not so much with matter as with manner. Chapter 6 presents the 'category' of Christian activity as such. This is 'hiddenness'. It is not primarily a visual quality, however; it is not the opposite of what can be seen, but an existential definition. Hiddenness means the death of vanity, self-glory and show. Anyone who wants to know what conversion to God (= repentance) means on the lips of Jesus, should study and meditate on Matt. 6.1–8, 16–18. Hiddenness means the field where my will breaks down and where my 'old man' dies (i.e., not just a part of me, but the whole of me). In hiddenness God breaks my will—in order to restore it to newness of life by looking graciously upon it. All human activity that seeks to stand before God must first meet such a death. All Christian activity is baptized by hiddenness, day by day.

Christian action takes place incognito, in humility and devotedness to the little ones (Mark 9.36–37; Matt. 18.1–9), in sacrifice (Matt. 19.23–36), in selfless, silent service (Matt. 20.20–28), in the quiet rejection of glory and show (Matt. 23.5–12), in the readiness to help anyone in the daily routine, none of which can be visibly measured by statistics, of course (Matt. 25.31–46). What is hidden belongs to God's creative sphere.

Finally, ch. 7 is again full of demands—injunctions (7.1–12) and warnings (7.13–27) of every kind. The threatening and promising indicatives of the future can be heard once again. Once more they are characterized as actions of God by the use of the passive mood and the neuter—the Jewish periphrasis for God's name which was not pronounced; God will judge you (7.1–2)—and also, God will give you, find you, open the door to you (7.8), and give you what is good (7.11).

Thus, in proclaiming the Gospel, Jesus declares this new righteousness. In fact, he provokes it by his teaching of the Law. His proclamation and his provocation go hand in hand. Those who are very familiar with their New Testament will have to suppress at this point certain questions which they have in mind from Paul and his teaching about the Law. We are not dealing with Paul at this point, however, and certainly not with the New Testament as a whole, but simply with Jesus, or more precisely simply with the synoptic Jesus.

6

THE EVE OF THE WORLD

AN UNPARALLELED saying of Jesus is recorded in Luke
(12.49–53). It hangs over the world like a storm cloud, dark and
threatening:

> I came to cast fire upon the earth;
> and would that it were already kindled!
> I have a baptism to be baptized with;
> and how I am straitened till it is accomplished!
> Do you think that I have come to bring peace on earth?
> No, I tell you, but rather division;
> for henceforth in one house there will be five divided,
> three against two and two against three;
> they will be divided, father against son and 'son against
>   father',
> mother against daughter, and 'daughter against her mother',
> mother-in-law against her daughter-in-law
> and 'daughter-in-law against her mother-in-law'.

An old prophetic saying (Micah 7.1–8) is being fulfilled; the
harvest is beginning. But neither grape nor fig is ripe. Good men
have disappeared from the land. Everyone thirsts for blood. Each
man traps his neighbour. Officials are corrupt, judges are bribed.
Caprice rules the world. Such is the state of things. And how
will it turn out? More terrible than before! The day of the seer,
i.e. the prophet, draws near. Judgement begins. Consternation
breaks out.

> Put no trust in a neighbour,
> have no confidence in a friend;
> guard the doors of your mouth
> from her who lies in your bosom.

God sits in judgement. Existing strife grows worse. God punishes sin with sin. Dissension leads to division.

Jesus ushers in the day of the seer—as the last seer himself. Yet how different is the dawn of the day! Does Jesus kindle a torch to set the world on fire? Does he reduce the earth to ashes? The Stoic doctrine of the world conflagration, by which a new cosmos is to arise out of the ashes of the old, does not accord with the day of his coming. Nor does Jesus prepare the world a destiny of eternal youth like that of the Phoenix. Yet he is no incendiary in the old style, such as the Baptist proclaimed. His fire does not mean destruction but decision. He has come to bring men home. When Matthew (10.34), in the parallel to Luke 12.49–53, makes Jesus say, 'I have not come to bring peace, but a sword', he is not making Jesus preach world-war or proclaim a crusade. The sword is his word. The prince of peace (Isa. 9.6) releases the revolt of the spirit and the spirits. If a literal sword of iron strikes, then it is not wielded by Jesus or his disciples. Rather, it is Jesus and his disciples who are struck and killed by it. The weapon is directed against the defenceless. Jesus will be the first one to be slain by the sword.

In the fire which he kindles on earth he is the first to glow with fervour. In the counter-fire, by which the world thinks to quench the flames of the spirit, he and his disciples are burned to death. This is the meaning of the profound saying about baptism. Master and disciples must be baptized with the baptism of death (Mark 10.35–39). It is not accidental that, looked at from a purely chronological point of view, Jesus' ministry is bounded by baptism and death (see pp. 114 ff. above). He shrinks from this baptism. But God has destined Jesus and his disciples for such a fate. He will be the first sacrifice of his mission.

By his death on earth he will reach out to the world. His failure —paradoxically—will prove the hope of the world. His death will be the evening sunset that heralds the new day.

1. *Who was Jesus?*

The question of Jesus' identity is meant first of all as a historical question. We shall examine the first three Gospels as we should examine any other sources about men of the past. Nevertheless, we must be conscious of the limitations of the question. In fact,

and modern fakirs and dervishes, whose powers are beyond dispute. Faith healers of our own day, such as Hermann Zaiss and Bruno Groning or the Americans Branham and Tommy Hixt, who fill their rooms and tents with thousands all the week long, can compete with the Galilaean charlatan (John 8.48).

Who was Jesus? (2) Jesus was a Jewish travelling preacher, a Rabbi who had risen from the artisan class. He had obviously not studied, nor had he been ordained. He gathered disciples round him like the Rabbis, he taught in the synagogues and engaged in argument with other scribes. But he never discussed freely chosen subjects like the Greek philosophers. He was prevented from conducting dialogues in Socratic fashion by the authority of 'the Law and the Prophets', which was the presupposition of his work. The truth which he proclaimed did not tolerate any human support. But he also rejected street-sermons, which the Hellenistic travelling philosophers of those days used to deliver before large audiences—like the orators at Hyde Park Corner. He did not regard it as his task to develop his ideas by means of artificial questions and objections in the style of the rhetorician; it was his task to declare God's truth by any means possible.

He differed from the scribes of those days, of course, by the way he restored authority to Scripture without resorting to exegetical proof. Jesus was no biblicist. Jesus embodied Scripture, as a spirit-filled person does. Because of his own personal authority a 'theological' reason for this or that expression, this or that decision, was unnecessary. 'For he taught as one who had authority and not as their scribes' (Matt. 7.29).

His manner of speaking is very human. The various parables and proverbial bits of wisdom with their appeal to wholesome reason prove this. One has only to think of the general truths in the Sermon on the Mount. 'Where your treasure is there is your heart' (Matt. 6.21); 'the light of the body is the eye' (6.22); 'no man can serve two masters . . .' (6.24); 'let the day's own trouble be sufficient for the day' (6.34); 'life is more than food and the body more than clothing' (6.35). How like a teacher of wisdom Jesus sounds, when he compares the relation of teacher and pupil to that of master and slave (Matt. 10.24), or when he tells one of his magnificent parables. A boaster wanted to build some huge farm buildings, but he miscalculated; now people laugh when they go past the half-finished, useless wall. A king had half prepared to go to war; now he has to surrender unconditionally. Hence one should weigh up whether one can afford the cost of discipleship. All such examples prove that Jesus is the representative of man. Man, however, though attracted by his call, lives under the Law —in the sphere of general truths. 'Human' freedom is man's best way of preserving his eschatological freedom (R. Bultmann).

What Rabbi ever set his own authority against other authorities in such an unguarded theological manner as Jesus did? He opposes not only the great interpreters of the Law, but the text of the Law itself! In the Sermon on the Mount the commands not to kill (Matt. 5.21–26) or commit adultery (5.27–30) or take oaths (5.33–37) make the existing Law more severe, while his words about divorce (5.31–37), retaliation (5.38–42) and loving one's enemy (5.43–48) emphasize certain conditions of the Law. All this takes place without any theological, in the sense of biblical, explanation; Jesus simply says 'But *I* say to you . . .'

Who was Jesus? (3) A prophet of the kingdom of God. This is what he is sometimes called by the people. 'This is the prophet Jesus from Nazareth of Galilee' (Matt. 21.11). Yet he refuses to give any proof that he is a prophet. A prophet must appeal to God and come forth in his name: 'This is the word of Jahweh'; 'Thus says the Lord' (Amos 6.14; Isa. 1.24, etc). Jesus is called and sent —at his baptism. But he never relies on it and he never seeks to make his message impressive by referring to special visions which he had. His word always carries its own weight. He always acts like someone possessing the highest authority.

His speech is characterized by its unique use of Amen (e.g. Mark 3.28; 8.12; Luke 4.24; Matt. 13.16). Amen means 'truly', and from time immemorial in ancient Israel it was the answer by which the community affirmed the word of God they had heard or the prayer offered on their behalf. If Jesus makes this final word into his opening word, this unusual mode of speech means that Jesus speaks as the one who replies to God (A. Schlatter). As the embodiment of God's presence Jesus speaks the word he has received in the manner of an oath. Where he speaks the hearer is listening directly to what God is saying.

One can easily imagine that what is recorded in the Gospels in this respect is not premeditated; the words are certainly extempore, as Jesus speaks them. Word and idea, idea and decision, are born together through contact with a person or group of people or a situation. But the ready wit with which it is always accompanied is an art which presupposes long and penetrating familiarity with God's word.

Jesus lives in the primordial Word which is developed in the Law of the Old Testament and which is constantly awakening the ear of the prophets; Jesus lives in the First Commandment. This 'Law' is written on his heart (Jer. 31.31). No stone with messages chiselled on it stands between him and God. No leather or papyrus scroll with letters inscribed on it stands between him and God. He and God talk to each other directly; theirs is communion 'in the Spirit'. Because their communion is such, Jesus' relationship with men is also direct. No stone or paper or institution—however holy—separates his humanity from that of men.

The same is true of his actions. Because Jesus lives in the primordial Word of God he can penetrate unhampered and directly into the lives of men with both demand and succour— in a way that the Old Testament either says or assumes only God can do. Where Jesus is at work the people involved are in direct contact with the activity of God. It is all very human: he takes an old woman who has a fever by the hand and sets her on her feet again—that is all (Mark 1.31). Some fishermen, with all hands busy on the lake, are called from their work without being given any reason or purpose—and they leave everything as it is (Mark 1.16–20). The sick are made whole, ordinary men are taken into service. The world which is out of joint is restored again. A wave of recovery surges through life. The world enjoys a sunset of great hope. Long before Easter Jesus is the hope of the world.

As the chosen one of God Jesus is the man of faith. He forgets himself for God. He summons men to have faith.

As the representative of men Jesus is the man of love. He forgets himself for man. He challenges men to love.

As the assailant of the world Jesus is the man of hope. He forgets himself for the world, into which he hurls his fire. He inspires men with hope in the midst of despair.

Who was Jesus? (4) He was the man in whom word and deed were a unity, in whom grace and judgement, present and future, were united. Jesus was the man who gave God what was God's and man what was man's. The fact that he did this simultaneously in one and the same action and utterance and not just consecutively

affirms that he was, in the language of the New Testament, the
Word of God. This is his chief distinguishing characteristic. 'It
is the ability of the Word of God to expose *and* forgive man's sin
that gives it its character of *God's* Word' (R. Bultmann). Jesus
was God's Word because he did precisely this (John 1.14).

Is that what he really was? Yes. And, therefore, he still is. He
is God's Word today as he was then. He will be so for all eternity
(Heb. 13.8). Was he always God's Word? We touch here on a
secret that we can only hint at on the basis of the first three
Gospels. The fourth Gospel, which was written later, has more
to say about this. Paul knew how to make the point even more
clearly. What the Synoptics prove is, by comparison, much 'less'.
They show us the Jewish travelling preacher at work; his activity
fulfils and bursts all previous norms. They invite us to understand
his person in terms of his work and to realize who he was by what
he did. His work is carried out in Galilee and Jerusalem, in a
country which changed overlords almost every century. His figure
is that of a Jew in the Hellenistic Roman period. But *in* his
activity—and not beyond it—the eternal destiny of the world is
decided (Mark 4.11–12). What has already been decided in heaven
is now being decided in, with and beneath chronological history.
What we said about the union of time and eternity when we were
thinking about the dawn of the kingdom of God is true of Jesus'
work and his person. It can only be understood by means of the
apocalyptic standard of reference (see the diagram on p. 141
above).

The later doctrine of the primitive Church tried to formulate
this secret in the dogma of the Trinity and the God-Man. The
kernel of christological dogma is the doctrine of the two natures.
It lies at the bottom of the Reformation creeds and catechisms:
Jesus Christ, truly God and truly man. Protestant orthodoxy of
the seventeenth and eighteenth centuries tried to think through
this doctrine and subjected it to a thorough examination. It did
so in intellectual documents of extreme subtlety and precision.
While using the terminology of the period it did not forget that
from very early days the dogma had had the twofold task, on
the one hand of shaping and explaining the truth about Christ,
and on the other of preserving its secrecy. Hence, orthodoxy
became a special type of discipleship of Jesus Christ: discipleship
in the form of rational understanding. It is part of the greatness

of orthodoxy that it never forgot worship in speculation. It respected the mystery of Jesus Christ.

It should not be forgotten, however, that this strange way of thinking cannot be repeated in precisely the same form. If we copy it today we are doing something basically different from what orthodoxy did in those days; we are evading the decision of faith, which has repeatedly to be made afresh—here and now. And then we cease to have to do with the living Lord; we are left with an empty concept of the past. We block the approach to the history of Jesus, which took place once for all in order that —paradoxically—it might be repeated in our lives. But in breaking through to the historical Jesus we meet God.

The Synoptic Gospels emphasize this fact by making Jesus speak as the ambassador of God. 'He does not come as a teacher with his own claims, but he speaks like an ambassador; it should be said that the fourth Gospel is quite correct in emphasizing this point of view: "my teaching is not mine, but his who sent me" (John 7.16)' (M. Dibelius). The first three Gospels express it through sayings about coming or being sent which have been preserved in the I-form: 'I have not come . . .' or 'I have come . . .'. We have already met such sayings in Matt. 5.17 (Jesus' relationship to the Law), and in Luke 12.49 and Matt. 10.34 (sayings about fire and the sword). These sayings are very pithy on the whole. 'I have not come to call the righteous but sinners' (Mark 2.17). 'The Son of Man did not come to be served but to serve and give his life a ransom for many' (Mark 10.45). 'I was sent only to the lost sheep of the house of Israel' (Matt. 15.24). The stylization of these and similar sayings is due to the influence of the early Church (cf. John 3.17; 9.39; 12.47; 18.37, etc.; I Tim. 1.15), but this does not mean their content is not Jesus' own. The words of Mark 2.17, Luke 12.49 and Matt. 15.24 are quite genuine.

But if these sayings are not isolated from Jesus' ministry as a whole, which includes both his work and his message, they accord admirably with the historical picture so far obtained. They correspond exactly to the consciousness of mission which lies behind everything Jesus says and is active in everything he does. The formula 'I have come' need not stem from a later period which is looking back on Jesus' completed work (as I Tim. 1.15). The Greek words simply mean, 'I am here'.

Jesus was known as 'the One who is to come', by the earliest believers (Ps. 118.26; cf. Dan. 7.13). This is a secret name in apocalyptic for the Son of Man (or the Messiah?). It is only possible to doubt that he could have understood himself as 'the one who had already come', if we leave out of account the underlying standard of reference, which makes present and future simultaneous. As God's rule is both future and present at the same time, so is Jesus the one who is to come and the one who has come. The fact that he is both is one of the things that distinguishes him from the Old Testament prophets. The Old Testament nowhere speaks of a prophet who is coming and has come. There is not one single prophet who enters on his ministry by saying, 'I have come'. The parallels from other religions (Egypt, about 1500 BC) are also insufficient. The formula bears unmistakable witness to Jesus' mission, in which according to a Jewish principle the sender himself is present. 'The person sent (i.e. the person commissioned and given authority) is as the man who sent him.' This is true of the disciples (Luke 10.16).

> He who hears you hears me,
> and he who rejects you rejects me,
> and he who rejects me rejects him who sent me.

Jesus is the one who sends because he is the one who has first been sent. As he is present in his disciples, so God is first present in him. Here is 'more' than a prophet.

This 'more' is explicitly or implicitly the token and pledge of the newness that Jesus brings and is. Here is more than David (Mark 12.37). 'Here is something greater than the Temple' (Matt. 12.6). 'Behold, something greater than Jonah is here . . . Behold, something greater than Solomon is here' (Matt. 12.41–42). Here is something greater than Moses, the highest divine authority (Matt. 5–7). The fourth Gospel will sharpen this difference into a contrast. It will provoke the question, 'Are you greater than our father Jacob?' (John 4.12) and dare the bold saying, 'Abraham, your father, rejoiced that he was to see my day; he saw it and was glad. . . . Before Abraham was, I am' (John 8.56 and 58). The correspondence of Moses and the Messiah becomes a contrast (John 1.17):

> The Law was given through Moses;
> grace and truth came through Jesus Christ.

This 'more', with which all the Gospels are concerned, does not mean an increase or strengthening in degree, but a difference in kind. It is not just that 'obedience is better than sacrifice' (I Sam. 15.22), but to love God and one's neighbour is much more than all 'burnt offerings and other sacrifices.' To the man who answers so 'wisely' Jesus says, 'You are not far from the kingdom of God' (Mark 12.33–34). It is not only the Johannine Christ who makes profound, self-revelatory statements (John 6.35, etc.). The synoptic Jesus also does so, in words of encouragement (Mark 6.50) or acknowledgement—'I am' (Mark 14.62).

2. *The Messianic Secret*

The question of Jesus' identity is framed differently by the scholar and the non-specialist. Scholarship has asked itself for a long time whether Jesus thought he was the Messiah or not. Ordinary Christians and others have asked whether Jesus was God's Son or not. The point of both questions is the same.

Today the first question—about messianic consciousness—is regarded as a false question: rightly and wrongly. Rightly, because the purpose of the evangelists is not to provide evidence for psychological reconstructions. Only a psychologically orientated theology could approach sources which witness to the end of time with this question. Wrongly, because Jesus was a man like ourselves. What he said and did arose out of what he felt himself to be. No one could think Jesus was so naive that he did not know who he was or what he wanted as a man with a definite identity. His self-forgetfulness which we have referred to on several occasions does not mean he had a diminished sense of personal identity.

The second question sounds less sophisticated, but is not so fundamentally. The term 'Son of God' gives rise to a whole group of questions. What is understood by 'son of God' in different religions? What does the New Testament mean by it? Does not Jesus speak of 'sons of God' in the Beatitudes (Matt. 5.9)? Does not the New Testament constantly use this expression of believers? Again, what do *we* understand today by the term 'son of God'? Does the expression still mean what it meant in the New Testament, or even in Luther? Does it mean anything at all to us, in fact? Question after question.

P

One thing should be clear in view of all that has been said so far: a name or title, even if we could find one on Jesus' lips would not, by itself, help us in the least. As long as we saw in it only a precious survival of the past, a sort of verbal holy relic, we should be no better off than before. Alternatively, if we really knew who Jesus was, we should be content to worship God without needing to look for names and titles used by himself or his disciples.

His words, 'Blessed is he who takes no offence at me', would then apply to us. But we should be capricious readers of the New Testament if we simply disregarded the names and titles given to Jesus. We want to find the historical Jesus. We should certainly not find him if we dismissed the question of his names. The person who has already satisfied himself as to who the historical Jesus is will put this question with a comparatively calm mind about its possible result. Our fate does not stand or fall with the number or authenticity of the titles, but with the man himself, the man called Jesus.

The Apostles' Creed begins the second article with the words, 'I believe in Jesus (1) Christ (2) God's only Son (3) our Lord'.

(1) *Was Jesus the Christ?* Did he set out to be the Christ? 'Christ' means the Anointed, the King, and is the Greek translation of the Graecized Hebrew word 'Messiah' which is the root of all the various meanings of the term 'Christ'. That Christianity has recognized Jesus as the Christ, ever since the first Easter, is an unimpeachable historical fact. Paul took over the term from the early Christian community. It is all the more remarkable, therefore, that the earliest tradition never attributes the word 'Christ' to Jesus himself. Jesus never said 'I am the Christ, the Messiah. Only believe that I am He! Woe to you if you do not believe it!' In the early sayings-source, which both Matthew and Luke draw upon, the word never once occurs. Jesus showed great reserve towards this title. This is obviously coupled with the fact that acceptance of the title would have necessitated direct political action against the Roman oppressors. Jesus never claimed this honour. In fact, he rejected it. The famous scene at Caesarea Philippi shows this clearly. Jesus asks his disciples what people think of him and what the disciples themselves think. Peter answers 'You are the Messiah'. Jesus forbids them to tell anyone (Mark 8.27–30). This can hardly be understood otherwise than

as a rejection of the name of the King who should appear at the end of time. He does not command them to keep quiet in the sense that they are to guard a secret. Rather he tells them very forcibly not to call him Messiah. The command of silence is thus meant very practically. The fourth Gospel preserves a similar tradition when it relates how Jesus fled into the hills away from the crowd, when he realized they wanted to proclaim him 'king' (John 6.15).

On the only occasion when Jesus raised the question of the Messiah of his own accord (Mark 12.35–37), he did so in a critical manner. By means of Psalm 110 he raises a problem of interpretation. David calls the Messiah 'Lord': how, then, can David's Lord be David's 'son'? The scribes make no answer to the question put to them. Jesus deliberately leaves it open. But this opacity really conceals a decision: although he is descended from the house of David, Jesus does not intend to be the Davidic Messiah. His silence conceals the 'messianic secret'. The messianic secret is taken over by Mark from the tradition. But Mark has understood it as a private secret, which is only open to those who have been initiated. This point of view dominates the account given in Mark's Gospel and makes it the 'book of secret epiphanies' (M. Dibelius). Time and time again Jesus forbids open publication of healings or cures of demon-possession (Mark 1.44–45; 3.12; 5.43; 7.36) or of his Messiahship (Mark 8.30) or Transfiguration (Mark 9.11). Only after Easter may the secret be revealed. The messianic secret goes back to Jesus, insofar as it meant for him not a theory but a practical decision. For him concealment meant suffering.

This choice of suffering was in turn, however, a rejection of political Messiahship. We have known for a long time that contemporary Judaism's messianic expectation was at least twofold. On the one hand, there was the 'official' expectation of a messianic war-lord; on the other, the 'esoteric' expectation of the Saviour whose path to glory would be through suffering. The discoveries in the caves at Qumran have confirmed this twofold expectation. In certain circles and groups two Messiahs were expected—the royal Messiah and the priestly Messiah, the Messiah from Israel and the Messiah from Aaron (see p. 90 above). This doctrine of the two Messiahs together with the prophetic figure of the 'teacher of righteousness' represents a very schematized messianic expectation. Apocalyptic did not possess a systematic doctrine

of the last days, least of all a unified messianic dogma. Jesus did
not, therefore, as earlier scholars assumed, have any opportunity
of linking himself as Messiah with a definite dogmatic position
already in existence. The question whether he thought of himself
as *the* Messiah is too narrow. The question today is whether he
thought of himself as *a* Messiah—and if so, which one? Jesus'
answer to this is not to be found in any theoretical judgement
but in his life; he saw that his life was at stake in his decision. By
his answer he decided neither for a dogma nor for a particular
portrait of himself, but for his life itself. In refusing to be the
Davidic king, he not only rejected a theory; he was also refusing
to become the ruler personally. It was very necessary for the
Davidic Messiah to be proclaimed. The priestly Messiah was
distinguished by the exact opposite of this—silence. The resolve
to be silent was so strong in Jesus that he avoided any messianic
expression—even in this direction. Although he chose silence, he
rejected both direct and indirect action and chose suffering instead.
He designated himself as the suffering and dying one. Out of this
decision and its consequences Mark has constructed an esoteric
doctrine which was intended for initiated disciples. Shining
through this curtain, however, is the historical fact that Jesus
lived the messianic secret. In fact, what is esoteric is Jesus'
decision to risk his life for God, for men and for the world. The
'mystery' of Jesus is his martyrdom. Later witnesses gave authentic
expression to this fact. He chose the shame of the cross (Phil. 2.6–8).
He who is the light of the world says quite paradoxically (John
11.9–10).

> Has not the day twelve hours?
> If any one walks in the day he does not stumble,
> because he sees the light of this world.
> But if any one walks in the night, he stumbles,
> because the light is not in him.

A 'gloomy saying' (J. Schniewind). Jesus, who brings the decisive
day, journeys into the night, where he stumbles and is killed.
His suffering is his disguise. His own death is the first sacrifice
in the 'category' which he discusses in the Sermon on the Mount
(Matt. 6.1–18). Secrecy means sacrifice. This is Jesus' choice—
passion instead of action.

His choice of the passion is so decisive that he even allows himself to be greeted with the Hosanna of the jubilant liturgy from Ps. 118.25–6 when entering Jerusalem with the caravan of Galilean festival pilgrims. But he rides on the foal of an ass, not on a war-horse (Mark 11.1–10). A king? Or a fool? Neither— but the poor, lowly Anointed who brings salvation according to the word of the prophet (Zech. 9.9; Matt. 21.5).

Finally, we come to the question of Messiahship in Jesus' trial. There is no cogent reason for regarding the high-priest's question to Jesus, 'Are you the Messiah, the son of the Most High?' (Mark 14.61), as a product of the early Church. Direct witnesses were excluded from the trial, it is true; but the hurried trial was too much in the centre of public interest to prevent the immediate circulation of important facts. In a period whose distinctive characteristic (according to Carl Jacob Burckhardt) was indiscretion, there is no need to doubt this. Jesus' answer differs in all three Synoptic Gospels. According to Mark (14.62) Jesus affirms 'I am'. According to Luke (22.67) he expressly denies it at first (contrast 22.70). According to Matthew (26.64) he leaves it undecided, yet in such a way that the emphasis seems to rest on an implied denial: '*You* say so'—not I. The difference of the answers reflects the variety of interpretations of the secret. Unanimity only appears when Jesus—going beyond the necessary, minimum reply—refers to the coming of the Son of Man in power on the clouds of heaven (cf. Ps. 110.1; Dan. 7.13). This constitutes the chief attack of God on the theocracy; the rejection of the political attack cost Jesus his life. Paradoxically stated, Jesus radically rejected radicalism. He maintained the secret of his identity to the last. He lives in the age of the earthly Augustus, but speaks of an incomparably different majesty—'not of the throne of David but of the throne of God' (M. Dibelius).

(2) *Was Jesus the Son of God?* Did he think he was the Son of God? From the evidence of the first three Gospels this question can be answered much more briefly than the question of his Messiahship, with which it is generally confused. In pre-Christian Palestinian Judaism the Messiah is never called 'Son of God.' Since the early prophets 'Son of God' is a title given to the people of Israel (e.g. Hos. 11.1) or the earthly king (Ps. 2.7; cf. Ps. 89.27). Angels, too, can be sons of God.

Jesus called himself 'Son' only once—to affirm that he did not know something: the Son does not know the day or the hour (Mark 13.32). The words spoken in the Spirit (Luke 10.21–22 = Matt. 11.25–27; cf. p. 135 above) come from the risen Christ rather than the earthly Jesus. The demons call him 'Son of God' (Mark 3.11; 5.7; 8.29), likewise the devil (Matt. 4.3, 6), and Peter (but only Matt. 16.16), the people in the boat (also once only: Matt. 14.33), the Roman centurion, who is in command of the men keeping watch beneath the cross (Mark 15.39), and even those who mock and jeer (Matt. 27.40, 43). The occasions are extremely rare, therefore, and the title is used almost exclusively by those who are not disciples.

It is remarkable that the title 'Son of God' is missing at the very point one would most expect it, namely in the stories of the miraculous birth (Matt. 1; Luke 2). This serves to show that the term is not to be understood in a physical sense. This is confirmed by the account of Jesus' most fundamental experience. At his baptism and transfiguration (Mark 1.11; 9.7) God addresses him as 'Son' and sets his choice upon him by his word. Election, however, always means separation for a definite task. Election is never an end in itself. God never chooses simply for the sake of choosing, but always for some purpose. Election and obedience, election and mission, have always belonged together. The election of Israel involves a commission to serve. The same is true of the election of its earthly king. To be elected means to be selected in a representative capacity. The term 'Son of God' denotes in the first instance not the origin of Jesus but his destination. In this sense Jesus did think of himself as God's Son. Further statements of the New Testament about the sonship of Jesus can be read elsewhere—and in the Church's confession of faith.

(3) *Was Jesus the Lord?* Did he think of himself as the Lord? The answer given by the Synoptic Gospels is again brief. The expression 'Jesus the Lord' receives its full content only in the confession of the early Church, Palestinian *and* Hellenistic. In the Graeco-Roman world there were many 'lords' (*kyrioi*), both earthly and heavenly. The boundaries separating them and their respective provinces of competence were fluid. Divine and human intermingled. We shall be hearing more of this in a later volume when we are concerned with Paul (but compare now I Cor. 8.5–6). The 'lords' not only claimed worship in the sphere of the cult

but also claimed obedience in the world. The New Testament speaks similarly of Jesus Christ in both respects: he is the Lord who is present in worship but who is at the same time the rightful Lord of the world.

But this was already known to Israel regarding Yahweh the Lord. The Septuagint translated the name of God—which was never pronounced and for which the word 'Lord' (Hebrew *Adonai*) was used instead—by the Greek word *Kyrios*, which is familiar to us from our liturgy and hymns. The word 'Lord' on the lips of Jesus did not possess such full significance. Though it emerges in the question put by Jesus, 'Is the Messiah David's son or David's lord?' (Mark 12.35–37), this is because Ps. 110 is being quoted. In the account of the preparations before the entrance into Jerusalem Jesus says, 'The Lord has need of the colt' (Mark 11.3). But the expression is used within the framework of the relationship of a Rabbi and his disciples, and is little more than the customary form of address. The same is true of the saying in the Sermon on the Mount about 'Lord, lord . . .' (Matt. 7.23). The repetition of the title was a sign of heightened respect in contemporary Judaism. The three occasions on which the expression 'Lord' is used by Jesus himself therefore tell us very little. According to Mark (7.28) Jesus is only once addressed as Lord—and then it is by the Syro-Phoenician woman.

All the three titles which occur in the Apostles' Creed, therefore—Christ, Son of God, and Lord—have their origin in words addressed to Jesus rather than in words spoken by him. Men and spirits, believers and non-believers can speak in this way to Jesus. God and the Church, too, can address him in this way. But they are most certainly not terms used by Jesus to describe himself. They belong not to the call he received but—apart from God's address to him (Mark 1.11; 9.7)—to the response he evokes, the response to his appearance.

3. *The Judge of the World*

The only title which can be attributed to the historical Jesus with any degree of certainty is one which was not used by the early Church and which did not find its way into any Christian confession of faith, either in the New Testament or in later doctrinal formulations. This was the term 'Son of Man'. It is the only phrase used by Jesus of himself. Was it a word which faded away into the void? Was it a call to which there was no answer? Apart from one instance in the Acts of the Apostles it occurs only in the Gospels—all four, for a change—sixty times! It is nowhere to be found in the rest of the New Testament. It is most unusual that Paul, who stood in such a close relationship to the early tradition and digested it so thoroughly, never used it.

The questions raised by this peculiar situation find their answer in the fact that the term 'Son of Man' (cf. 'Man') does not describe an outgoing message which expected no answer. The expression is not so much a title as a description of the nature of Jesus. That is why it only occurs on his own lips. Basically it cannot be predicted of him; it can only be embodied by him. It enshrines so much that is distinctive of Jesus that it can never be used by others without losing its meaning: 'Man' is the word used by Jesus himself. It unites his person and his work. The complete absence of the term (apart from Jesus' own use of it) reflects the fact that the New Testament, Paul, the early Church and the later Church refrained from using it because they understood that Jesus was the 'Man'. We shall not enumerate and evaluate all the Son of Man passages individually, but will content ourselves with a summary statement: in the Gospels they fall into three groups dealing with the future, the present, and the suffering 'Man'.

The 'future' sayings tell of the coming of the 'Man' on the clouds of heaven (e.g. Mark 8.38; 13.26; Matt. 24.27; Luke 18.8). They reveal most clearly the colour of apocalyptic expectation about the end. In pietistic circles and revival groups people were awaiting this heavenly being to judge the world (cf. p. 58 above). But only one of these passages is historically reliable—the testimony of Jesus in the presence of the High Priest (Mark 14.62). The crux of the mystery is that to sit at the right hand of God and to come in judgement seem to be mutually exclusive. Probably Jesus was not speaking of his coming—generally referred to as his 'Second Coming'—but his exaltation from the lowliness of earth.

The 'present' sayings speak of him as having come, or, better, of the presence of the 'Man' and his power to act. 'The Son of Man has power to forgive sins on earth' (Mark 2.10). 'The Son of Man is Lord of the Sabbath also' (Mark 2.28). 'The Son of Man has nowhere to lay his head' (Matt. 8.20). These words bear witness to a well-attested tradition. They all refer to the earthly Jesus—all 'too earthly' (Matt. 11.19) and their historical probability is confirmed by the narratives about Jesus which are incontestable. The use of Son of Man as a term to describe the earthly Jesus has its origin in the preaching of Jesus.

The most obscure sayings are those concerned with the suffering Son of Man who is to rise again. It is natural that the influence of the early Church was strongest at this point. From the preaching of the primitive Church and its relation with the world it is easy to understand that these words of Jesus were later altered and elaborated. 'The Son of Man is to be betrayed into the hands of men' (Luke 9.44) is the basic original saying of Jesus. It was from this, or, more precisely, from those words of Jesus about himself which developed from it and became part of the tradition, that the three prophecies of suffering, already stylized in Mark, arose (Mark 8.31; 9.31; 10.33). The connection of the first 'prophecy' with Peter's previous confession of faith seems to be historically reliable. Jesus refuses the title of Messiah, forbids that he should be proclaimed Messiah and replaces the title by his own description of himself as 'Son of Man', a title which excludes every public reference and designates him as the one who must suffer. Men will despise and betray the Son of Man, 'as is written of him' (Mark 9.12; 14.21, 41). Thus, the Son of Man is the sign of the judgement which is to take place on earth, as Jonah was once a sign for his generation (Luke 11.30). The days of the Son of Man are like those of Noah before the great Flood; the people were eating and drinking, marrying and being married, as if life were nothing more than amusement and not the prelude to and beginning of judgement (Luke 17.22, 26). All this represents the office of the Son of Man in relation to the world. The most obscure of all the Son of Man sayings, however, remains to be noticed. 'The Son of Man did not come to lord it over slaves, but to serve and to give his life as a ransom for many' (Mark 10.45). The saying is so isolated and unique in content that it has been doubted whether it is a genuine utterance of Jesus. Moreover, the word 'ransom' is not to be found anywhere else in the whole of the New Testament. This fact could also favour the exactly opposite conclusion. A number of factors, indeed, speak for its authenticity. Not so much the Palestinian and Semitic character of the expression 'ransom' and 'the many' (in the sense of 'all'), but the directness and boldness with which it is used. The fact that scriptural proof is lacking—precisely the same is true of other words referring to the Son of Man (Mark 9.12; 14.21)—and that the image is not fully explained, points in the direction of Jesus' sovereign style of speech. It is striking that the cultic picture of a sacrifice that effects atonement is left vague. The question of when the ransom is paid remains open. At the final judgement? But is not the final judgement already under way? Equally open is the question, who receives the ransom. Satan? Definitely not. The last thing Satan wants is suffering (Mark 8.33). God? But the Son of Man is chosen to fulfil God's plan. God is involved in the work and passion of the Son of Man as subject, not as object. The recipient of the ransom is—deliberately?—unnamed. Everything is as untheoretical, untheological and undogmatic as possible. Could such a sentence, formulated in such unguarded language and left to carry such a tremendous weight of meaning, be attributed to the early Church? These words of Jesus are among the great 'fighting value-judgements'. The historian, Ernst Troeltsch, who made the most extensive and large-scale investigation into 'the distinctiveness of Christianity and the history of religion', said of them, 'Experience shows that there are few such value-judgements and that real revelations of new spiritual ideals have been very rare . . . Those who have had something new to say to men have always been few in number and it is surprising how few thoughts men have, in truth, lived on'.

Jesus' saying about ransom, however, is not only a thought or a value-judgement. In it Jesus verifies for us his whole existence. There is a union of speech and action in it. Jesus chooses suffering even as he speaks about it. His decision to suffer *is* itself the beginning of his passion.

At this point the most distinctive fact that we know about Jesus—his rejection of all titles of political Messiahship—becomes clear. He chose instead the word which originated in the revival groups, a word which had close associations with the frontiers of heresy, the word 'Son of Man'. He did not take it over just as it was, however; he altered it decisively. He brought the Son of Man down from the clouds of heaven to the rude earth of present realities. He brought the distant near. And he brought the Coming Messiah out of the future into the present. In and through Jesus the Son of Man became the homeless *Man*. But what does it mean to be a man? Joseph Weinheber knows what it means when he writes these somewhat pathetic but sincere lines about himself:

> I, a man among men,
> Buffeted and standing on an abyss,
> Lonely and helpless in face of the world's chaos,
> That breaks on me blackly
> Like a pack of thieves on a deserted house.

As the Son of Man Jesus is man in his frailty—helpless to the last degree. He is ready for suffering and death not only in the general sense in which they come to all men. He prepares himself to suffer and die as a condemned man—a criminal. The friend of sinners becomes the accomplice of criminals. The judge of the world is arraigned before an earthly tribunal. He is condemned by the judgement of men to suffer death upon a common cross. The representative of man maintains his bond with men until the very last. He intercedes for guilty men until (in the eyes of God and the world) he is identified with them—with all that this involves. He dies for 'the many'.

The 'many' in the Qumran community are the associates of the pure, priestly community which is separated from the world, the children of light. The 'many' on the lips of Jesus are—as in Isa. 53.11—*all* men. In the monastery-barracks of those who had withdrawn into the desert, particularistic and exclusive modes of thought prevailed. In the midst of the world of stirring life the thought of Jesus is universal and inclusive.

It is clear from this that the 'Son of Man' is the end of the 'Messiah from Israel'. The two are different in origin and mission. The political Messiah comes as a man from Israel, as a descendant of the old royal family; he is sent only to Israel, in order to free it from dominion of Rome. Everything is narrowed down to one particular nation's existence. The Son of Man, however, comes from the wide, open spaces of the divine world and sets to work as God's messenger to the world. In this case everything takes on an all-embracing aspect. In the midst of the unsettled Hellenistic-Roman world with its developing imperial consciousness he quietly goes his way: to a world whose basic law is self-seeking he gives the rule of self-surrender (Luke 17.33):

> Whoever thinks to save his life will lose it,
> And whoever loses it will preserve it.

He is the first to put his own rule to the test—without reserve. He opposes the desire for world-conquest by the surrender of his rights as a man. It is not God exacting a price. Nor can the devil demand one. But *human life* as such expects one—a 'neutral' power, which includes every area in which life meets us day by day. Jesus pays the price to life itself: in self-surrender he finds himself.

What is united and integrated in Jesus—self-surrender and self-preservation—breaks apart in our existence. The paradox of his life and suffering disintegrates for us in the problems of daily decisions. Bonhoeffer has outlined the problem in a letter from prison (dated 21.2.1944): 'I have often wondered where the border lies between necessary *resistance* against "fate" and equally necessary *submission* to it. Don Quixote is the symbol of resistance carried to the point of absurdity and madness—like Michael Kohlhaas who insisted on his rights until it became his own undoing. In both cases resistance in the end defeats its own object, and vanishes into illusion and fantasy. Sancho Panza is the type of complacent and sly accommodation to things as they are. I am sure we must rise to the great responsibilities which are peculiarly our own, and yet at the same time fulfil the commonplace tasks of daily life. We must sally forth to defy fate—I think the neuter gender of *Schicksal* (fate) is significant—with just as much resolution as we submit to it when the time comes. One can only speak of 'providence' on the other side of this dialectical process. God encounters us not only as a Thou, but also disguised as an It; so in the last resort my question is how we are to find the Thou in this It (i.e. fate). In other words, how does fate become providence? It is impossible to define the boundary between resistance and submission in the abstract; both are necessary and both must be exercised. Faith demands this elasticity of behaviour. Only so can we stand our ground in each situation as it comes along, and turn it to gain.'

This is the secret of the Son of Man. For him resistance and submission form an indivisible unity.

4. *The Disguise of God*

The saying about 'ransom' (Mark 10.45) shows signs of contact between two different traditions, that of the Son of Man and the

Servant of the Lord from Isaiah 53. Jesus himself only quoted Isaiah 53 once. Luke attached the unique saying to the conversation round the table at the Last Supper (Luke 22.34–38). Jesus is looking back and reminding the disciples of the time when they were first sent out—without lacking anything. But the turning point has arrived; a time of persecution is coming. Times are drawing near when the poorest will be lucky to get away with his life; it is better to renounce clothing than weapons of defence such as a sword. The reason why Jesus does not encourage them in any limited form of self-defence is to be found in the reply 'It is enough', which he makes to the production of the two swords (this is the basic passage for the doctrine of the two swords in the Middle Ages). The seriousness of the situation—immediately before he was condemned to death—should be obvious enough to them. The disciples belong to a proscribed Master. For the words from Isa. 53.12 are to be fulfilled in him, 'He was numbered with the transgressors.'

Apart from this there are only indirect references to the great hymn about the suffering and triumphant Servant of God. Such references as there are, therefore, are all the more notable. This is the case with Mark 10.45. It does not contain a direct quotation from Isaiah 53, but it is 'a response to it' (P. Volz). Its terminology and ideas, its style and emphasis cannot be understood without Isaiah 53. 'The many' occurs once more in Mark's account of the Last Supper (Mark 14.24). Moreover it may be noticed that Jesus constantly has Deutero-Isaiah (Isa. 40–55) in mind. We do not usually make direct quotations from sayings or writings which are part of us. The more they are part of us, the less likely we are to quote them. A quotation always presupposes distance. But where a saying has grown up with us it moulds what we think and say. The Suffering Servant Songs were part of Jesus, just as the First Commandment, God's basic word, was.

The most important fact, however, is that he not only gave a silent, living and suffered commentary on Isaiah 53, by the way he lived, but he also brought together the two figures of the Son of Man and the Servant of God. He did not do this within the framework of a theological or prophetic scheme; he did not add or combine the Son of Man from Daniel 7 and the Book of Enoch and the Suffering Servant of Isaiah 53. Jesus was not a 'composer' like the evangelists, particularly Matthew. He achieved the union of the two hitherto separated figures in the 'exegesis' of his historical life. In his unique figure and by his unrepeatable methods Jesus brought the two traditions of the Son of Man and the servant of God to interpret each other in turn.

The attempt has occasionally been made to classify Jesus as a poet. To a certain extent this is quite feasible. For his sayings and discourses permit the conditional application of aesthetic standards. Jesus is the poet of his parables in the highest degree— irrespective of the later alterations and additions to the tradition. Even as they are, they are such an unmistakably living expression of his message that we no longer feel that the lost son, the good Samaritan, the generous vineyard owner, or the farmer who goes to bed and finds his seed thriving without any effect on his part, 'never really lived'—to use a rather banal expression. They are all figures of a poetry that reflects real life, of course, but in a stylized way. The greatest 'poem' of Jesus, however, and the one most fraught with consequences, was his own life story. This is most succinctly expressed in his combination of the Son of Man and Servant of God in the one poem—his life—by his simply being what he was.

It is quite certain that the tradition did not always understand this; it is equally certain that the reflection of this fact is not uniformly and powerfully visible. Matthew has not fully perceived this. By means of his customary scriptural proof he has twice made reference to Isaiah 53 (Matt. 8.17; 12.18–27). The clearest example is Mark's fusion of the Servant of God from Deutero-Isaiah with the Son of God (i.e. the righteous one) from Psalm 2, Wisdom of Solomon 2–5. Not only his Passion narrative drew on this figure; the theme of his Gospel, 'the Messianic secret', also came from the same source.

The fact that the evangelists were able to fit the individual *pericopae* of the tradition into such a 'framework' is not the result of capriciousness on their part but of their recollection of the man who united in himself the dominant figures of eschatological expectation not theoretically but existentially. The historical significance of Jesus of Nazareth's achievement is reflected in their fragmentary clauses as well as in some of their outlines.

Finally, then, let us ask why Jesus united these two figures— the Son of Man and the Servant (cf. Son) of God—rather than

any others. A brief answer under several headings would be as
follows:

(*a*) Both figures are thoroughly untheological. It is true that
the Son of Man is the object of lay speculation, but no
uniform, dogmatic sketch exists. The prophecy about the
Servant of God was scarcely understood by late Judaism,
and had certainly not been elaborated theologically.

(*b*) Both figures are peculiarly ambiguous. Each of them can
describe either an individual or a community (cf. 'Israel'
in Isa. 44.1, and 'the people of the saints of the Most
High' in Dan. 7.27). Both figures have the power, therefore,
to accommodate two destinies—that of the Chosen One
and that of the chosen ones.

(*c*) Both figures deal with a wide horizon from the beginning—
unlike the official Messianic expectation. The origin and
mission of both these messenger figures are universal.

(*d*) Both figures are linked with expressions of divine glory.
The Son of Man receives it prior to his appearance, the
Servant of God attains it through his suffering. The great
hymn about the Suffering Servant begins (Isa. 52.13–15)
and ends (Isa. 53.12) with the Servant's victory.

(*e*) Both figures permit the possibility of their bearer experiencing a real history—the path to exaltation through humiliation. Jesus understood the Son of Man in the light of the
Servant.

(*f*) Both figures, as they fade perceptibly in Jewish tradition,
call out for concrete manifestation and a man who would
express them in flesh and blood.

(*g*) Both figures have their place in an encroaching divine plan
of salvation, the saving decree of divine election. This finds
expression in the way the Gospels refer to 'as it is written'
in connection with both figures.

This brings us to the heart of Jesus' message. As the chosen
and beloved Son—Son of Man and Servant simultaneously—
Jesus embraces the will of the Father utterly and completely;
and, at the same time, he embraces the side of man completely,
although the world is in rebellion against God. He does this not
in the style of the Emperors who rule the Roman Empire, but

by the sacrifice of himself. The law of this world is the murder of millions and millions of unfortunate although not innocent victims. The law of the world which Jesus introduces is self-giving to the last. Augustus mounts the Capitol in order to celebrate High Mass for the gods of the Empire in the Temple of Zeus for four nights long. Jesus goes to Golgotha. No plays, no weeks of theatrical celebration follow as in Rome.

The fourth Gospel shows Jesus being examined by the Roman procurator before his execution (John 18.33–37). Pilate asks, 'Are you a king?' Jesus replies, 'My kingship is not of this world; if my kingship were of this world my servants would fight, that I might not be handed over to the Jews: but my kingship is not from the world.' Pilate said to him, 'So you are a king?' Jesus answered, 'You say that I am a king. For this I was born and for this I have come into the world, to bear witness to the truth. Everyone who is of the truth hears my voice.' Pilate said to him, 'What is truth?' In his own way John has made the Christ state expressly what the historical Jesus achieved by his resolve to suffer as Son of Man and Servant of God. The evening of the world is here.

Everything occurs in hiddenness. The disciples misunderstand him. Their ambitious spokesmen quarrel. The people flock to him and pass on their way again. Within a few days, almost in the same breath, they cry 'Hosanna' and 'Crucify'. The disciples flee. Judas betrays him. Peter denies him. The leaders of the theocratic state have him arrested. The Roman equestrian, Pontius Pilate, gives way to the wishes of the mob and orders his execution. The most decisive event in the world takes place. But it is hidden beneath its opposite—concealed and disguised. No wonder if Pilate—according to John—displays a tired and somewhat *blasé* scepticism. Who really knows what truth is? And yet everything is done as if truth existed and men could know what truth is. Men live in a world of make-believe (as if . . .). What appears necessary is folly and accident. Truth is the work of subordinate spirits with an exaggerated sense of their own importance.

In the midst of accident and folly, however—cutting across the vast and yet pitiably small theatre of the world—the necessity of God's eternal plan of salvation is found. Jesus bowed to the will of the Father. He did not subject himself to any apocalyptic world-law. Now men may meet the will of the Father in everything; the 'It' reveals the eternal 'Thou'. About the turn of the last century it was still believed that monism could confer freedom from dogmatic compulsion on men. The masses took up the battle-cry, 'We no longer believe in miracles; we believe in the un-alterable laws of nature.' But this was jumping out of the frying pan into the fire. An old compulsion was exchanged for a new one. Men stepped out of an alleged bondage into a real one. For the old bondage left open the possibility of appealing to God against dogma. The new bondage, however, confronted men with a silent, brazen Leviathan, the mechanical workings of which were in-exorable—or it included men in an energetic self-sufficient whole, in whose vortex the individual was drowned.

The old apocalyptic gave way to a new one. The place of a mythology which was still able to examine its contrast in its idea of God was taken by a new mythology, which abolished trans-cendance in the name of knowledge and regarded 'finite self-sufficiency' (P. Tillich) as absolute. All this could have been tolerated to a certain extent, if there had been a realistic aware-ness of the new position by men. But men succumbed to the illusion that the new world with its new standards and new categories and values was the ultimate newness of the enlightened spirit. In fact, what was happening was the expression of some-thing irrevocably old.

Anyone who meets the historical Jesus, who as Son of Man and Servant of God does the will of the Father, and becomes his disciple, is given a new consciousness of the world. His world is enlarged. He sees it in depth in the variety of its dimensions. The 'times of refreshment' (Acts 3.20) do not only refer to personal life; they also include the relationship of men to the vast, intractable environment of social and physical forces. The discoveries in the sphere of atomic physics have not only evoked feelings of pride or a sense of liberty in men. It is not necessary to paint the devil of atomic war once more on the world's wall of destiny. It is sufficient to think of the peaceful uses of atomic energy, which modern atomic physics have discovered, or the new possibilities of understanding the world in greater detail and ruling it on a wider scale. Does the knowledge that the arm of knowledge and technology extends a million times further into the world than ever before really make us happy? Is it not rather disheartening

Q

for man, seeking to maintain his humanity, to see how the world
is beginning to shrivel together?

> The world is perfect everywhere
> Unless tormented man appear,

says Schiller. This perfection of the world, which is identical with
its freedom, is being progressively lost.

The only remedy is the encroachment of an incalculable power
of goodness, such as makes a person's heart beat. It meets us in
the lowliness of him who as Son of Man is our brother man. The
humanity of Jesus of Nazareth is the focal point in a world that
has lost its mystery. Jesus is the secret messenger of God, 'who
was with God and was God and could have had great joy, but
who thought of the wretched people in prison and came to them
clad in the uniform of wretchedness in order to free them by his
blood' (Matthias Claudias). Whenever a man meets Jesus, God
in disguise, he knows that the world is no prison. The world is
not a giant concentration camp, in which man is held captive by
the whim of some despot. The world is God's creation, a place of
freedom for its Creator. It is also, however, a place of freedom
for all those who recognize God's rule over the world and God's
glory in the world. Who are these men? All those who have heard
from Jesus that God's freedom means election.

Jesus gives back the world its mystery, Jesus gives back to
modern men capacity for hope. The simple, historical recollection
that a man by the name of Jesus passed through this world without
losing his mystery, could preserve the world from the extremities
of despair.

5. *The Call-up*

The question we started from—who was Jesus?—excludes a
number of answers which attempt to describe his character,
either alone or in company with his disciples. The first three
Gospels make a number of points clear.

Jesus was no religious virtuoso, in the way that the early
Schleiermacher thought. Nor was he, as the later author of *The
Christian Faith* thought, the 'archetype' of the Church, for the
Church to emulate and model itself on. He was not, so to speak,
the perfect holy man, in whom 'the full force of God-conscious-

ness', the 'actual being of God within him', was developed within the community of the devout.

Jesus was not the founder of a school like the Jewish Rabbis or the Greek and Hellenistic philosophers. He did not aspire to a theological system. He possessed neither a system of ethics nor teachings of practical morality.

From the point of view of comparative religion, Jesus was not the founder of a religion who established Christianity as a new religion, parallel to or opposed to other religions such as Buddhism or Zoroastrianism, or who wanted to enter into competition with the mystery religions of the Roman Empire of those days.

Yet all these answers do conceal a correct observation. Jesus cannot be considered in isolation—like any other thinker in history. As soon as his name is mentioned, one is reminded of the community which he began to form. Otherwise it is no longer Jesus of Nazareth, even historically, who is being discussed. This immediately raises the question whether Jesus founded the Church. This is denied by many Protestant scholars. The word to Peter (Matt. 16.17–19) is unmistakably a later community formation. But, even apart from this, it is said, founding a Church does not fit in with Jesus' 'historical consciousness'.

There is a grain of truth in both criticisms. Jesus did not intend to 'found a Church' in the sense that the term 'Church' evokes nowadays. He neither planned nor organized a Church, which could be compared sociologically with the institution of the temple-state or the synagogue or the Qumran community. Such an organization really would contradict his historical consciousness.

If we guard against introducing later concepts or later ways of formulating questions, a different interpretation might suggest itself. Neither textual criticism, nor literary criticism, nor form criticism have any essential objections to bring against Matt. 16.18 and 18.17, where the same word *ekklesia* occurs in two different senses—the Church as a single unit and the Church as a community of individuals. Moreover, the uniqueness of the text speaks for rather than against its authenticity. The historian will have to guard against unconsciously reading into the texts the experiences of a later period which were the result of the Roman Catholic understanding of Peter and the Church. There is no need to understand the texts by reference to an institution. The Church,

indeed, is not an institution, although it always possesses traits
which are characteristic of institutions because it is a community
of people in the world. Apart from the Semitic colouring, the
choice of expression and terminology, which gave rise to puns
that are not obvious in translation—*Petrus/petra* (Rock-man/rock)
—is evidence of the age and authenticity of the saying. In Matthew
Jesus' word is the immediate conclusion to Peter's confession of
faith in Christ. It is sometimes regarded as a compliment paid by
Jesus to his disciples for faith in him. But this is most certainly
not so. Jesus says,

> Blessed are you, Simon Bar-Jona!
> For flesh and blood has not revealed this to you,
> but my Father who is in heaven.
> And I tell you, you are Peter,
> and on this rock I will build my church
> and the powers of death shall not prevail against it.

Does this seem like a return compliment? It is true that Matthew
does not show Jesus immediately forbidding Peter to proclaim
him—as Mark 8.30 and Luke 9.1 do. This does not occur till a
little later in Matthew (Matt. 16.20). He puts the saying about
the Church in between. Whether this is the original historical
context or not is doubtful. But this says nothing about its authenticity. The possibility that Jesus intended to intercept and cut
short Peter's Messianic confession by his saying about the Church
is not excluded. In promising the establishment of the Church
he reveals the new sphere in which testimony to the Christ has
its proper place, without the danger of being misunderstood and
abused politically.

At any rate, it should be noted that the saying about the Church
concerns a promise for the future ('I will build') and that all the
active verbs in the next verse (Matt. 16.19) which determine the
content of the mission are in the future tense. It is the risen Lord,
not the earthly Jesus, who builds the Church. Even then it is
Peter—and only Peter—who executes Jesus' command. There is
no mention of a successor or line of successors such as the Roman
popes.

Jesus makes no promises or guarantees about a firmly established
institution cradled in external security and settling down in
complacent tranquillity. Rather, he sets the Church in the sphere

of eschatological temptations, where danger threatens life itself. He makes sure, however, by his word that as 'his' Church it shall not be overwhelmed in the midst of the struggle by the powers of death. This archaic language belongs to the earliest period when the catastrophes which were breaking over Jesus directed his gaze to the future. It should certainly not be given a Protestant interpretation!

It agrees excellently with Jesus' historical consciousness. Jesus knew himself as the chosen Son of God, the Son of Man and the Servant of God. He was conscious of being sent because he was conscious of having been chosen. According to apocalyptic expectation—of whatever kind—the appearance of the Chosen One coincided with the gathering of the chosen ones. The 'Man', the righteous one and the righteous ones, belonged together— like the Messiah and his companions (cf. p. 60 above). They are both pre-existent together; they will both be revealed together.

The decision about the gathering of the community of chosen ones was made as soon as Jesus was conscious of being the Chosen One. Of course, he gathers this community by his call—how else? The promised Church, which is also to be built on the 'rock', Peter, will also be built by his call. We are also to understand by the metaphor of the house that the Church is the eschatological people of God or, as the Old Testament put it, the eschatological levy. The levy, however, is for fighting with 'the powers of death'. It is called out by the Chosen and Righteous One who goes the way of humiliation and suffering. Both—the Jesus who suffers and the Jesus who establishes the Church—belong together. Or, more briefly: Church and Cross, Cross and Church.

It is clear that anyone who thinks of the monastery of Qumran and the barracks of the 'army of salvation' and their spiritual 'manual of exercises' will get a wrong idea about the Church which Jesus builds and the community which he gathers. He certainly ought to! For there are no regulations, in this case; everything is improvised. A 'world church' in any organizational sense is not in his mind at all; it is a fighting fellowship of men of faith, life and hope.

The call of the disciples is the gathering of the final levy. The accounts of these calls are very different (cf. Mark 1.16–20 with Luke 5.1–11). The number twelve appears to be old. The twelve disciples correspond to the twelve patriarchs. The latter are

the ancestors of the ancient people of God; the former are the
ancestors of the new people of God. As the college of the twelve
does not play a decisive role later, though it is presupposed by
Paul (I Cor. 15.5), good tradition lies at the base of it. The rules
of the Qumran community are also familiar with a council of
twelve, alongside three priests. A table of the twelve disciples is
to be found in Mark 3.13-19 (= Matt. 10.1-4= Mark 6.12-16).
All three agree with each other and with the catalogue in Acts 1.13
in general outline, but they differ in details of names and their
order. The three leading disciples, Peter, John and James, appear
at the head, except that Matthew and Luke place Andrew next
to his brother, Peter. These three belong to the circle of the
twelve, however, in contrast to the three priests at Qumran, who
are additional to the twelve. They are the trusted witnesses—
at the little girl's deathbed (Mark 5.37), on the Mount of Transfiguration (Mark 9.2), and in the Garden of Gethsemane (Mark
14.33).

All three evangelists make it clear that the choice of the disciples
was a free decision or selection—he called those 'whom he wanted'
(Mark 3.13)—and that they were endowed with charismatic gifts
by the prime possessor of such gifts, Jesus (Matt. 10.1). The
twelve are to be the future princes of the new Israel; they are to
'sit on twelve thrones judging the twelve tribes of Israel' (Matt.
19.28). Quite apart from temperament and peculiarity of character
they form a motley group. Side by side stand the fisherman and
the farmer, the 'patriot' Simon (Luke 6.15) and the tax collector,
Levi (Mark 2.13-14) or Matthew (Matt. 9.9). In view of these
extremes the circle is anything but a 'pure' community in the
sense of the priestly ideal. Probably it was not so closed as the
stylized lists imply. We have already seen that there were women
among Jesus' followers (Luke 8.1-3). Luke is acquainted with a
tradition that Jesus appointed 'another seventy' disciples (Luke
10.1-20) alongside the twelve (Luke 9.1-16=Mark 6.7-13).

All this gives the impression that Jesus had no positive principle
of selection. In particular cases his response was purely negative.
He rejected requests or offers of discipleship (Mark 5.18-19)
roughly and in part unheard. His words to the aspiring disciple
are very discouraging. 'Leave the dead to bury their own dead',
he says; and he forbids another person to say farewell to those
at home (Luke 9.57-62). Here is more than Elijah (I Kings 19.20).

A more cutting, piercing wind blows through the sayings about the obligations of discipleship (Mark 9.33–37), giving offence (Mark 9.42–48), salt (Mark 9.49–50) and the advice, warnings and threats which Matthew has brought together in larger units. The demand is most sharply expressed in Mark 9.43–47:

> And if your hand causes you to sin—cut it off;
> it is better for you to enter life maimed
> than with two hands to go to hell
> to the unquenchable fire.
> And if your foot causes you to sin, cut it off;
> it is better for you to enter life lame
> than with two feet to be thrown into hell.
> And if your eye causes you to sin, pluck it out;
> it is better for you to enter the kingdom of God with one eye
> than with two eyes to be thrown into hell,
> where their worm does not die and the fire is not quenched.

The community of disciples chosen and challenged in this way forms a single large family. Organization and members' roll are not decisive; much more important is the practical response to God's call to action. When Jesus' mother and brothers come to call him, he says, 'Who are my mother, and my brothers?' And looking around on those who sat about him, he said, 'Here are my mother and my brothers! Whoever does the will of God is my brother and sister and mother' (Mark 3.31–35). The Church is formed wherever Jesus can be heard. Wherever Jesus looks he can see God's family. It is no brotherhood in the old, Pharisaical style, no revival group or movement of apocalyptic rank, no order of stricter or laxer discipline, but the family of God. The Father begets his own children—from those who listen and obey. They are united and bound together by the decree of God. This family is constituted as a family with its own rights at the Last Supper on the night before his death. The word of challenge is completed by the meal which satisfies hunger and creates the covenant. 'The Last Supper marks the founding of the Church' (M. Dibelius).

Just as Jesus 'called up' the disciples without any apparent principle, so he sends them out to serve in exactly the same way. Was Jesus responsible for the mission to the Gentiles, then? Like the question about the Church the answer must be 'No', if the issue is confused by modern, preconceived ideas. If we understand the Church on the model of the institutional Roman Church or the liturgical Orthodox Churches or the preaching Protestant Churches together with all their constitutional practices and machinery of government, then Jesus did not found the Church. Nor did he have in view an ecumenical organization such as the World Council of Churches, as a possible means of uniting and co-ordinating the churches. And if we understand 'mission' on the model of modern missionary work at home or among the 'younger churches', then Jesus neither instituted nor encouraged mission. But this answer would be as misleading as the answer to the question about the Church.

Mission, like the Church, was the natural corollary of his election; universal mission, of course. Jesus' rejection of the title 'Messiah from Israel' prepared the way for it. His election as Son and his awareness of being God's Servant were his first steps on the way. The Servant of God of Deutero-Isaiah had undertaken his office for the sake of the whole world from the beginning. He was chosen to call the many, and to bring the wisdom and truth and righteousness of God to the furthest shores, 'the islands'. The 'coastlands' wait for the new order of the Lord God (Isa. 42.4). The nations (the Gentiles) are waiting.

But the Servant of God is also the criterion of the mission which God expects him to inaugurate. The view expressed by the salvation-oracles of Deutero-Isaiah and presupposed in the Synoptic Gospels is different from that held by the churches today, which are hives of activity. In this they resemble all too closely the synagogue of Jesus' days with its programme of religious propaganda. It is precisely this 'mission' that Jesus rejected: 'Woe to you, scribes and Pharisees, hypocrites! for you traverse sea and land to make a single proselyte, and when he becomes a proselyte you make him twice as much a child of hell as yourselves' (Matt. 23.15).

Who is not reminded by these words of many of the methods of European missionary activity, which have brought the 'blessings' of Western civilization—not only 'between the Nile and the Caucasus'—to nations where the indigenous culture has been uprooted in the process. For the Old Testament and for Jesus himself mission is the eschatological miracle. When the time is ripe, the waiting nations of the world will awake. They will set

out of their own accord and come to the place of salvation. There
is no need, therefore, of any organization or any 'missionary
work'. All that is needed is to give the alarm. We may call this
view naive. But it is the view of the prophets and the view of
Jesus.

Accordingly he sends the disciples out—because *he* is here. He
teaches them to take the first step and to go to the lost sheep of
the house of Israel, not to hurry after the Gentiles, not even to
enter a Samaritan city (Matt. 10.5). But it would be wrong to
derive from this the principle that the mission to the Gentiles is to
be rejected. This would mean subordinating Jesus to principles!
The verse is part of Matthew's special material and should not be
overemphasized; to be more precise, it should be understood
within the total framework of Matthew. The theme of Matthew's
Gospel is as follows: the Messiah who is to come from Israel and
for Israel (Matt. 1) will be rejected by this same Israel—and be
accepted by the nations! This rejection is foreshadowed early in
the Gospel by the brutal Herod (Matt. 1). But the eschatological
miracle of the rousing of the nations occurs; the plan is corrected
and ultimately, in fact, fulfilled. The Magi came from the East
on the silk-roads of the former empire of Alexander (Matt. 2).
Although Jesus classes the Syro-Phoenician woman with the
'dogs', she will not be rejected (Matt. 15.21–28). In this way the
Roman centurion forms his own estimate of the miraculous healer
from Capernaum (Matt. 8.5–13). Jesus himself is taken by surprise;
'Truly I say to you, not even in Israel have I found such faith'
(Matt. 8.10). Linked with this is the indication that the prophecy
of Deutero-Isaiah is now beginning to be fulfilled (Isa. 49.12;
59.19). It is not until the end of the Gospel that the ascended
Lord gives the command to go out into all the world, to 'all'
nations (Matt. 28.19). The overall framework is obviously the
work of Matthew. The interpretation which he thus gives to the
work of Jesus is a consequence of the later expansion of the
mission to the Gentiles by the Jews. Nevertheless the dialectical
tension of Israel and the Gentile world reflects a movement which
may have had an effect on the activity of the historical Jesus. But
Jesus took the first step before taking the second. This was
provided for in the mission-oracle of Deutero-Isaiah (Isa. 49.6ff.).
There is nothing to suggest that Jesus, who made the words of
this prophet part of himself, did not take seriously the command

given to the Servant of God. It also corresponded to his own understanding of reality.

Luke also emphasises the universality of the Gospel, but he does not make Jesus suppress the pre-eminence of Israel at all. It is not accidental that the bent woman is 'Abraham's daughter' (Luke 13.16) and the chief tax collector, Zacchaeus, is 'Abraham's son' (Luke 19.9). But it is equally certain that Jesus' gaze goes beyond the borders of the theocracy. The Samaritan village is spared (Luke 9.51–56). Of the ten lepers who are cured only the 'foreign' Samaritan returns to thank Jesus for his help (Luke 17.11–19). It is not accidental that the good neighbour is a Samaritan (Luke 10.29–37). All this is deliberately stressed. According to the fourth Gospel one of Jesus' most universalist sayings occurs in conversation with a Samaritan woman (John 4.24). The tradition could not have said all this, if it had not observed Jesus himself turning to the world of the Gentiles. If Jesus had forbidden the mission to the Gentiles in principle, this limitation would have been bound to have had political repercussions in view of the existing situation. This would have meant Jesus recanting his work as Servant of God and Son of Man.

6. *The Attack*

Jesus was not the founder of a religion. Jesus did not set out to spread 'Christianity' in the world. He was not responsible for the arrival of 'a Christian era', which could subsequently be secured by 'an era of Constantine'. He liberated us from the nightmares which a generation ago disturbed the Anglo-Saxon world particularly; it was feared that since the world had renounced its alliance with the Church in modern times, a 'post-Christian era' had arrived. All this is pure fantasy; it is not the more real for being a pious fantasy.

Jesus called the Church, the eschatological people of God, to arms. The disciples form the fighting core of the new 'covenant', the sworn companions of their Master. Jesus, however, is the 'oath of God' in the flesh; he guarantees that the world will come to a good end (Blumhardt Junior). They gather round their sworn Master. They wear no uniform, though by his own 'uniform of wretchedness' he identifies himself with all mankind. They do not march in step. They follow him. But to be a disciple means to fight and be tempted. The moving principle of the call-up is not expansion but conflict.

Jesus takes the attack. His attack is the 'attack of grace' (Karl Barth). Jesus does not doubt the world, and, above all, he does not despair of it. He sets his hopes on it; he has great hopes for it. Men of hope are never 'radicals'. Radicalism is a product of torment and despair. But Jesus is a man of hope. If he had been a radical, in either a religious or political sense, he would hardly have caused the offence he did. It is an old experience that in the history of the world the radicals usually make the running. The more radical they are, the more successful they are! Radical leaders usually seduce the followers of the moderates. It is no different in the sphere of religion. Young people and intellectuals usually follow the 'most inspiring' spirits. Somersaults of thought, excessive demands and absurdity in any shape or form stimulate the articulate and non-articulate. Radicalism is the world's acknowledgement of its own hopelessness, the performance of a dialectical shadow-play of despair.

Jesus has nothing to do with any of this. He and the Baptist please no one. His contemporaries appear to him like children playing at theatres. They sit in the market place and play at weddings and funerals. This is their whole repertoire. Anything more is beyond them. But the little that they can do they are emphatic about. They have no flair for nuances. Yet they are spoil-sports, who are not willing to abide by the rules of minor comedies and tragedies. They call out to one another:

> We played the flute—but you did not dance!
> We wailed in lament—but you did not weep!

John was a grim preacher of repentance. It was said he had a demon. Jesus came and lived a normal life. It was said he was a glutton. The wish for something out of the ordinary is never satisfied. The messengers of God please no one (Luke 7.31–35). If Jesus had played the radical they would have followed him or let him go on his way, according to their taste. But the Jews, at least, would not have persecuted or murdered him.

It was not his excessive demands that provoked his contemporaries. It was his generous goodness that caused offence. This seems to have been so from the beginning. The 'gracious words which flowed from his lips' challenged his enemies (Luke 4.22).

The grace of God which he preached gave offence (Matt. 20.1–16). He brought the 'easy yoke' (Matt. 11.29). Rabbinic expectation went further. When the Messiah comes, they believed, his 'days' will be a time of zealous study of the Law. The theatres and circuses of the Roman Empire will be converted into lecture-rooms for the Torah. Even the academies of the Babylonian Jews will be transplanted to Palestine. The Messiah will be the chief teacher of the Law in this centralized republic of scholars. But *he* came differently. He established the Torah, God's command, in the sense of Deutero-Isaiah's 'Servant of God'. Matthew realized that the manner in which he established justice did not correspond to the ideal of the Pious and the scribes (Matt. 12.18–21＝Isa. 42.1–4):

> Behold, my servant whom I have chosen,
> my beloved with whom my soul is well pleased.
> I will put my spirit upon him,
> and he shall proclaim justice to the Gentiles,
> He will not wrangle or cry aloud,
> nor will any one hear his voice in the streets;
> he will not break a bruised reed
> or quench a smouldering wick,
> till he brings justice to victory;
> and in his name will the Gentiles hope.

Is this to be the new Law? Will he not break his staff over those who are accused? It is no accident that in the days of the 'Third Reich' it was at this point that the attack of grace was felt to be a danger to the state. The text for the Twelfth Sunday after Trinity—Matt. 12.20—was once seized by the secret state-police. Its circulation had brought agitation against the state's legislation for euthanasia. It is true that the justice which Jesus brings is not a political law; but, as God's justice, it excludes all 'justice' that conflicts with humaneness. The destruction of 'valueless life' cannot be justified by the attack of grace. Such a concept does not even exist before the judgement throne of grace. Every life has value for God's justice which Jesus brings. The enemies of Jesus understood better than his followers that Jesus embodied the provocative attack of grace.

The world perceived he was an enemy. His own family thought he was out of his mind (Mark 3.21). The Pharisees and the

Herodians lay in wait for him and involved him in disputes (Mark 2.16; 3.6; 8.11). The central authorities in Jerusalem kept a watch on him by means of officials from the circles of the scribes and Pharisees (Mark 3.22; 7.1). He himself warns his disciples of the 'leaven' of the Pharisees and Herod Antipas (Mark 8.15). He reserved his sharpest criticism for the existing religious and secular powers because they act as agents of destruction. What Matthew makes Jesus deliver as a concentrated attack (Matt. 23) may represent a collection of sayings which were uttered on different occasions. But, even where they reflect the later differences of the Church with rabbinic legalistic piety, they bear the stamp of the original conflict.

Jesus also came into conflict with the Sadducees (Matt. 16.6). The quarrel was begun by the party of the priestly aristocracy. It showed how little Jesus attacked his rivals with radical arguments of an eschatological sort. They tell him the queer story of the woman who married seven men in succession in accordance with the Law. Whose wife, then, would she be in the resurrection? The question assumes that the Sadducees were looking for a theological *reductio ad absurdum* of the doctrine of the resurrection, which was not attested in the Law. Jesus is not disconcerted. He produces a strange 'scriptural proof' from the Law. He does not set off any eschatological fireworks. He replies on the level of his opponents. But even so he defeats them by his unusual quotation of the words of God's self-revelation from the story of Moses' call. God made himself known to Moses at the burning bush with the declaration, 'I am the God of Abraham and the God of Isaac and the God of Jacob' (Ex. 3.6). If God names the deceased patriarchs in the same breath as his own name, then his name is qualified by the names of the patriarchs and the dead share in his life. Curious logic? Yes—in its method, at any rate. But concealed behind it is a living experience of God. God's name is his nature, just as man's name is part of his nature. And just as God links his nature in such a way with those long dead, so his breath of life fills them with his vitality. 'He is not the God of the dead but of the living. You are quite wrong' (Mark 12.18–27).

At this point the possiblity emerges that Jesus expected not only a coming resurrection of the dead, as the apocalyptists had done previously. The indication is that he knew of an unbroken life of man which death could not destroy. This need not be understood in the sense of the Greek view of the 'immortality of the soul'. Jesus was not a philosopher and he knew nothing of an isolated soul which is a never-dying substance of man, so to speak. Immortality was not a predicate of man or of a 'higher' part of him in Jesus' view, but part of the glorious nature of God. He knew of God's living word to man and its superiority to death. God, who is the Creator of the world, speaks in creative realities. As he speaks he acts. In the course of addressing man he draws him through death and gives him a share in his heavenly life. His *word* is immortal. Just how immortal is shown by this story. Jesus kindles the sparks of the Gospel from the hard stone of the Law. The fundamental issue is the First Commandment, or, more precisely, its preface 'I am the Lord, thy God'. Water springs from the rock of the Law; 'thy God'—the meaning of the Gospel. Through this word God gives eternal life here and now.

The words recorded by Luke in the parable about the rich man and poor Lazarus (Luke 16.19–31) are probably to be understood in the sense of this present eternal life experienced here and now. The same is true of Jesus' word to the repentant thief. 'Truly, I say to you, today you will be with me in Paradise' (Luke 23.43). These two texts were given rough treatment in the previous generation. After the First World War the idea of judgement was given new life by a theology which was extremely eschatological in outlook, in contrast to a shallow idealism which taught the immortality of the soul. There was an attempt to interpret these sayings in a radically eschatological manner. This was only possible, however, by means of a mistaken etymology. It is true that body and soul are not distinguished in either of the two passages, nor is it stated that the body is mortal, the soul immortal. The whole man is meant throughout. But man is told that salvation or judgement is present. The statements about the present and the future nature of eternal life are not calculated systematically. The statements conflict. Each excludes the other for all normal purposes of thought. They may, however, be validly combined in paradox, as the present and future of God's rule or the mutually exclusive indicative and imperative of the Sermon on the Mount.

This was not sufficient, however, for the modern theology of judgement and its radical outlook. It was concerned about the seriousness and purity of Christian teaching about the resurrection.

It did not see that even on this plane Jesus employed the attack of compassion. It wanted to decide everything by 'the last things' and forgot that our present certainty of life is encompassed within the here and now, which is 'prior to the last things'. It attributed promises that man is already going through death and judgement to the Johannine Christ (John 5.24), but not to the synoptic Jesus. Luther did not only think of God coming, but of God already active in his word. Consequently he discovered what our two texts are saying. 'Wherever God speaks to a man, whoever he is— whether in wrath or in mercy—that man is truly immortal. The nature of the God who speaks and the word that he speaks make it clear that we are creatures with whom God desires to speak till eternity, in his own immortal way.'

Jesus does not attack the world with abstract 'seriousness' but with the eternal compassion of God and the compassionate promise of eternal life. The world cannot bear this attack. It makes the attacker the attacked. It makes him—and his followers —suffer. For us attack and suffering are separate. For him they conceal each other. His suffering does not follow his attack. His attack is made in the form of humiliation and suffering.

7. *The Preparation*

Jesus' sufferings begin long before the dark and bitter experiences of the last days of his life, which are described in the Gospels and which are usually grouped together under the term 'Passion'. His suffering begins with his baptism, or rather with his election as Son at his baptism. The Gospels give no indication of a process of development. The final Passion is foreshadowed very early in his public ministry. Fairly near the beginning Mark records that after the second Sabbath-conflict the Pharisees held a conference with the Herodians, at which it was decided to 'destroy' him (Mark 3.6). According to Luke there was an attempt to lynch him in the usual Jewish manner by throwing him down from the edge of a cliff and stoning him—after his first sermon in Nazareth (Luke 4.28–29). Meanwhile Jesus is informed by some Pharisees that Herod Antipas is after him. When warned and urged to flee, Jesus answers, 'Go and tell that fox, "Behold, I cast out demons and perform cures today and tomorrow, and the third day I finish my course. Nevertheless I must go on my way today and tomorrow and the day following; for it cannot be that a prophet should perish away from Jerusalem" ' (Luke 13.31–33).

In the so-called predictions of the Passion it is possible to hear something of the unrest of Jesus' life. All the synoptic Gospels record these sayings, even if in slightly different forms. A comparison of the texts with one another (cf. Mark 8.31; 9.31; 10.33–34) shows that not only the number 'three' is stylized, but their form also is determined by the viewpoint of the early Church. The details are too precise (e.g. Mark 10.34), in spite of some inaccuracies (e.g. Mark 8.31 and 9.31 speaks of the resurrection 'after three days'; Matthew and Luke 'on the third day'), for them to be absolutely true as they stand. The fact that the terminology is influenced by testimonies of the expected Son of Man (Dan. 7) and the Servant of God (Isa. 53) does not exclude them from having a historical kernel. If Jesus united what were originally two unrelated expectations, we should have had to do with the expression of this direct consciousness of mission in the sayings which were influenced by the early Church. Jesus was conscious of having been chosen as Son, Son of Man (i.e. the Righteous) *and* Servant of God. It is difficult to imagine that he had no foreknowledge of his violent end. If in former times a prophet's destiny meant suffering, to be the chosen Servant of God meant it even more. The way was foreshadowed for Jesus by all three figures:

> Many are the afflictions of the righteous;
> but the Lord delivers him out of them all (Ps. 34.20).

If this was true of the pious as such, then it was especially true of the eschatological deliverer.

At any rate, it is important that suffering is understood as an experience both for the righteous (Ps. 34.20b; Wisd. 2–5) and for the Servant of God (Isa. 52.13–53.12). Isaiah 53, as is well known, sets out to be a hymn of victory (Isa. 52.13; 53.10–12):

> Behold my servant shall prosper,
> he shall be exalted and lifted up,
> and shall be very high . . .
> Yet it was the will of the Lord to bruise him;
> he has put him to grief.
> When he makes himself an offering for sin,
> he shall see his offspring, he shall prolong his days;

the will of the Lord shall prosper in his hand;
he shall see the fruit of the travail of his soul and be satisfied;
by his knowledge shall the righteous one, my servant,
make many to be accounted righteous;
and he shall bear their iniquities.
Therefore I will divide him a portion with the great,
and he shall divide the spoil with the strong;
because he poured out his soul to death,
and was numbered with the transgressors;
yet he bore the sin of many,
and made intercession for the transgressors.

The Righteous One, the Son of Man, the Servant of God, takes the path of humiliation to exaltation by God. It would be curious if Jesus, living in a world of such realities, had only known about them theoretically. His knowledge compelled him to put his election as ambassador into effect. His rejection of the official messianic ideal was the logical sequence of his assent to the electing call of God (cf. the change of key in the account of Mark 8.27–30 and 8.31–32).

This gives rise to an important principle for our investigation. The fact that humiliation and exaltation are never spoken of separately is understandable from the tendency of the divine promises and from Jesus' answer. The texts reproduce a very credible situation both historically and psychologically. The supposition that Jesus predicted his death but not his victory would be meaningless. Only the circumstance that God's promise of his election contained within it the equally certain promise of victory over death loosened his tongue to utter these predictions of his Passion. This does not mean that Jesus predicted the future like a clairvoyant. The possibility that, living at the summit of existence as he did, he may have had such knowledge of a higher sort is certainly not excluded. Nevertheless, such a possibility would not be of great weight. The important fact is that he expected his death as an event which was a necessary part of the mission which God had given him. By virtue of God's promise, however, this death was 'swallowed up in victory' (Isa. 25.8; I Cor. 15.54). One cannot separate God's call and Jesus' response any more than one can separate the texts about death and resurrection from each other; nor can one isolate the New Testament

R

message of Good Friday from that of Easter Day. Both together constitute one and the same promised event. The world is given hope.

The Gospels consider it important to know about the inseparability of humiliation and exaltation. For the life of Jesus of Nazareth manifests the pattern which the lives of those who regard him as the final messenger is to take. He is dependent on the service and witness of his followers. He and his followers share a common fate. The law of his existence is the law of their discipleship (Mark 8.34–38).

> If any man would come after me let him deny himself
> and take up his cross and follow me.
> For whosoever would save his life shall lose it;
> and whoever loses his life for my sake and the gospel's
> will save it.
> For what does it profit a man, to gain the whole world
> and forfeit his life?
> For what can a man give in return for his life?
> For whoever is ashamed of me and of my words
> in this adulterous and sinful generation,
> of him will the Son of Man also be ashamed,
> when he comes in the glory of his Father
> with the holy angels.

Suffering means self-denial. Self-denial means the end of oneself. Only if one is ready to aim at this and maintain this beneath the cloak of everyday life can one know who Jesus really is.

From the beginning, to share in Jesus' life as a disciple means to share in his death. Hence the dismay of over-impetuous candidates. Hence, too, the warning and reminder which constantly attends the life of the disciples and the searching questioning of the existence of his 'novices'—'Can you drink the cup which I drink; or be baptized with the baptism with which I am baptized?' (Mark 10.38).

But this question is not the result of the principle which lies at the root of a pessimistic view of the world. It stems, rather, from a man who guarantees in his own person the new world of God. Jesus stands between the extremes of abstract radicalism, between abstract possibility on the one hand and abstract necessity on the other. Unconditional, abstract possibility is Satan (cf.

p. 129 above); this is the possibility of breaking through all restrictions at will and out into the far corners of the world. It was against this that Jesus promised to secure his chosen followers (Matt. 16.18b). Absolute, abstract necessity, on the other hand, is the legalism which sees only the restrictions of life and prefers to have it so, even if it means raising restrictions where God himself set none. The basic expression of this in religion is asceticism. Jesus, in contrast to the Baptist, was no ascetic (Matt. 11.19). He and his disciples did not submit to any rule of fasting; in fact, Jesus' presence meant a marriage-feast for them (Mark 2.18–19). Fasting (Matt. 6.16–18), at all events, was to be supplemented by giving practical help, and by breaking the curse of evil by which men are afflicted (Mark 9.29). Jesus rejected both abstract possibility and abstract necessity in choosing naked reality; this is the will of the Father, to which the will of man is able to respond. For Jesus this naked reality means the Cross. Jesus was able to require his own followers to take up their cross because he knew about the one who had commissioned him, and who had sent both him and them into a world of wolves (Matt. 10.16):

Behold, I send you out as sheep in the midst of wolves;
so be wise as serpents and innocent as doves.

His followers are not to do as Rome does when in Rome. To 'accept' the world does not mean to capitulate to it. Solidarity with the world can only be realized in separation. Only in resistance is acquiescence permitted. To say the right word in such a situation the spirit of God himself is needed. But the disciples do not need to seek it. In such times of need the Spirit will be given them; the Spirit of the Father will speak through them (Matt. 10.19–20). The disciples enter the battlefield of the world as victors, though unrecognized (Luke 6.22–23):

Blessed are you when men hate you,
and when they exclude you and revile you,
and cast out your name as evil on account of the Son of Man.
Rejoice in that day and leap for joy,
for, behold, your reward is great in heaven;
for so their fathers did to the prophets.

Reward? Yes, reward. Men cannot earn it, but God gives it to his own, who know they are dependent on his mercy (Matt.

20.1–16). God is God. Do we wish to restrict his goodness? The
life of faith is a fight. Are the picked band of soldiers only to fight
but never conquer? The reward which is spoken of in the Gospels
is never something that can be calculated or earned, of course. It
is the triumph of the new world. It is divine grace. It is the kingdom,
and the power and the glory of God.

8. *The Sacrifice*

But triumph is preceded by struggle, attack and suffering—
not just in theory but in reality. Events follow one another in
rapid succession. Anyone who wants to know how God makes
history should read Mark 11, 14 and 15 consecutively.

Jesus decides to go up to Jerusalem for the Passover. His
intention is to challenge Jerusalem, both theocracy and populace,
to decision. Strange presentiments thrill through the inner circle
of followers. 'They were on the road going up to Jerusalem, and
Jesus was walking ahead of them; and they were amazed, and those
who followed were afraid' (Mark 10.32).

Jesus enters Jerusalem (Mark 11.1–10). The crowds of pilgrims,
who are going to celebrate the festival commemorating Israel's
deliverance from Egypt, flock together to David's city from every
land in which there are communities of the Jewish Diaspora. The
Galilaean pilgrims are intoning the traditional, ancient psalms
of the liturgy. The rest of the crowd joins in. There does not appear
to have been any question of a messianic demonstration on the
crowd's part; there was certainly no question of an armed rising
to make Jesus Messiah. Jesus forestalled any such proclamation
by his choice of animal on which to ride into Jerusalem. The ass,
the poor man's animal, does not carry David's heir, but the servant
who wears the uniform of wretchedness.

More important than Jesus' entry is the first thing he does—
usually called 'the cleansing of the Temple' (Mark 11.15–19).
The fourth Gospel places it at the beginning (John 2.14–17) of
Jesus' ministry, which, it is suggested, lasts two or three years.
This position gives the event special emphasis. In fact, it must
have been an unheard-of attack by Jesus on the rights of the
temple-state. It is true that Jesus does not penetrate into the
temple-buildings, but only into the 'forecourt of the Gentiles',
where the money-changers who have been authorized by the

priesthood exchange foreign money into the old Hebrew currency, which is used in the temple-area. He drives these people out of the forecourt along with those who are selling sacrificial animals, without interference from the temple-police or the Roman security guards. Jesus is not acting here as a reformer of the Jewish cult. How improvised everything is and how unsystematic and ineffective in view of the intricacy of the cult system. Jesus' attack is an eschatological sign, to which, for one awful moment, the proper authorities could find no effective counter-measure. People expected that the time of the Messiah would be a time when the Temple was renewed. In other religions, also, a king's entry into power was linked with the ritual cleansing of the Temple. The Babylonian New Year festival and the Hellenistic myth of the Emperor regard the cleansing of the Temple as the omen of a new era. There is a lot to be said for the supposition that Jesus, by what he did—which went far beyond the scope of prophetic authority—aimed to break the particularism of the theocracy and declare the Temple a universal place of prayer, as a late prophecy had promised would happen in the last days (Isa. 56.7). All four Gospels show the high priests countering this eschatological demonstration with the question of his 'authority' (Mark 11.27–33).

Jesus challenges the responsible leaders of the theocratic state to come to a clear decision either for or against God's kingly rule —the theme of his message and from the beginning a threat to the foundations of the theocracy. This decision is made. It is made in silence. Public opinion, which is still uncertain, makes open arrest by the temple-authorities appear too daring. On the other hand, the coming festival urges them to dispose swiftly of the uncomfortable Galilaean who cannot be fitted into any existing category. Hence the decision to arrest him unobtrusively (Mark 14.1–2). A suitable helper is found in Jesus' closest circle—the disciple Judas Iscariot (Mark 14.10–11). The motives behind his offer to betray Jesus are as obscure as his name. If his first name denotes that a village of southern Judaea was his birthplace, this would make him the only non-Galilaean. If it means that he was an Assassin, a terrorist, his unreliability is intelligible. According to the fourth Gospel he was the treasurer of the disciples and acted from avarice (John 12.6). All conjectures, however, verge upon fantasy, even those which suggest he wanted to compel

Jesus to take direct political action at last by his gamble. The tradition is incomplete at this point, but its silence is a guarantee of reliability. Legend would be much more verbose. Matthew records the sum of the blood money—thirty pieces of silver (Matt. 26.15). This is the price of the penalty for damages which had to be paid for a slave if he was killed by an ox (Ex. 21.32).

While the net is being spread Jesus holds his Last Supper on the Thursday evening. The preparations for the meal in a house in Jerusalem (Mark 14.12–16) are as mysterious as the preparations for the entry into Jerusalem (Mark 11.1–6—the foal of an ass). According to the Synoptics this Thursday was Nisan 14, in other words the afternoon prior to the evening when the Passover began. The Last Supper, therefore, was a Passover meal. According to John the Thursday was Nisan 13. John's chronology suits the course of events better than the synoptic view. A number of factors are against the synoptic view: on the Passover festival night Jesus goes to Gethsemane; the guards and some of the disciples are carrying weapons; there is a sitting of the Sanhedrin during the night of the Feast; Simon of Cyrene is coming from the field (i.e. work). All this and much else besides could hardly have taken place after the commencement of the Passover night; this seems to favour the Johannine chronology, which puts these events a day earlier. In that case the Last Supper would not be a Passover meal and one could see in the anticipation of the meal Jesus' intention of characterizing the new order by means of a new calendar and a new meal.

More important than the date of the meal, however, is what took place at it. We have three accounts of the Last Supper (Mark 14.17–25; Matt. 26.20–29; Luke 22.14–23) plus the recitation of the words of institution in Paul (I Cor. 11.23–25). We shall forego a complete discussion of the literary, historical and theological questions and content ourselves with brief suggestions of a general nature together with an exposition of particular motifs connected with the meal.

Firstly, then, the four texts have a liturgical rather than a historical character. The formal character of the words of institution conceals the ancient character of the tradition. The differences are to be explained by the sacramental practices of the primitive Christian communities. Obviously, this same factor makes it more difficult for us to ascertain what Jesus actually said. Critical study and comparison of the texts, however, has established that two forms of tradition are presupposed—the Marcan text on which Matthew is dependent and the Pauline text to which Luke is similar. Little can be said about the age of the two forms. If Mark is posited as a basis, this suggests that the Lord's Supper originated in the very much richer context of a house liturgy, which was divided into four parts, and at each of which a cup of wine (i.e. four cups altogether) was passed round after prayers (i.e. blessings). Our accounts say nothing of this. But they permit the reconstruction of what Jesus did at that time. Following the grace before the main Passover meal, Jesus probably spoke these words of interpretation over the bread: 'Take, this is my body.' Separate from this, following the grace after the meal, he spoke these words of interpretation over the third of the four cups: 'This is my blood of the covenant which is shed for many.' During the feast the *Hallel*-Psalms (hymns of thanksgiving)— at first only Psalm 113, but later Psalms 114–118—were recited (Mark 14.26).

It is important to remember that our celebration of the Lord's Supper today represents only a fragment of a much richer liturgical formula. The two words of institution (over the bread *and* the wine) have been brought closer together and have thus received a meaning which they did not have in their original setting. Even so, however, it is easy to see—especially if one compares the formula of the Pauline account—that there is no interest in 'holy substances'. None of the texts makes the equation, bread = flesh or wine = blood. Rather, they all speak of the body (i.e. the person) of Jesus, and of the blood of the covenant, which in Paul and Luke is related not to the wine, but to the cup (and its contents, of course). No holy materials are administered, but a transaction is completed and interpreted.

What, then, is this transaction, which is recorded in these different ways, meant to affirm? There are three main themes. Firstly, the death of Jesus is announced (i.e. proclaimed)—to those who share in the meal. What this death—as the Son's end which is in accordance with the will of God—achieves, is made available to men. The representative of man gives his life for this. He takes our place and by his sacrifice makes possible the forgiveness of sins. Secondly, God makes a new covenant. The covenant-meal, of which Ex. 24.9-10 speaks (Moses with three companions

and the seventy elders—cf. v. 8), is renewed. At this table-fellow-
ship God's chosen band is finally stamped with the character of his
family. Jesus' eating and drinking with sinners finds its permanent
expression here. Thirdly, the future messianic banquet is antici-
pated. This is why eschatological jubilation prevails (Mark 14.25).

> Truly, I say to you, I shall not drink again of the fruit of the
> vine, until that day when I drink it new in the kingdom of
> God.

Whereas Matthew and Mark close with this, Luke provides the
same eschatological viewpoint *before* the words of institution—
with the addition of a sentence about future eating.

The questions posed by the Reformed churches—both Lutheran
and Reformed—in their teaching about the Lord's Supper move
on a plane where the New Testament texts do not really permit
a straightforward answer. It is time to let the texts speak for
themselves more forcibly. Only if they mediate their gift with
new power once more shall we be able to appreciate the Reformers'
motives and understand the words as a stimulus instead of
repeating them mechanically. The gift of the Lord's Supper
is none other than the living Lord himself. His sacrificial death
incorporates us in the new world order, the pact of God, and
allows the victorious world of God to dawn in the figure of his
disguised Son. The material nature of this event conceals the
existence of the living Lord. The sacred meal seals the present *and*
the future of God's kingly rule. It is its paradoxical unity. . . .

What follows defies description. It is best to read the Gospels
themselves. Jesus goes to the Garden of Gethsemane (Mark
14.32–42). He wrestles in prayer with God over the final certainty
of his path. His fear and trembling in the face of death and his
offering of himself enable us to catch a glimpse of his very real
humanity. What is it that makes him afraid? Death and its
physical pain? Certainly Jesus, as a man, is afraid of this. But far
more terrible for him is the fact that death comes to him to
execute the judgement of God. Gethsemane is the answer, in
fact, to the question of Psalm 90:

> Who considers the power of thy anger,
> and thy wrath according to the fear of thee?

Who, indeed, considers the power of God's anger in death? No one. We are all aware of death as something terrible, because it brings pain with it, because it separates us from one another, because it puts an end to our plans and our activity, and because it is incalculable. But that God's anger is executed in it is something we do not consider. We do not believe it. At the most we are indifferent to it. In fact, most men would laugh at it. The question of Psalm 90 is lost in emptiness. Only once has the question been taken seriously. In the Garden of Gethsemane Jesus was aware of the power of God's wrath. He trembled before it. He wrestled with God, therefore, that God might spare him this dreadful experience. His final prayer is as paradoxical as the reality he introduces, as paradoxical as his whole earthly existence.

> Abba, Father all things are possible to thee;
> remove this cup from me;
> yet not what I will, but what thou wilt (Mark 14.36).

The critical hour of Gethsemane is Jesus' final temptation. The crowd of guards approaches, led by Judas, with swords and cudgels (Mark 14.43–52). Jesus is arrested. And the disciples? They 'all forsook him and fled', including the one who tried to strike out wildly at random (v. 50). Jesus' picked band, which has just been made God's family by the Last Supper, disperses —at the first appearance of danger.

The trial of Jesus begins. We possess no legal records of what happened during it. There might never have been any. The Gospels offer none and have no desire to. The possible recorders had fled. Only Peter kept quiet in the background, where it was possible to hear something—but only very little—at second-hand. We do not know how the account of the trial, which mentions two hearings and two sentences, arose. What happened later in public could have been witnessed by many people. But what took place indoors could only have become known later. Moreover, at the time events tumbled over each other too rapidly. The trial was conducted in the form of a summary jurisdiction. Jesus was condemned according to martial law, so to speak. But by whom? By the Jewish Sanhedrin or by the Roman procurator? Or by both? Scholars are still divided on this issue even to the present day.

According to the Gospels Jesus was tried by both Jews and Romans. The trial before the Sanhedrin (Mark 14.53–72) was followed by the trial before Pilate, which resulted in Jesus being condemned by the procurator (Mark 15.2–15).

Lietzmann's suggestion still seems the most illuminating. 'We may affirm fairly confidently that the council (the Sanhedrin) did not arrive at any legal condemnation on the ground of blasphemy; if it had, it would have had to put Jesus to death by stoning on its own authority. This was prescribed in the Law and was still carried out, as we see in the case of Stephen (Acts 7), for instance. It is a mistake—shared, of course, by the Gospels and encouraged by them—to think that the Sanhedrin did not possess the right to pass and execute the death penalty. But the recorded sequence of events, which we ought undoubtedly to accept, shows rather that the Jewish authorities—probably for very good reasons—refused to settle the matter by means of a religious trial and preferred to hand Jesus over to the Roman authorities on a charge of sedition. This is clear from Mark 15.1.' The leaders of the theocratic state refused to accept responsibility. In this way they avoided any violation of a major festival and at the same time ensured that the whole affair should be thoroughly cleaned up.

The trial before Pilate was hastened by a special circumstance. 'As it happened, the man known as Barabbas was then in custody with the rebels who had committed murder in the rising. And the crowd appeared asking for the usual favour.' Roman justice allowed an accusation to be quashed on the occasion of a special festival and an appeal for mercy to be allowed. In addition, there was the Jewish custom of the Passover amnesty. The initiative came from the people. From the very beginning Barabbas—a Zealot and a 'patriot'—was the chief character as far as they were concerned. The case of Jesus was a most inconvenient interruption in their eyes; it threatened to frustrate, or at least to complicate, the plan they had prepared some time ago. But the demonstrators gained their objective, and the political prisoner was released. Jesus took over the destiny of this man, who was called 'Son of Abbas' after his father, or Jesus Bar-Abbas according to the special tradition of Matthew (27.16). More important than the idea that here one Jesus meets another Jesus is the fact that here substitution in the literal sense of the word takes place. Barabbas is the only man of whom it can be literally said that he received his life back afresh, because Jesus suffered death in his stead.

Pilate handed Jesus over to the Roman guards to be whipped. This initial punishment was so barbaric that many a condemned man hardly survived it. He was led inside the barracks and dressed in a soldier's cloak, and a crown of thorns was coiled on his head. The soldiers were delighted at the possibility of swearing allegiance to a real 'king'—the king of fools!

Luther summed up the events of this night in the following words. 'Thus our dear Lord Christ suffered, not in secret nor through those who had no authority, but publicly and through those who occupied seats of public authority, in order that we might not be troubled when we see that both forms of authority, spiritual and secular, are against God. Christ's Passion means, as we confess and say in the Christian faith, "I believe in Jesus Christ, suffered under Pontius Pilate." Hence, it has always happened and still happens today that Christians and righteous martyrs are put to death by the accepted authorities, both spiritual and secular. . . . Prophets are murdered not by conspirators, but by those who sit in authority and have been duly elected. All blood that is shed for Christ's sake is shed by those who are kings, princes, judges, senates, etc., of secular power, and by bishops, preachers, etc., of spiritual power. A prophetic death is one that is ordered by the accepted authorities' (Sermon of 22.3.1534).

9. *The End*

The narrative that follows, telling how Jesus was led away to Golgotha and was crucified there, has the character, even more strongly than anything else in the Gospel records up to this point, of a preached message rather than a literal report. This does not mean that the whole episode is historically unreliable. On the contrary, the most important statements—the entry into Jerusalem, the cleansing of the Temple, the Last Supper, the arrest and trial, the interplay of spiritual and secular authorities and the condemnation itself—are among the best attested data of historical writing in late antiquity. The general trend of events is reproduced not only by the first three Gospels but also by John—a unity seldom attained elsewhere in the Gospels. In detail, however, the Synoptics not only give a different picture from John, they also give different pictures from each other. Our habit of overlooking the differences in detail is the result of the general tenor of the narrative. The Gospels owe this to the early Church, which saw the sufferings, death and resurrection of Jesus not only predicted but also foreshadowed and prefigured in the great texts of the Old Testament. Psalms 22, 31 and 69 and the Suffering Servant passage, Isaiah 53, formed the basic texts by means of which the terrible experiences of Jesus' Passion were given new colour and meaning. Meditation on the 'Gospel of the Passion' in the Old Testament in the light of these experiences, combined with meditation on the events in the light of the old prophetic texts, ensured that unity of scriptural word and historical event which we are always coming across in the person and work of Jesus of Nazareth. The witnesses who proclaimed this history and the hearers who accepted it were certain that God himself was at work in the suffering and death of Jesus.

This uniform certainty, nevertheless, gave the individual evangelists sufficient scope for each one to impart his own emphasis to his account. Because of the general parallelism in the different accounts and because of the Gospel-harmonizations, such as we find in our hymn-books, we are accustomed to even out the differences. As a result not only a great deal of historical light and shade but also a great deal of the originality and freshness of the various different accounts is lost. Regard to the variety and differences of the evidence enables us to recapture the original richness of the tradition. All the accounts are dealing with the same man and they all understand him as the one who by his death restores lost hope to the world. But they proclaim him in different ways.

Simply to ask 'what actually happened' would result in a whole heap of contradictions. For example, according to Mark and Matthew the two robbers who were crucified with Jesus agree in cursing and blaspheming, together with those passing by (Mark 15.32). According to Luke, on the other hand, only the one blasphemes, while the other rebukes him for his words and turns to ask Jesus not to forget him when his kingdom arrives (Luke 23.32–42). Historically the two accounts do not overlap. Nor are they complementary. They are mutually exclusive. Put pointedly, Luke is talking about quite different people from Mark and Matthew, as far as historical reporting goes. But it is precisely in this way that the special message of each evangelist is brought out. Mark and Matthew are saying that Jesus died between two hopelessly impenitent criminals. This was the way Jesus silently maintained his brotherhood and solidarity with them—to the bitter end. Luke, on the other hand, wants to show that Jesus fulfilled his vocation of Saviour not only during his lifetime but even in death, and that even in the closing minutes when there is nothing more to hope for those who repent can find forgiveness.

Moreover, the words of Jesus on the cross cannot simply be added together with the help of the fourth Gospel to form the 'seven words' which we are familiar with. At all events, if we do that we do not receive a historically reliable picture. Every word leads its own life, basically. The whole Jesus is some-where in every word. And every word helps the bloody events on Golgotha to take on a new aspect for us. We should try to read and understand each Gospel on its own first of all, as if there were no second, third or fourth Gospel beside it. Only then do we hear the full tones which the chorus of voices singing anti-phonally—or polyphonally—makes it possible to hear. According to the first two Gospels Jesus dies with the cry from Ps. 22.8, 'My God, my God, why hast thou forsaken me?' (Mark 15.29). This has often been understood as an expression of deepest despair. Luther regarded this expression and the 'cry of death' which follows it as signs that Jesus experienced the hell of God-forsakeness and even rejection by God. The reference to Psalm 22 by the evangelists affirms a great deal more however; Jesus dies in harmony with God's will as he prays Psalm 22, a hymn which resounds in praise of God. According to Mark and Matthew Jesus said nothing on the cross but this. This one episode is enough for the complete understanding of his death. According to Luke, however, Jesus prays first of all for his executioners (23.34); he then promises the repentant evil-doer that he will be received into Paradise (23.43). After the words of Ps. 31.6, 'Father, into thy hands I commend my spirit', Jesus breathes his last (23.46). Jesus dies with the normal evening prayer, said by every pious Jew before going to sleep, on his lips (23.46); it is the evening of the world. According to John Jesus utters three further words: the charge to his mother and the beloved disciple (John 19.26–27); the word in fulfilment of Scripture (Ps. 22.16; 69.22), 'I thirst' (19.28); and, finally, 'It is finished' (19.30). All three sentences are pregnant with meaning and rich in association, especially the last, which marks the conclusion of the divine work of salvation.

A great number of legendary embellishments have been incorporated in the tradition. What is felt to be legendary, however, is usually the forcible declaration of what is really most important but can no longer be expressed by a literal, historical account. What a good thing the evangelists were still at home in a charismatic climate and did not produce learned historical studies! Jesus hangs on the cross for six hours, from nine in the morning till three in the afternoon—a comparatively short time considering that those crucified were often tortured to death for several days by the burning heat of the sun and the cold of the night. During this period, the evangelists report, strange things happened. About midday darkness settled 'over the whole land' for three hours (Mark 15.33). The world hid its face in sadness, as was prophesied in Isa. 13.10 (cf. Mark 13.24) of the day of God:

> The sun will be dark at its rising
> and the moon will not shed its light.

Amos (8.9) had prophesied that the sun would set at midday. Yahweh's day is here! Good Friday is the day of the Lord in the strict sense—the day of his coming. *Dies irae, dies illa!* This is the day of judgement *and* mercy, final judgement and final mercy. This day begins with sunset. What the world experiences as its end is in fact its beginning. That midday is the eve of the world.

When Jesus dies the curtain of the Temple is 'torn in two, from top to bottom' (Mark 15.38). According to Matthew (27.52–53) there is even an earthquake, rocks split and graves open. 'And many bodies of the saints who had fallen asleep were raised, and coming out of the tombs after his resurrection they went into the holy city and appeared to many.' This is clearly a later interpolation. The death of Jesus breaks the curse of death, so that even before Easter those who have been awakened rise from their tombs. Later still another reader saw the contradiction and 'corrected' it: it was only 'after Jesus' resurrection' that they appeared in Jerusalem. Is this a reference to the descent of Christ into Hades, which only occurs in later writings (I Peter 3.19; 4.6)?

Mark concludes his account with the words of the Roman officer who is in command of the guard: 'Truly, this man was a son of God!' (Mark 15.39). The High Mass of Golgotha, the antithesis in some ways to that High Mass which Augustus celebrated on the Capitol at Rome in the year 17 BC, is over. Pontius Pilate and the leaders of both the theocratic state and the Roman Empire are the acolytes at the Mass. But the priest is not any Pontifex Maximus of Roman or Jewish origin, but Jesus himself. Priest and sacrifice are here identical. This priest offered himself for the world. Another paradox! No less paradoxical is the fact that the eternal God was active in the activity of the Son.

Are we beginning to find ourselves in the region of religious fantasy? No! This is not the dying god found in the myths and mythologies of other religions. This is the death of a historical person. The stake on which he is hung—only John mentions nails and the print of the nails—is rammed firmly in the ground. The torture which the victim has to endure—he was scourged beforehand and spat on—is terrible. But the torture of loneliness is the worst. Deserted by his followers, he has to witness the collapse of his work, even before it has been properly established. All this is historically true, like any other earthly event which can be verified.

Historical parallels spring to mind. Is the death of Jesus like that of Socrates? No, neither in intent nor in fact. Socrates' whole work is one long experiment. By his philosophizing he aims to test the correctness of the Delphic Apollo's oracle, stating that no one was wiser than Socrates. Both Jesus and Socrates were put on trial, but the course of the Attic trial was properly regulated and Socrates was allowed to defend himself at great length. The punishment, also, was humane; Socrates was allowed to drink the cup of hemlock in his private cell, surrounded by friends and disciples, conversing philosophically. He went to his death gladly, knowing that death would release him from the fetters of the body and open the true life to him. The imprisoned bird would fly out through the doors of death into the eternal world of the gods. In Jerusalem, however, everything is the exact opposite. Jesus is arrested in a police-raid as a common criminal. His case is dispatched with great haste. The trials hardly deserve the name of trials. At the crucial moment everyone deserts him. The barbaric punishment of crucifixion is good enough for him. It is the most inhuman form of execution. It was taken over by the Persians from the steppe-dwellers of Asia and inherited by the Hellenistic rulers. The Romans used it for slaves and rebels. In fact, they made frequent use of it. Cicero made it clear he loathed the practice and was ashamed of it. It was not so much the physical torment that was the dreadful thing about it, but the humiliation and affront which was inflicted on men's natural, human feelings. Jesus died such a death; this is one of the facts of history.

There are a number of fixed points in the tradition that provide further historical reference. The disciples were with him right up to Gethsemane. Peter followed him, albeit furtively, even into the court of the High Priest. An anonymous disciple left his garment behind in the hands of the soldiers during the flight from Gethsemane (Mark 14.51). Who it was, we do not know. Perhaps Mark himself? At all events we may surmise that this figure who is otherwise quite irrelevant to what is taking place was an eyewitness. The same is true of Simon of Cyrene who was returning from the fields when he was press-ganged by the soldiers into carrying Jesus' cross. He is expressly described as 'the father of Alexander and Rufus' (Mark 15.21). In Paul's letter to the Romans (16.13) a Rufus and his mother are mentioned. This link in the tradition, like Mark's Gospel, points to Rome.

On the evening of that day a pious member of the Sanhedrin, Joseph of Arimathaea, dares to present a petition personally to Pilate and ask for Jesus' corpse. This brave man is only referred to at this point in the tradition, but his name is given in all four Gospels. Probably he was one of Pilate's personal circle. His motive is not stated. He appeals to the Romans to let Roman custom prevail and to hand over the corpse of the condemned man to his relatives or friends. By doing this he prevents the otherwise unceremonious disposal of the body. He has the body placed carefully, but without any rites of mourning, in a tomb in the rock. A stone is rolled in front of the entrance to the tomb so that neither animals nor men can get in. Two women, Mary of Magdala and Mary the mother of Joses, who had belonged to the Galilaean followers of Jesus, observed where Jesus was laid, after they had watched the crucifixion from a distance (Mark 15.42–47; cf. 15.40–41). Is this a pious legend? The discrepancies with Isa. 53.9 tell against such a view. Be that as it may, Joseph the Jew stands alongside the Roman centurion: they represent the two nations under whose authority Jesus lived and died.

The Greeks stand and live apart. But the peculiar prophecy which is to be found at the end of Plato's *Politics* sounds like a Greek prediction of Jesus' death. The prophecy contrasts the good and the bad. It is said of the good that, because he lives among the bad, he is 'whipped, tortured, put in chains and blinded in both eyes; finally, after suffering every abuse he is dragged to the cross and is at last brought round to the view that—in this world, at any rate—he ought not to be good, but only *appear* so'. Can the teachers of the early Church be blamed for seeing in this unexpected word about the Cross an oracle of the philosopher referring to Jesus? Socrates did not meet such a death. Socrates' death did not fulfil the requirement of the Platonic myth . . .

The stake rammed in the ground on Golgotha is empty. The corpse of the criminal is removed. So swiftly does the scene change. Only an inscription tells who died here a few hours ago. It is the normal 'title' which was fastened on the cross, giving the reason for the condemnation. It is recorded in all four Gospels. The inscription reads, 'The King of the Jews' (Mark 15.26). This reliable statement summarizes the events of the last day; the Jews had given the Procurator a realistic translation into Latin of the messianic title claimed by Jesus. Pilate must have agreed to act in order to nip the new religious revolt in the bud. But the abbreviation required by the inscription turned a messianic pretender into a Jewish Messiah. John's Gospel (19.19–22) made the scorn which lay in this abbreviation the occasion of a protest on the part of the High Priest, who wanted the words to be altered. But Pilate refused to yield. In addition, John has given the inscription a new form. It is supposed to have been expressed in Hebrew, Latin and Greek, and to have read:

Jesus of Nazareth, the King of the Jews.

When the initial letters of these Latin words are written down one after the other this produces the well-known I N R I. The expansion of the inscription is a Johannine commentary on historical fact. It describes the importance of Jesus' death on the cross for the world in which Jesus lived. We have come to know this world under the three aspects which are represented by the official languages on the inscription—the theocratic state, the Roman world-Empire and the Hellenistic world of 'modern' man.

s

Bultmann says that, according to John, 'this inscription is not only Pilate's revenge on the Jews, who forced him to pass the sentence he did and whom he is now insulting in return, but far more significantly it is a demonstration that the condemnation of Jesus is also the judgement of Judaism, which has abandoned the very hope which gave meaning to its existence, and the judgement of the world which surrenders its future for the security of the present. The judgement does not simply consist in the fact that Judaism has lost its king, however, or the fact that the world has lost its future. In that case, the crucifixion would be surrounded with a certain sense of tragedy; instead of which it is permeated by deep wrong. For the crucified Jesus really is the King. The kingship of hope is not destroyed as such, but re-established in a new sense. In fact, the Cross is Jesus' exaltation and glorification. Hence Pilate, like Caiaphas (John 11.50–51), has unwittingly and unintentionally become a prophet. The fact that his inscription, which reveals the price paid by the accusers, is to be understood as a prophecy is shown by the declaration that it was written in three languages (19.20); in other words, the Cross is an event that involves the whole world, and the King of the Jews is the Saviour of the world (4.42).'

10. *The Easter Event*

Mark's Gospel breaks off with a brief account of how the above-named women, who had watched the crucifixion from a distance and had marked the tomb where Jesus' body was laid, had gone to the tomb very soon after the end of the Sabbath, about sunrise, in order to embalm the corpse. As they went along they discussed, 'Who will roll away the stone for us from the entrance to the tomb?' When they looked in the direction of the tomb, however, they saw the huge stone had been rolled away. A vision of an angel had exhorted them in their terror, 'Do not be amazed! you seek Jesus of Nazareth who was crucified. He has risen, he is not here; see the place where they laid him. But go, tell his disciples and Peter that he is going before you to Galilee; there you will see him, as he told you.' At this the women fled from the tomb trembling and astonished and said nothing to anyone, because they were afraid (Mark 16.1–8). At this point Mark's Gospel comes to an end. This is the end of the story of Jesus of Nazareth for

Mark. There are three supplementary endings in later manuscripts. They affirm that Jesus has been exalted to be Lord and Ruler on the throne of God. He is not a dead figure of the past, but a living person of the present.

The evidence of Easter is that 'God has raised Jesus from the dead. God has exalted him as Lord over all the world. God has revealed him to his Church as the Living One.' This conviction sustains all the statements of the New Testament. Without the certainty of Easter there would be no New Testament—not one single line. Just as the earliest preaching of the Church is Easter preaching, so is the faith of Christianity Easter faith from the very beginning. It is not the message of Christmas but the preaching of the Resurrection that stands at the beginning of the history of the Church. If there were no Easter there would be no Christian Church.

If the account of Jesus' death had been the last word about him, then everything that is included in the ambiguous term 'Christianity' would be extinguished—the Christian festivals, the Christian Sunday, Christian worship, Christian doctrine, and Christian action both individual and social. Even more important, however, would be the extinction of that inward quality that Christianity has engendered and nourished, preserved and maintained—God's creative utterance, which rings out in preaching and is the theme of the sacraments of Baptism and the Lord's Supper. This affirmation is supported not only by the believing Christian (cf. I Cor. 15.17) but also by the critical scholarship of the historian. It is an unassailable position.

Because Christianity stands or falls by the evidence of Easter, we shall have to examine the statements in which it is formulated very carefully. We shall have to distinguish within the corpus of evidence between the Easter message, the Easter narratives and the Easter event.

The Easter *message* is older than the Easter narratives of our Gospels. It is to be found in its oldest form in Paul and in some primitive texts, which are preserved for us in the speeches of Peter in the Acts of the Apostles. In contrast to the Easter narratives the Easter message is uniform and unequivocal, although it has various forms and formulas. The New Testament allows us and, in fact, requires us to speak of the Easter message in the singular. There is only *one* message. The most concise expression of it is by Paul in one of the oldest passages of the New Testament: 'We believe that Jesus died and rose again . . .' (I Thess. 4.14). Paul took over from the early Church at Jerusalem—probably through the mediation of the Hellenistic community—the old, reliable credal formula, which he passes on as the kernel of preaching and faith (I Cor. 15.3-4):

> Christ died for our sins in accordance with the Scriptures,
> and was buried,
> and was raised on the third day in accordance with the Scriptures.

From the beginning Jesus' death and resurrection are understood as two moments in one and the same event. That his death as well as his resurrection was 'in accordance with the Scriptures' is confirmed by two facts. Firstly, God is active in both cases, realizing his eternal plan of salvation through them. Secondly, both events are elements in the efficacious word of God, by which he seeks to address mankind uniquely once and for all and to invite all the world to be saved. Both events have decisive significance for everyone who understands them. What 'was written' is true. It is true without a shadow of doubt for those who ratify it in faith, i.e. for those 'who believe in him that raised from the dead Jesus our Lord,

> who was put to death for our trespasses
> and raised for our justification' (Rom. 4.24-25).

Jesus' death and resurrection are not related in the form of a historical report aimed at spreading knowledge about a man's fate. His fate is published in the form of a message which comes from God and which aims to involve men and open their hearts to God's will.

The original existential aim of the Easter message is also evidenced by the primitive Easter formulas in the speeches of Peter in the Acts of the Apostles, a book which from the viewpoint of literary history is much later. These primitive formulas or Easter summaries are to be found in the speeches made by Peter before the people at Pentecost (Acts 2.22-24, 31-33, 36), upon the healing of the lame man at the Temple (3.13-15, 26), before the Sanhedrin on two separate occasions (4.10-12; 5.30-32), and in the house of the centurion Cornelius at Caesarea (10.37-43).

In addition there is a similar sort of Easter summary included by the Acts of the Apostles in Paul's preaching at Pisidian Antioch (13.28–31, 36–37). The important elements of the Easter message are these: its connection with the preaching of the crucifixion, the fulfilment of Scripture, the challenge to believe and repent. Here again in different ways those who were spectators become involved. The message 'cuts them to the heart' and sparks off the concrete question, 'What shall we do?' (2.37). It makes them wonder (4.13), but it also makes them very angry (5.33). When the message is heard, the Holy Spirit overcomes those who are listening (10.44). When it is understood it produces liberating joy, although it also excites contradiction and persecution (13.48–50). At all events, it is never simply a factual report; it is always an invitation which produces decision.

The primitive formula used by Paul in I Cor. 15.3–4 links the statements of Jesus' death and resurrection by means of an intervening clause 'and he was buried'. It is striking that the words 'in accordance with the Scriptures' are missing, although burial possesses a much more obvious scriptural basis than death and resurrection—one has only to think of Isa. 53.9. By its simplicity, however, the clause underlines that the death of Jesus was a real death and that his death, humanly speaking, was final and irrevocable. Paul (i.e. the tradition which he found already in existence) is obviously well aware of the idea of resurrection (i.e. the resurrection is understood as creative intervention by God, as a result of which a new situation is brought about—life instead of death). In the circles of the Pharisees it was believed that at the end of time the graves would open and the dead would walk out. Paul's earliest letter shows that he shared this view (I Thess. 4.16). The belief that Jesus' resurrection from the dead establishes the coming resurrection of those now dead occupies the whole of I Corinthians 15.

Alongside this view, however, stood another form of expectation: the Son of Man will come from heaven in majesty. If Jesus of Nazareth was regarded as the Son of Man, hidden in the form of the Servant of God, it was only a short step to hope that he would be transported from the humiliation of his earthly disguise into heavenly glory. This idea may have taken the crucifixion for granted; but unlike the idea of resurrection it did not contemplate the grave. Possibly even in the pre-Pauline period there was a belief that Jesus was exalted directly from the Cross to God. In this case resurrection and exaltation coincide; there is no interval between Good Friday and Easter Day. There is certainly no necessity for a special ascension. A faint suggestion of this view appears in the pre-Pauline hymn to Christ in Phil. 2.9, as in some of the primitive passages in the speeches of the Acts of the Apostles. 'God has made him both Lord and Christ, this Jesus whom you crucified' (Acts 2.36; 2.33). 'The God of our fathers *raised* Jesus whom you killed by hanging him on a tree. God *exalted* him at his right hand as Leader and Saviour' (5.30–31). This peculiar identity of resurrection and exaltation can be supported by scriptural proof (cf. Ps. 110.1 in Acts 2.34) as, for instance, Luke 24.56, which is unique in its context, shows. This same scriptural proof was later used by the author of the Letter to the Hebrews in giving evidence for the atoning work of Jesus Christ by reference to the prophets and Psalms (Heb. 1.3–13). As eternal High Priest Jesus sat down at the right hand of God's throne, after making purification for sins (1.3; 8.10; 10.12). He entered the heavenly shrine with his own blood (9.12), 'now to appear in the presence of God on our behalf' (9.24). Through the curtain, that is through his flesh, he has opened a new and living way to God for us (10.20). Christ's self-revelatory discourses in the fourth Gospel—a late work—speak of the Son going to the Father; exaltation is understood in a twofold sense—of the Son of Man being exalted *to* the Cross as well as *from* the Cross to the glory of the Father (John 3.14; 8.28; 12.32–34). Such statements are greatly modified in the narrative of the Passion and Easter (John 19–20).

But, although we are not able to pick out the historical connections of the tradition in detail, it is quite definite that the standard creed preserved by the Easter message was influenced not by the view of exaltation but by that of resurrection. There is a possibility, in fact, that the historical events which are so well known to us through the account of the burial—and other events whose historical point of reference is the tomb—gave greater precision to the statement about exaltation by linking it with the idea of resurrection from the tomb.

The Easter message awakened Easter faith, and this expressed itself in the *Easter narratives*. The variety and difference of these narratives stands in stark contrast to the uniformity and unequivocalness of the message. Every reader of the New Testament

who makes the slight effort of comparing the Easter narratives
in the six chapters Mark 16, Matt. 28, Luke 24, John 20–21 and
I Cor. 15—perhaps with the help of a home-made synoptic table
—is aware of this fact. The very first glance reveals that these
narratives do not transmit a uniform historical picture to any degree.
In the course of the Enlightenment, about two hundred years
ago, Reimarus, fragments of whose writings were published by
Lessing (1777), gave what one might call a complete list of the
contradictions and improbabilities of the Easter narratives. His
criticism is not rendered insignificant by the fact that he burdened
it with the absurd supposition that the disciples had freely
invented the resurrection of their Master for their own ends. A
group of liars would have acted rather more subtly and would
have arrived at more uniform results. Lessing, in fact, pointed
out that the contradictions of the reports do not prove conclusively
that the resurrection was impossible.

Nevertheless, the contradictions cannot be denied or harmonized
away. They are all the more surprising in view of the fact that all
four Gospels provide a comparatively uniform account of Jesus'
Passion, whereas the contradictions in the Easter narratives run
right through the synoptics themselves and even through the
separate Gospels. There is only one exception: the story of the
women (Mark 16.1–8; Matt. 28.1–10; Luke 24.1–11) or woman
(John 20.1–18), who found the tomb empty, is recorded almost
unanimously.

We shall content ourselves with a few reflections. What is
demonstrably the oldest tradition of the Easter message—in Paul
—contains the seeds of the fuller Easter narratives later. Paul
knows—obviously on the basis of well-attested tradition—of
appearances of the risen Lord to different people. 'He appeared
to Cephas (= Peter), then to the twelve. Then he appeared to
more than five hundred brethren at one time, most of whom are
still alive, though some have fallen asleep. Then he appeared to
James, then to all the apostles. Last of all, as to one untimely
born, he appeared also to me' (I Cor. 15.5–8).

In other words the tradition spoke of resurrection appearances,
i.e. Jesus the risen Lord became visible. Paul uses a Greek word
which occurs elsewhere, as, for instance, in Luke 24.34 or Acts
13.31 and 26.16. In each case 'he appeared' means 'he was seen'.
His becoming visible is on each occasion an act which depends

on his initiative. It is not the subjective observation but the objective visibility that is emphasized. Human perception, i.e. what is termed 'vision' in the history of religion or psychology, is not passed over. It is a case of vision, but this does not mean that what is seen is the result of a psychological compulsion; what is seen is not a product of the imagination or intellect. In his vision man sees objective reality, which confronts him from without. Thus, Paul attests that he has really seen the living Lord, or more accurately, that the living Lord has really revealed himself to him in a unique personal encounter. He assumes the same of the visions of the other individuals and groups mentioned above. They, too, did not see a figment of their imagination, but the risen Lord allowed them to see him quite visibly.

The individual details of these occurrences are not disclosed by any texts in the New Testament. There can be no doubt, however, that for the inhabitants of late antiquity the certainty of their faith did not depend on a subjective experience, but on an objective occurrence. Paul himself, without wasting words on the problem that confronts us here, underlines that the same Lord made himself visible to many others in the same way. Not only his two eyes have seen him. Jesus revealed himself to over a thousand eyes as the Lord exalted to be the Christ of God. Paul has only seen him once—on the road to Damascus. This was enough for him to believe in Jesus as the heavenly Lord. Moreover, this was his authority for becoming an apostle of the Lord, like Simon Peter and the other apostles. This one appearance empowered him to put the definite question, 'Have I not seen Jesus, our Lord?' (I Cor. 9.1). He was the last one to whom Jesus appeared in this way; he was the last eyewitness.

Paul makes it clear that Jesus was visible to his followers on different occasions, in different places and at different times. But he met everyone in person in his own way and he gave everyone his special task. For those who did not see him personally in those days, the validity of the message depended on the numerous eyewitnesses.

These visions of the first eyewitnesses are, from our point of view, the last events that we can examine with any confidence of historical reliability. From God's point of view they are the first events that he permits men to see. The historian may well prove that this is the authentic interpretation of the Easter witnesses of the oldest block of tradition. But he cannot prove the truth of this faith to anyone. He can say that the oldest witnesses recognized Jesus as the exalted Lord through the occurrences of Easter. He met *them* in the form of these visions. They understood these visions as acts of Jesus and acts of God for themselves and for all the world. But no one else can answer for us as to whether *we* see Jesus and God himself at work in their Easter experiences or not. We must answer this ourselves. One thing only is certain: just as historical research cannot give us Easter faith, neither can it take it away. In fact, the reality of what happened at Easter cannot be disputed by historical knowledge, but only by a pre-historical (i.e. non-historical) prejudice, which is generally of a philosophical sort—as with Reimarus of old, the 'rational wor-shipper of God'.

The Easter narratives display a variety of originally independent traditions, which there were attempts to harmonize or combine in the course of time. The unity of these varying narratives, however, is not only the product of artificial combination, but the presupposition of the one Easter message. The variety of the narratives, which indicates historical contradiction, is to be seen at the following points.

First, Jesus' resurrection-body. All the accounts agree on the basic concept of the new existence of the Lord (what happened at Easter is not concerned with the revival of a corpse but a new heavenly form of existence); but the picture of its nature is different. According to Paul God gave the dead Jesus a new body of glory; by means of this he reveals himself directly from heaven to his followers on earth. In the Gospels, however, the dominant view is that Jesus returned temporarily to a transformed earthly existence. Relations with Jesus are pictured materially with all the distance he maintains in speech and conduct towards men. He walks with the disciples and talks with them (Luke 24.13–35). The women touch his feet (Matt. 28.9). The command not to touch him (John 20.17) is paralleled by the request to do so (John 20.27); the print of the nails in his hands and the wounds in his side are proof of his identity and reality (John 20.24–29). Likewise the fear of the disciples at the appearance of a spirit is pacified by the proof of his palpable, bodily form and the fact that he consumes a piece of cooked fish (and honey?) before their eyes (Luke 24.36–43).

Secondly, the witnesses. All the accounts agree that Jesus appeared only to a limited circle of people, 'not to all the people but to us who were chosen by God as witnesses' (Acts 10.41). The persecutor, Paul, is the great exception that proves the rule. Only the apocryphal Gospel of Peter tells the extravagant legend of Jesus appearing to his enemies also, Romans and Jews alike. The number and names of the witnesses varies, however. The statements of Paul (I Cor. 15.5–8) and the narratives of the Gospels are certainly not contradictory, but neither are they identical. The Gospels do not say anything about a mass-appearance before five hundred people. The latest stratum of the tradition is aware that the Gospels give only a selection of stories about Jesus (John 21.25). This allows room for the suggestion that the variety of the narratives reflects the variety of the appearances. Obviously the variegated nature of the events of Easter does not permit the reconstruction of a comprehensive historical picture.

Thirdly, the place. All the accounts agree that Jesus appeared to his followers in the historical places of his earthly ministry. Here again Paul is an exception (Acts 9.3–9). But the statements about the places of his appearances differ in detail. Mark and Matthew locate them in Galilee (Mark 14.28; 16.7; Matt. 28.7, 10, 16–17), Luke and John in Jerusalem and its surroundings (Luke 24; John 20). The supplement to the fourth Gospel tries to harmonize the two views (John 21).

Fourthly, the time. All the accounts agree that the appearances of Jesus began shortly after his death, from the second day after Good Friday, and were limited to a period of a few weeks. Once again Paul is an exception. But the particular accounts describing the time of day when the empty tomb was discovered and Jesus' first appearance are different; views on the length of time between burial and resurrection, on the one hand, and the first and last appearances, on the other, vary. Luke 'historicizes' his Easter narratives, by including them according to a calendar of salvation-history within the sequence of forty days; this period closes with what was originally a narrative peculiar to Luke about the bodily resurrection (Luke 24.50–52; Acts 1.9–14). Apart from Luke, there is little interest in precise chronology. The oldest tradition places the resurrection on the third day after the death and burial (I Cor. 15.4). '*On* the third day' is found in Jesus' predictions of the Passion in Matthew and Luke. It stands to some extent in contrast to Mark's 'after three days' (Mark 8.31; 9.33; 10.33), but in Matt. 27.64 the two phrases have already been combined. This is incompatible with Matt. 12.40, according to which the Son of Man, like Jonah in the belly of the whale, is to spend 'three days and three nights in the heart of the earth'. The early dating of the resurrection on the 'third day' was certainly influenced by Hos. 6.2, which originally related to the fate of the nation. The Greek text of the Septuagint reads:

> After two days he will revive us;
> on the third day he will raise us up
> that we may live before him.

It would be very difficult to derive the date purely from this passage, however. The primitive tradition, that Jesus had already risen from the dead during the second night after his death, could only have been brought into line with the prophetic dating, if the passage in Hosea had the very general sense of 'after a short time'. The later Jewish Targum, however, shows that Jesus' resurrection 'on the third day' was regarded as the fulfilment of Hosea's prophecy by Christians at a very early date; it erased the precise chronological reference 'after two days' and 'on the third day' and replaced them by the more general phrases 'in the days of consolation' and 'on the day of resurrection', in order to exclude the Christian interpretation.

Fifthly, the tomb. All the accounts agree that Jesus died on the Cross and was exalted to a heavenly life. We have already discussed the way the simple statement of exaltation became a more precise testimony to resurrection. The statement about the tomb belonged in essence to the Easter message from the beginning (I Cor. 15.4). The empty tomb is not discussed in detail but assumed and taken for granted. For a person in late antiquity it was as self-evident as the fact that objective realities were to be met with in visions. Paul did not believe '*in* the empty tomb' or '*in* the emptiness of the tomb'—how could one do this, in fact?—but in Jesus Christ, whom God raised from the tomb. The clause 'he was buried' belongs to the ancient credal formula. This is not a reference to the object of faith, but to the accompanying data of faith. In other words, Paul knows about the tomb of Jesus because he believes in him. To attribute to Paul knowledge of the resurrection of the dead but not of the tomb being made empty by God is to force him into the Procrustean bed of our abstract logic and to make him responsible for thinking something absurd. Paul is not the philosopher of the absurd, however, but the witness of the para-doxical activity of God, who creates life from the dead. Obviously, the empty tomb is not what is preached or believed in. For Paul it is not even a means of proof. It is simply part of the shape of events. It underlines the reality of this death at one end of the scale and the reality of this resurrection at the other end. The statement that Christians are buried with Christ (Rom. 6.4) silently assumes this view. Only in the legendary narratives of the Gospels is it possible to trace a line which seeks to make the empty tomb the first place of evidence to prove the resurrection. But here, too, the reserve is noticeable; the empty tomb is not made into the object of faith. The message of the angels expressly forbids treating the tomb independently. 'Why do you seek the living among the dead? He is not here, but has risen' (Luke 24.5–6).

Modern scholarship has tried to make the historical course of events at Easter intelligible, on the basis of the discovery of the empty tomb seeing that this tradition is so old. This is very sensible. The legendary character of the narratives does not tell against the historicity of the empty tomb as such any more than the unusualness of the resurrection tells against its reality. But the service which archaeology can render towards confirming the historicity of the empty tomb is limited, if not altogether doubtful. An inscription found in Nazareth, probably stemming from the early Roman Empire and threatening those who violate and rob tombs with the penalty of death by virtue of an imperial edict, may be quite genuine. But even so it says nothing about the historicity of the empty tomb, except to confirm the disputes with the Jews and their malicious aspersions, presupposed in Matt. 28.11–15 and John 20.11–28. The attempt to trace back the tradition of Jesus' tomb, which was discovered in the year 326 under the Emperor Constantine and is still honoured as such today, to the first decade after Jesus' death is equally problematical. Even if it were possible to prove the existence of a Christian cult of Jesus' tomb at this early period, all it would prove is that even at a very early date there were those who not only believed in the living Lord and allowed themselves to be led by him, but also there were those who forgot the meaning of the Easter message and began to practise idolatry in the name of Jesus. Completely wide of the mark and in a completely different category from the serious enquiries based on reason are the 'fantastic attempts that are made from time to time with regard to the Turin Shroud by producing expert 'authorities'. They completely obscure the fact that the truth of the Bible lies in its message of God's grace and judgement and not in any department of antiquities.

At first glance the historical substance of the narratives seems to be slight. The disciples have fled to Galilee. Jesus appears to them and summons them back to Jerusalem—to the city where the irrevocable decision was made. They receive concrete instructions from him. The first person to whom he appeared may have been Peter (I Cor. 15.5; Mark 16.7; Luke 24.34; John 21). He is appointed the shepherd of the flock (John 21.15–17). They all receive the universal commission to proclaim salvation (John 20.22–23) and to embark on a mission to the whole world (Matt. 28.16–20). World-shaking events are approaching 'silently, on the wings of the dove'. They are foreshadowed in the narratives of Easter.

This brings us to our final question, that of the *Easter event*. We have seen (cf. p. 280) that the last event we are able to examine historically is the visions of the eyewitnesses. Do these visions and the events recaptured in the Easter narratives point to a primordial event? To put the question is to answer it in the affirmative. The contrast between the unified message and the varied narratives is only intelligible on the basis of a primordial event which extends over the variations. Both message and narrative depend on this event. It is the substance of the message; in fact, the message recalls this unique event. *The* event occurs in the events.

But what event are we actually talking about? We are talking about the resurrection of the Son by the Father prior to and apart from the message, prior to and apart from the events which are described in the narratives. We cannot say very much about it because both Paul and the Gospels, like the rest of Scripture, are silent about what happened. The actual occurrence of Jesus' resurrection by God is nowhere described for us. Only the apocryphal Gospel of Peter describes the actual event—and, what is more, in the presence of unbelievers and even before the disciples have been informed! In the New Testament, on the other hand, we stand to a certain extent in front of an abyss, at this point; we are at the edge of a crater, caused by something striking vertically from above. Historical research is also aware of this crater. If it had shut its eyes to this or if it had acted as if it had never seen anything it would have abandoned its royal calling. In fact, it knows much more than it allows. The historian would do well if he were to try refusing for a period to be dictated to by the theologian as to how far he might go in his investigations. In the last century the belief which F. C. Baur expressed as follows has gained ground: 'The nature of the resurrection as such lies outside the scope of historical consideration. . . . As far as history is concerned the necessary presupposition for all that follows is not so much the fact of the resurrection as belief in the resurrection.' But this observation is only true in a limited sense. And the fact that it has been repeated in various forms up to the present day does not make it unconditionally true. In fact, it would be false to try to distinguish at this point between the task of the scholar and the believer.

It is true that knowledge and faith are to be distinguished from each other, but they both have the same object in this case. The believer who was no longer willing to pursue truth or make historical investigation would be threatened by the danger of disobedience. The believer does not see more than the scholar. Only the unbeliever could see more. What the believer sees is the same, whether he looks from the standpoint of faith or of knowledge. He sees the great gap, the crater—surrounded by the fragments of the tradition in the form of the different irreconcilable narratives. They form the crumbling edge of the powerful stroke of judgement which the New Testament describes in these words, 'God has raised Jesus from the dead.' The believer is constantly being challenged and asked afresh, whether he will dare—in the light of this historically verifiable disaster—to believe afresh that God was active here.

Both the message and the narratives presuppose that God was active in his Son *before* he was active in men. The Easter event is not the product of the message and the visions. The truth is just the opposite; they are the result of the event. Jesus was not resurrected in the message or the visions or in faith. Jesus was raised by God and exalted to God. Paul does not say in I Cor. 15.17 that 'If the Easter message is not proclaimed, your faith is futile', but 'if Christ has not been raised . . .' It is true that God brought about this resurrection in the sight of men, but he did so by raising his son to his heavenly world. The fact that this activity of God cannot be examined objectively is what constitutes its genuine historicity, which seeks to be believed *and* known. What genuine historical fact could the historian treat perfectly objectively, anyway? Droysen, who described the phenomenon of Hellenism historically and gave it the name it still retains today, wrote in a letter of 1838 to Perthes the remarkable words, too rarely considered, 'The true fact is not in the sources.' The saying is directed against the naïve positivism of the historical school, which set out with the aim of establishing 'how it actually happened'. The historically important fact can never be examined and scrutinized directly but only indirectly. It is in this sense that the event of Jesus' resurrection from the dead can confront us today; it is in this sense that it can be accepted, believed and known by us.

But what is it that can really be *known*? There are three things that can and ought to be known. These three facts are the content of the message which abides even when the glimpses and rumours from the period of the first witnesses have faded into the past (cf. I Cor. 13.8–13). Ever since Easter it has been known what the Easter event means for God, for man and for the world.

God has revealed himself as God by the resurrection of the crucified Jesus of Nazareth. He has done this in such an unrepeatable fashion that he can no longer be thought of or believed in or prayed to apart from the resurrection. God has involved himself so deeply in the destiny of Jesus of Nazareth who was executed as a criminal that the name 'he who raised Jesus Christ from the dead' (Rom. 4.24; Eph. 1.20; I Peter 1.21; cf. Rom. 4.17; II Cor. 1.9) is the true name of God henceforth. Anyone who continues to speak of God without qualifying what he says in the light of God's resurrection of Jesus Christ from the dead is speaking of something else—perhaps an idea, perhaps a phantom, but not God. God revealed himself at Easter as the Creator. He demonstrated his divinity. In doing so he made true faith possible.

God has also revealed himself as the God of man by the resurrection of the crucified Jesus of Nazareth. He has accepted the Jesus whom men men rejected and whom he chose for service and suffering. He has brought him out of shame into a position of honour. He has rejected men's rejection of the Son. Ever since Easter it has been quite plain what he took upon himself in the humiliation of the earthly life of Jesus and his ignominious end on Good Friday. Only after the resurrection can it be understood what the crucifixion on Golgotha meant. We are on the brink of an almost inexpressible secret which will occupy us again later: the Cross means that God himself rejected Jesus—not for his sake but for our sake. This is the secret of 'representative action'. The message which promises us this affirms the forgiveness of sins (cf. Rom. 4.25). In Jesus' whole destiny—in Cross and resurrection—it becomes clear that God revealed himself at Easter as the reconciler. He revealed his humanity. In doing so he made true love possible.

Finally, God revealed himself as the God of the world by the resurrection of the crucified Jesus of Nazareth. He has given 'all power in heaven and on earth' (Matt. 28.18) into the hands of him who was subject to the power of death. Jesus Christ is exalted to be the Head and Lord of his Church and the unseen ruler of the world. In him the whole universe in all its parts has been given its Lord. Paul knows that, 'if we believe that Jesus died and rose again, even so, through Jesus, God will bring with him those who have fallen asleep' (I Thess. 4.14). This new freedom is offered to all the nations in the world (Matt. 28.19–20). In fact, every creature—including the animal creation—waits with longing and sighing and travail for the day when the disguise of the children of God will be done away with and changed into majesty (Rom. 8.19–22). God revealed himself at Easter as the Redeemer. He revealed his openness to the world. In doing so he made true hope possible.

THE RESCUE OF SISYPHUS

THE EASTER EVENT, which first of all really occasions the message and the narratives, and subsequently expresses itself and appears in them, is the universal theodicy (i.e. the final justification of God and of man and of the world). The great question, which is the unseen but disturbing problem of all history, is already posed in the Old Testament—in Job—but it only attains its full force in the preaching of the Gospel. In modern times the problem has been reformulated by Leibnitz as follows. How is metaphysical, moral and physical evil compatible with the rule of the all-wise, all-good God over the world? The question agitated the whole eighteenth century. The answer given by Leibnitz—this world is the best of all possible worlds—was a noble one. But it did not meet the needs of the day; one need only think of the Lisbon earthquake in 1755.

The answer given by the Easter event, on the other hand, is proof against crisis. For it is itself born of the greatest crisis that the world has ever experienced—the outrageous execution of the Son of God. It is an answer which not only has catastrophe in mind, but has it for its central theme. It says, in fact, that God only acts through catastrophe. Catastrophe in any shape or form is not evidence against God but for God. The suffering of God, the suffering of man and the suffering of the world are so entwined in the crucifixion and resurrection of Jesus of Nazareth that the age-old question is given a completely new answer. What Leibnitz called metaphysical, moral and physical evil is not an excusable irregularity of God's universal rule, but an essential moment in the divine activity itself. Since Easter suffering has become the signature of meaningful existence *par excellence*.

In the course of the nineteenth century the question of a theodicy gradually disappeared from modern man's general consciousness of the world. The flood of nihilism envisaged and conjured up by

Nietzsche seems to have washed it away. If God is dead, as 'Zarathustra' maintains, he can no longer be brought to trial and accused or defended, condemned or acquitted. Together with the question of God the question of the theodicy, the question of God's justification, is also extinguished. Man himself has taken over the functions of world-ruler. He creates himself and atones for himself and redeems himself. He alone is responsible for dealing with the metaphysical, moral and physical evil. Where he is not able to master it, he puts himself or—what is substantially the same—others on trial. He prepares his own 'Mount of Olives' and his own 'Gethsemane'. Absolute this-worldliness, where the world and men are only concerned with each other and have no need of God, is powerfully expressed. The French writer, Albert Camus, hit upon 'the absurd' as the ambiguous category of existence and consequently interpreted life and reality by means of it. The word of Oedipus, 'I find that everything is good', 'drives out of this world a God who had invaded it with discomfort and the desire for useless pain. He makes destiny a human affair which is man's responsibility.'

In his *Myth of Sisyphus* Camus has raised the vigilant conqueror of his own fate into the symbol of the contemporary ideal man. 'The gods have condemned Sisyphus to roll a large boulder up a mountainside all his days. The stone is constantly rolling down from the summit of the mountain. They have decided, with some justification, that there is no more terrible punishment than the performance of something useless and without prospect.' Who would deny that this brief sentence is a true expression of our present fate? We all live in the grip of 'work that is useless and without prospect', absolute emptiness both inward and outward, completely lacking in meaning.

This diagnosis may stand. Everyone today, including the Christian, is asked whether he is prepared for this. It is true that the churches have carried out their task in different ways ever since the days of Jesus and the apostles and they seek to fulfil their task in all seriousness. But has their message the ring and the power of the early period? It is true that Christians think it has and work hard to make it so. But does their faith have the joy and the freedom which activates and shapes life? We only need to put these questions to know that the answer is no. What we say and hear, what we do and suffer, is perhaps not only objectively but also existentially serious and sincere. But an overall picture, in which every experience has meaning, is lacking. We, too, live in the world of make-believe, in which Pilate and his contemporaries lived. We need to examine ourselves as to how much in our Christian thinking, speaking and acting is only inherited and at best adopted, but not personally won and independently made our own. We need to do this all the more seriously because we live in a world which does not pretend to possess any metaphysical, let alone religious, 'antennae'; and perhaps, indeed, it does not possess such antennae any more. Shall we ourselves possess any tomorrow—assuming we do so today?

This world of ours is not only presumptuous but also sincere in refusing to have recourse to God as a general hypothesis of existence. It realizes that if there really is a God, then it is not permissible to use him as a means to solve spiritual and material questions and needs. In all of this the world observes the traditional remains of 'religion', which today are only needed as a spiritual narcotic, in order to be able to endure the constant pain of existence.

How can we find our way in a world, which absolutely refuses even to ask the essential question about the meaning of life? How can we help the world? The first answer may lie in the reflection that Sisyphus' question about the meaning of life is by no means settled. It has only been displaced, to return again in a new form. For Sisyphus it means, 'is life worth it or not?' Its sharpness is expressed in the statement, 'There is only one really serious philosophical problem—suicide.' Behind both question and statement the old problem of the theodicy is concealed in a new form.

How, then, does Sisyphus solve his questions? He does so in such a way that in descending into the valley he consciously affirms the uselessness of the previous ascent. On the return journey, in the 'hour of awareness', he rises above his fate. 'He is stronger than his boulder. This myth is tragic, because its hero is aware of what he is doing. Where, in fact, would be the punishment if at every step hope of success were to result in new power? Today the worker does his job throughout his life under the same conditions, and his fate is just as absurd. It is tragic, however, only in the few moments that the worker is aware of it. Sisyphus, the powerless, rebellious offspring of the gods, knows the whole extent of his unhappy position. He thinks

about it during the descent. This knowledge, which is the source
of his real distress, at the same time completes his victory. There
is no fate that cannot be overcome by contempt.' We wait,
listening inwardly: does the sound not seem strangely familiar
to us? Only the person who has no knowledge of the history of the
human race could see in this Sisyphus a new type of conqueror
over life. In fact, Sisyphus is only a new variation of a very old
type, which is characterized by its desire to stand the test of life.
Sisyphus makes the attempt to subdue fate 'by means of his own
reason and strength'. It is the attempt into which men have always
lapsed as soon as they have turned their back on the gods or have
considered abandoning them. This attempt seems so attractive
and promising that even devout Christians and devotees of other
religions have not always escaped it. The great monks built it
into the discipline of their ascetic practices, by affirming what is
contrary to life and by overcoming this by every means that their
religion allowed.

Not even the fact that Sisyphus overcomes fate by means of
contempt is new. This was done in antiquity before him (e.g. the
Cynics) and in modern times (e.g. the Romantics). Lenau's three
gypsies showed the poet how men 'dream away, smoke away
and fiddle away their life—and disdain it three times over'. Of
course, Sisyphus is fully aware and radical; consequently he
loses his way, from beginning to end. He consciously affirms his
pain, which is new every morning and which he scorns anew
every morning. 'The absurd man says yes, but his troubles can
no longer be ended. If there is such a thing as personal fate, then
there is no fate set above men's heads—or at least only one that
is full of doom and contemptible. . . . Convinced by the purely
human origin of everything human, he is always on his way—
a blind man who would like to see but knows that the night has
no end. The stone rolls again. . . . I leave Sisyphus at the foot
of the mountain. His burden is one that men are constantly
assuming. But Sisyphus teaches us the greater loyalty which denies
the gods and rolls the stone.'

We, too, must leave Sisyphus, but in another way. For Sisyphus
lives in us all—as a constant threat to our existence. He survives
in every heroic attempt to master life in our own strength. He lives
in the remarkably resilient mistake of men who will rely on nothing
but themselves. Sisyphus will not consider it true that to be human

means first of all to receive. He does not believe that man can only act after having received. Consequently he runs the constant risk of betraying humanity into the hands of a barbarism of higher pedigree in the name of man! This barbarism consists in man's self-reliance and self-involvement, man's total surrender to himself so that he is constantly sunk in himself. Sisyphus is, ultimately, this self-imprisoned, self-centred man. He is his own God and his own Satan: at war with heaven, embittered with earth, and contemptuous of hell. That is the peak of modern, demonic insanity. It is also the peak of absurdity. Absurdity can no longer see through itself in actual life and in its own activity. It is condemned to denying its humanity in the name of man!

Sisyphus must be rescued from himself—from his misunderstanding and his abuse of his humanity. He must be delivered from the dark delusion of the 'greater loyalty which rejects the gods and rolls the stone'.

The Gospel of Jesus of Nazareth declares that Sisyphus has already been rescued from himself. It happened at Easter. The stone has been rolled away (Mark 16.4) by the invisible hand of a stranger. It was not Jesus who rolled it away. Someone else rolled it away for Jesus. This someone has also rolled it away for Sisyphus—once and for all. The legend which reports the resurrection of the dead is stronger that the myth of Sisyphus. For the legend proclaims a unique, unrepeatable event, while the myth whispers a perpetual circle. If Sisyphus were able to understand its call, he would reject his 'greater loyalty'. He would cease to roll his stone in the previous way. He would even believe in refusing to do this work. He would see that since Easter man is no longer free to leave the question of the meaning of life open or closed. He would feel the abolition of this question to be an outrage against God and man. All this would be open to him, if he chose to exist historically instead of mythologically. Men begin to live historically as soon as they meet the historical Jesus, whom God has raised from death to life.

Of course, the stone with which we have to do day by day has to be grappled with day by day. But this is different from what Sisyphus was accustomed to doing. It is no longer an act of fear, but an act of freedom based on faith; no longer an act of hatred, but an act of willing love; no longer an act of despair, but an act of confident hope. Defiance of God, bitterness against men and disdain of fate would be overcome. In mythological terms, Sisyphus would no longer be Sisyphus. In the language of the New Testament, man would be free from the curse of the Law and brought under the blessing of the promise (Gal. 3.13–14).

Sisyphus need no longer fear that the rejection of his heroic conception cheapens the real issue of life. In a certain sense it is even easier to persevere in a meaningless world where there is no longer anything important to hope for. Easter, however, declares that Jesus' resurrection cannot be separated from his crucifixion— nor can ours. We are to accept it willingly, not disdainfully. We pray, at any rate, that this might be so. Since Easter we know that the world is not meaningless, as long as it is a place of suffering —as long as we suffer in it and for it and as long as the suffering creation waits for our help.

Jesus' resurrection does not put an end to his suffering for the world. Easter day unlocks Good Friday and makes it effective for us. The eyewitnesses of what happened at Easter recognized their risen Lord because they recognized in him the historical Jesus of Nazareth. They were able to see both the earthly and the heavenly in him because they knew the word of the Old Testament promise was fulfilled in him.

Living by Easter faith we take up the stone anew each morning 'with joy', as the hymn says. This Easter faith does not mean believing in the correctness of certain narratives and assertions or in the reality of certain events. In fact, strictly speaking, it does not even mean believing in *the* resurrection, but in the Risen One— personally. But, precisely because we believe in him as a person, we can never disregard his history. Like every other man—albeit some- what differently—he brings his history with him—the history of his earthly life and suffering, and the history of his people which is part and parcel of his own history. In his 'day'—the day of Easter—the 'thousand years' of the Old Testament are present. In him the One

> in whose sight a thousand years
> are but as yesterday when it is past
> or as a watch in the night

is present. In his 'day' relentless death relents. In him life which is lost beyond recall is recalled. In him the world in which there is no leave-taking is begun.

BIBLIOGRAPHY

BIBLIOGRAPHY TO ENGLISH EDITION

SOURCES AND COMMENTARIES

Old Testament and Judaism

Das Alte Testament Deutsch, ed. V. Herntrich and A. Weiser, 1939 ff.

The Old Testament Library, ed. J. Barr and P. R. Ackroyd, 1960 ff. Already published: G. Von Rad, *Genesis*; M. Noth, *Exodus*; A. Weiser, *Psalms*; other volumes in preparation.

The Apocrypha and Pseudepigrapha of the Old Testament, ed. R. H. Charles, 2 vols., 1913

The Dead Sea Scrolls in English, translated by G. Vermes (Pelican)

C. Westermann, *A Thousand Years and a Day*, ET, 1962

New Testament

Das Neue Testament Deutsch, ed. P. Althaus and G. Friedrich, 1933 ff., esp. J. Schniewind's commentaries on Mark (1933) and Matthew (1937)

Black's New Testament Commentaries, ed. H. Chadwick, 1957 ff.

The Apocryphal New Testament, tr. M. R. James, 5th imp. corrected, 1953

The New Testament Background: Selected Documents, ed. C. K. Barrett, 1958

OTHER WORKS

D. Bonhoeffer, *The Cost of Discipleship*, ET (complete edition), 1959

G. Bornkamm, *Jesus of Nazareth*, ET, 1961

J. Bright, *A History of Israel*, 1960

R. Bultmann, *Jesus and the Word*, ET, 1935; *Primitive Christianity in its Contemporary Setting*, ET, 1956; *Jesus Christ and Mythology*, 1960

M. Dibelius, *Jesus*, ET, 1949; enlarged British ed., 1963

E. C. Hoskyns and F. N. Davey, *The Riddle of the New Testament*, 1931

K. Jaspers, *Die grossen Philosophen* I, 1957

J. Jeremias, *The Parables of Jesus*, ET, revised ed., 1963

J. Klausner, *Jesus of Nazareth*, ET, 1929

W. G. Kümmel, *Das Neue Testament, Geschichte der Erforschung seiner Probleme*, 1959

E. Meyer, *Ursprung und Anfänge des Christentums*, 3 vols., 1921-23

R. Otto, *The Kingdom of God and the Son of Man*, ET, 1938

N. Perrin, *The Kingdom of God in the Teaching of Jesus*, 1963

R. H. Pfeiffer, *History of New Testament Times*, 1949

M. Rostovtzeff, *History of the Ancient World*, ET, 2 vols., ed. 2, 1928-30; *Social and Economic History of the Hellenistic World*, ET, 3 vols., 1941

A. Schweitzer, *The Quest of the Historical Jesus*, ET, 3rd ed., 1954

E. Stauffer, *Christ and the Caesars*, ET, 1955; *Jesus and his Story*, ET, 1960

J. Wellhausen, *Prolegomena to the History of Israel*, ET, 1898

G. E. Wright, *Biblical Archaeology*, 1957

INDEX

INDEX